PHILOSOPHY
RHETORIC
AND
ARGUMENTATION

PHILOSOPHY

RHETORIC

AND

ARGUMENTATION

Edited by
Maurice Natanson
and
Henry W. Johnstone, Jr.

Foreword by Robert T. Oliver

The Pennsylvania State University Press
University Park, Pennsylvania
1965

ACKNOWLEDGMENTS

The editors are indebted to the following authors and publishers who have generously granted permission to reprint material used in this book:

The Speech Association of America (Hoyt H. Hudson, "The Field of Rhetoric," *Quarterly Journal of Speech Education*, IX, 1923, pp. 167-180; Maurice Natanson, "The Limits of Rhetoric," *Quarterly Journal of Speech*, XLI, 1955, pp. 133-139; and Maurice Natanson, "Rhetoric and Philosophical Argumentation," *ibid.*, XLVIII, 1962, pp. 24-30)

The Speech Association of America and Donald C. Bryant (Donald C. Bryant, "Rhetoric: Its Functions and Its Scope," *Quarterly Journal of Speech*, XXXIX, 1953, pp. 401-424)

Le Centre National de Recherches de Logique (Henry W. Johnstone, Jr., "Some Reflections on Argumentation," *Logique et Analyse*, VI, 1963, pp. 30-39)

Philosophy and Phenomenological Research (Henry W. Johnstone, Jr., "A New Theory of Philosophical Argumentation," *Philosophy and Phenomenological Research*, XV, 1954, pp. 244-252; and Ch. Perelman, "A Reply to Henry W. Johnstone, Jr.," *ibid.*, XVI, 1955, pp. 245-247)

The Henry Regnery Company (Richard M. Weaver, "The *Phaedrus* and the Nature of Rhetoric," which appeared as Chapter I of *The Ethics of Rhetoric*, Chicago: Henry Regnery, 1953, pp. 3-26)

The *Journal of the History of Ideas* and P. Albert Duhamel (P. Albert Duhamel, "The Function of Rhetoric as Effective Expression," *Journal of the History of Ideas*, X, 1949, pp. 344-356)

The University of Chicago Press and Ch. Perelman (Ch. Perelman and L. Olbrechts-Tyteca, "Act and Person in Argument," *Ethics*, LXI, 1951, pp. 251-269)

The Pennsylvania State University Press (Henry W. Johnstone, Jr., "Persuasion and Validity in Philosophy," which appeared as Chapter IV of *Philosophy and Argument*, University Park, Penna.: The Pennsylvania State University Press, 1959, pp. 42-56)

NOTE: Full citations of all the works referred to in the text of this volume will be found in the Bibliography.

The essays comprising this book are arranged in such a way as to present a philosophical problem. The Introduction constitutes one approach to the problem. The main sequence of ten chapters is another approach, in the sense that it is the sequence itself, rather than the individual chapters, that adumbrates the problem and some suggestions as to its solution.

This book is intended as evidence that a new field of philosophy has appeared—a field in which the concepts of rhetoric and argumentation, including the rhetoric and argumentation of the philosopher himself, are subjected to philosophical scrutiny. The book traces out connections between this new field and the more traditional treatments of rhetoric and argumentation, as well as developing the field in its own right.

CONTENTS

FOREWORD

PHILOSOPHY, RHETORIC, AND ARGUMENTATION: CONGENIAL OR CONJUNCTIVE?

The question which gives special pertinence to the grouping of topics covered in this volume is whether rhetoric, philosophy, and argumentation are related in ways that may be pleasant or mutually convenient or add to the efficient operation of one or all of them—or whether, on the contrary, they are in some manner conjoined so essentially that without a genuine mutuality of relationship one or perhaps all of them would be significantly, if not fundamentally, incomplete.

The hypothesis of this collection of essays is that neither rhetoric nor philosophy nor argumentation can exist independently of the other two; that each depends for the achievement of its own function upon the unique or special contributions of the other two.

The meaning ascribed to *rhetoric* has not always been uniform. Generally in these essays it means a mode of thinking that considers an object in terms of a purpose concerning it which is to be accomplished in the form of a specific reaction from one or more auditors. The purpose might be to persuade or to inform or even to entertain. An individual is thinking rhetorically when he considers race relations, for example, in terms of the facts that will serve his purpose in effecting agreement or understanding or enjoyment by selected auditors. The rhetorical procedure is to determine what the speaker wishes to accomplish in influencing the behavior of particular listeners concerning a specific subject.

Aristotle, rather narrowly, defined rhetoric as "finding all available means of persuasion." The rhetoric which interested him and which formed the subject of his discourse was specifically a rhetoric of persuasion. This is not at all to deny, however, that there is also a mode of discourse which aims to procure understanding, in which instance the rhetoric employed would be designed for the "finding of all available means of enlightenment." Nor can we ignore the fact that some discourse aims to create enjoyment, in which instance the rhetoric is designed for the "finding of all available means of heightening interest."

It may be maintained that rhetoric is a term specifically significative of what Aristotle defined as rhetoric and that if any further or different meaning is intended, a different term or terms should be employed to designate these intended meanings. Such a contention, however, is already lost in the confused progression of history—for rhetoric has too often been employed to mean too many different things. In this collection of essays "rhetoric" can be understood as a mode of thinking which seeks to determine the relationships that exist between the truth of the matter under consideration, the purpose or personal goals of the one doing the considering, and the needs or susceptibilities of those who are to be influenced in their attitude toward the subject.

It should be noted that in terms of this conception (as also in Aristotle's) rhetoric is a mode of thinking or a mode of "finding all available means" for the achievement of a designated end. Accordingly, rhetoric concerns itself basically with what goes on in the mind rather than with what comes out of the mouth. To state the matter simply, one may be just as fully occupied rhetorically while seated alone at his desk as when standing before an audience of listeners. Rhetoric is concerned with factors of analysis, data gathering, interpretation, and synthesis. Rhetoric involves any and all conceivable types of thinking and feeling, with the single and essential proviso that they must be directed to the triad of relationships that bind the subject, the aim of the speaker, and the reactions of the listeners into one indissoluble unity.

Since the user of rhetoric is seeking to accomplish his own purpose in terms of the susceptibilities of a target audience, he may on occasion do violence to the facts. Sometimes he does this in order to utilize misrepresentation as an aid toward the achievement of his aim. This is unethical; but the rhetorical mode of thinking comprises unethical as well as ethical methodologies. A philosopher, on the other hand, claims to pursue the truth regardless of whether the latter is persuasive or palatable. Sometimes the facts may be misrepresented by oversimplification. Here the "rhetorician" needs to be reminded by the "philosopher" that to sacrifice subject matter in an effort to help the auditor is really to do damage to both of them.

Various of the possible meanings and dimensions of rhetoric are explored in the essays constituting the first half of this book.

The old and simple meaning of philosophy is the love of wisdom. Philosophical thought is aimed comprehensively and explicitly at determining the real nature and form of the object under consideration. As such, the use of philosophy to rhetoric is obvious. Philosophy so defined is an indispensable handmaiden to rhetoric, as it is to any inquirer who seeks or needs, for any purpose, to know what is true. But philosophy not only supplies truths that can be rhetorically communicated; it also investigates the truths presupposed by the effective use of rhetoric itself. Among these are truths regarding human nature and the nature of language. Philosophy must even ask to what extent it must make use of rhetoric in presenting its own arguments. It is considerations and questions of this sort to which the second half of this book is largely devoted.

It may, in fact, be suggested that philosophy becomes operant only when it is rendered rhetorical. This is to say that a given process of philosophical thought attains a possibility of being meaningful when it investigates a realm of subject matter in terms of a particular purpose with the aim of achieving intelligibility for a specific kind of recipient mind. A philosopher no less than a rhetorician might and indeed must say to himself: I shall analyze such-and-such a subject in terms of a particular preconception with the view of rendering it meaningful within the context of such-and-such reaction possibilities.

In recent decades students of meaning have come into general agreement on certain conceptions which, if they are indeed valid, mean that rhetoric and philosophy are much more than congenial affiliates—that they are in a general sense conjunctive; they cannot function apart.

One conception is that mind comes into meaningful relationships with its environment only through a process of *symbolic transformation;* that is, no object in itself can be introduced into the nervous system of an observer. He receives and interprets a symbol representative of the object and must deal with it in the awareness that it is only a representative symbol and not the object.

Another conception is that what we notice in the environment and how we notice it are both predetermined to a significant degree by how we are prepared to notice this particular type of object. Walter Lippmann, in his early book, *Public Opinion,* put it this way: "For the most part we do not first see and then define, we define and then see." Cultural anthropologists point out that given acts and objects appear vastly different in different cultures, depending on the values attached to them. Psychologists investigating perception are increasingly insistent that what is perceived depends upon the observer's perceptual frame of reference.

A third conception is that meaning does not inhere in a given symbolic pattern but in the behavioral or introspective response of the observer. What such-and-such *means* is not determinable by defining the symbolic context in which it appears but in observing the reactions of those who are stimulated by it.

Finally, one more currently influential conception is that knowledge is and must be anthropocentric (meaning both egocentric and, more broadly, ethnocentric). Michael Polanyi put this view into neo-orthodox form when he wrote, in *Personal Knowledge:* "For, as human beings, we must inevitably see the universe from a centre lying within ourselves and speak about it in terms of a human language by the exigencies of human intercourse. Any attempt rigorously to eliminate our human perspective from our picture of the world must lead to absurdity."

These four conceptions, singly as well as cumulatively, lead to the conclusion that philosophy is in itself a form of rhetoric. Philosophers should not merely try to "use" rhetoric as a means of making what they

xi

have to say more intelligible or more attractive to their auditors. To conceive of rhetoric as mere decoration or artifice, is to violate its true nature. But philosophers, while engaging in their own essential work, *must* think in the rhetorical fashion of viewing their selected object in terms of their own purpose and the susceptibilities of their particular audience.

Both rhetoricians and philosophers are required to set about their business by asking, How can I present this selected subject both truly and consistently with my aim to discuss it for a certain kind of recipient? This is, of course, not to deny that in some (or many) instances the intended recipient might be mankind itself.

So far as argumentation is concerned, it clearly derives from philosophy (logic) in accordance with the demands of rhetoric. Logic professes to detail kinds of inevitable relationships between objects. Logic becomes argumentation when it undertakes to detail those relationships in ways that will be convincing to selected auditors. For argumentation the aim is rhetorical: to depict that truth which serves the purpose of the speaker in a manner that suitably affects the responses of the auditor. The situation is not fundamentally different for those kinds of argumentation that are directed not to a specific but to a universal audience —for then the arguments are phrased in forms presumably applicable to human nature in general. Meanwhile, the obverse of the relationship is that philosophy is and must be developed and communicated in the mode of argumentation. It must stand and confront all challenges.

Two thousand years ago the indissoluble nature of the relationship that does and must exist among rhetoric, philosophy, and argumentation was scarcely open to question. Aristotle and Plato, in their very different ways, both clearly were ever-conscious of listeners who had to be convinced of the validity of their philosophical speculations. Perhaps theology must bear some responsibility for splitting the three apart, as first Augustine and then Aquinas sought to prove with a cosmic finality that God's truth is true, in and of itself, for anybody or nobody, under any or all conceivable contingencies. By the time of Descartes, many professional philosophers were inclined to speculate about knowledge as though it were abstractable from the contamination of time, place, and human motives. With the advent of William James, Charles Peirce, Hans Vaihinger, John Dewey, and Alfred North Whitehead, as well as the Existentialists, philosophers once again began to make clear their own understanding that their own work could only be accomplished within a rhetorical context. One of the functions of the essays in the second half of this book is to evaluate this context.

Meanwhile, for many centuries rhetoricians clung to a gradually attenuating system of stylistic development as the center of their concern. This interest in style began largely through emphasis upon the Aristotelian concept of *inventio*. But as the fountainhead of this inspiration faded further into the past, without significant renewal, other than mere re-interpretations, rhetoric became weak enough to be largely displaced by elocution. Students of speech became, for a time, less concerned with the *modes of thought* requisite for their specialization than with *methods of presentation* by which some kinds of thought (their own or that of others) might be attractively transmitted to listeners. The theories of elocution for a time prevailed. But as the essays brought together in this book suggest, rhetoric has begun to come into its own again.

Significantly, argumentation, likewise, separated from both philosophy and rhetoric, in the *disputations* of the Middle Ages, became little more than an intellectual game. Sometimes—as in contemporary debate tournaments—it still has an appearance of remoteness from the ordinary concerns of life. In recent years, however, when argumentation is discussed as a species different from logic, it is generally characterized precisely by its philosophic concern with the nature of its subject matter and its rhetorical concern with adapting the presentation so that the speaker's purpose may prove to be acceptable to the target audience.

As the essays in this volume indicate, both philosophers and rhetoricians (with students of argumentation included in both groups) have come to insist once again upon the communality of their interests and even, to a significant degree, of their methods and aims. Not that the distinctive characteristics of each group are not sustained. Indeed, it is precisely their complementary differences which make them indispensable to one another. So, we believe, it is also true that philosophy, rhetoric, and argumentation are functional because of and in terms of their close interrelationship.

Whether or not the readers of this volume may agree that the case is made by the essays that follow, we hope at least that the question will prove inviting for continuing examination and consideration. These essays are presented not as dogmatic statements but, in their spirit and so far as may be in their arrangement within the volume, in the form of dialogue. I hope that this collection will encourage the continuation of that dialogue.

Robert T. Oliver

HENRY W. JOHNSTONE, JR.

SOME REFLECTIONS ON ARGUMENTATION

When we wish to control the action or belief of another person, but either lack an effective means of control or have an effective means that we nevertheless do not wish to use, we argue with the person. Argument is therefore not effective control. To argue with another is to regard him as beyond the scope of effective control, and hence is precisely to *place* him beyond the scope of effective control, provided he is a person capable of listening to argument and knows how it is that we are regarding him. We give him the option of resisting us, and as soon as we withdraw that option we are no longer arguing. To argue is inherently to risk failure, just as to play a game is inherently to risk defeat. An argument we are guaranteed to win is no more a real argument than a game we are guaranteed to win is a real game. An adept arguer can feel certain that he is going to win an argument against someone, but if the certainty is an objective consequence of the very procedure he is using, then this procedure is not an argument.

I do not mean to suggest that the nonargumentative control of action or belief is necessarily infallible. We can command the obedient child but not the disobedient one. But our failure to command the disobedient child is not the result of our regarding him as beyond the scope of effective control. His resistance does not arise from our having given him the option of resisting. It arises from a technical shortcoming on our part. Perhaps with further research we can find the procedure that will guarantee the child's compliance. If we cannot, we may even have to turn to argument.

Argument is a pervasive feature of human life. This is not to deny that there are occasions on which man can appropriately respond to hypnotism, subliminal stimulation, drugs, brainwashing, and physical force, and occasions on which he can appropriately control the action and belief of his fellow-man by means other than argument. But only the sort of person whom we would characterize as inhuman would take pleasure in a life spent controlling the behavior of others through nonargumentative means, and only an idiot would willingly obey him. We do not even exercise power over people when we merely manipulate them. We can exercise power over them only by treating them as people.

One typical way of exercising power is by means of threats. A threat is a form of argument because whoever uses a threat in the attempt to obtain action of a specific sort runs the risk that the other will choose to accept the threatened reprisal rather than to act as desired. It is only a person who can respond to a threat, and when we threaten a person we at least treat him as a person. We treat him as capable of envisaging the consequences of noncompliance. Perhaps some animals are capable of responding to threats. This would imply the capacity to comprehend a conditional proposition. To the extent that we actually can deal with animals in this way, we are certainly treating them as persons.

A threat is, however, a degenerate form of argument. It is degenerate because its appeal to the person is only momentary. Once the threat has been uttered, there remains only to carry it out, or, if it has succeeded in bringing about the desired action, to break off contact. The one who is threatened has no occasion to treat the propounder of the threat as a person at all unless he can utter a counterthreat.

Commands are sometimes of a mixed status. They are usually efforts to control behavior and sometimes belief by nonargumentative means. Sometimes a command carries an additional implicit threat, however, and so is partly an argument. This is much more likely to be the case when the command is addressed to a human than when it is addressed to an animal. The automatic, unquestioning compliance that we expect of an animal is the response to a more purely nonargumentative technique than any we would ordinarily use when dealing with a human being.

Arguments are often contrasted not only with commands but also with assertions of fact. No doubt there are conceptions of argument that imply such a contrast. But the present conception does not, since only the arguer regarded as absolutely authoritative could avoid the risk of failing to produce through the assertion of facts the desired alteration of belief in the mind of another. The effectiveness of an assertion of fact is relative to the authority of its source, and there is no source that does not have its disparagers. We see, then, that the present conception of argument is broad enough to include most assertions of fact. But like threats, such assertions are degenerate forms of argument because they are not conducive to the maintenance of personal relationships.

Not only the arguer takes a risk; the person to whom the argument is addressed may or may not elect to run the risk of having his behavior or beliefs altered by the argument. By closing his mind to the argument, he can avoid the risk altogether. Then anyone wishing to control his behavior or beliefs must resort to nonargumentative modes of control if he is to have control at all. There are issues to which all of us must, to some extent, close our minds. We cannot argue everything out, or always be available to arguments addressed to us. But we cannot always have closed minds, either, for the person with the totally closed mind cuts himself off from the human race. Such a person is inhuman, although he is not beastly, for we do not accuse animals of having closed minds, any more than we say that their minds are open.

On the other hand, the person willing to run the risks involved in listening to the arguments of others is open-minded and, to that extent, human. The differences between man and the animals are typified in man's open-mindedness. Open-mindedness is not merely an added means of accomplishing what the animal can to some extent already accomplish by other means. It is an entirely new possibility. In making himself available to arguments, man transcends the horizons of his own perceptions, emotions, and instincts. Within these horizons the risks of argument do not occur; there is no arguing over what I immediately see, feel, or do. No arguer can take away from me what I immediately experience or feel, because this bears no relation to the conclusions for which he is arguing. These conclusions consist of argued beliefs, evaluations, and lines of conduct, and they can come into conflict with my views only to the extent that these are themselves argued rather than immediate. Immediacy makes no claim, and where nothing is claimed nothing could be submitted to the risks of argument.

Knowledge and morality are possible only to the open-minded person who has transcended the horizons of immediate experience by taking the risks implicit in argument. The animal perceives and expects, but has no knowledge because it cannot expose to argument its interpretation of what it perceives or its reasons for expecting. The animal cannot behave morally because it cannot argue for its conduct. The animal, in short, has no world. The world is revealed only to an open-minded person.

I have spoken of open-mindedness as involving a risk. The risk that the open-minded person takes is that of having his belief or conduct altered. This risk, of course, is strictly correlative to the risk the arguer takes that his arguments might fail. The question arises whether it is necessary to characterize the possibility that the arguer might fail or that his interlocutor might be persuaded, as a *risk*. Is it not sufficient to characterize it as a *possibility*, and say simply that the open-minded person faces the *possibility* that argument might alter his belief or conduct?

The difference between a risk that a person takes and a possibility that he faces is that he has an interest or stake in the outcome of activity in which he is taking a risk, whereas he is unconcerned with the outcome of activity that he merely supposes to present various possibilities. To say that it is merely a *possibility* that argument might alter his belief or conduct is to suggest that the person plays a wholly passive role in the transaction—that "he couldn't care less." It is to suggest that he has resigned from the control of his own action and belief—that he has transferred this control to the hands of the arguer, saying, in effect, "You must decide for me." But what such a person has done is simply to withdraw from the argument. And having withdrawn from it, he brings the argument itself into question. For it now appears that the arguer possesses direct control over the belief and conduct of the person with whom he is arguing. The former takes no more of a risk than the latter. Thus the argument itself collapses into a nonargumentative type of control.

Thus genuine argument can occur only when the respondent is neither impassive nor passive to the utterances of the arguer. It can occur only when the respondent is himself interested in the outcome of the argument; that is, where the respondent takes a risk, and thus forces a risk upon the arguer. What, then, is the interest that the respondent has in the argument? We might be tempted to say that it is an interest in maintaining his own belief and conduct. To some extent such an interest does account for the risk a person takes in allowing himself to become involved in an argument. He takes the palpable chance that his belief or conduct may be exposed as questionable and overthrown. But this cannot be the whole story. For one thing, it is not clear why anyone should feel any resistance to the abandonment of his position once its defects have been revealed. Why does he not cheerfully say "good riddance" and adopt the recommendations of the arguer? For another thing, there can be risk in arguments over issues concerning which a person has no prior opinion. In this situation there is no present belief or conduct to be maintained. What, then is the risk? It is that the respondent, in his belief or conduct, may have to take account of something that he has not had to take account of before. What he would like to maintain is the relative simplicity of his own position. And in general the risk a person takes by listening to an argument is that he may have to change himself. It is the self, not any specific belief or mode of conduct, that the arguer's respondent wishes to maintain. But his interest in maintaining it cannot be absolute, for if it were he would be presenting a closed mind to the argument.

The open-minded person, then, is one in whom there is tension. On the one hand, he wishes to maintain himself. On the other hand, he must expose himself to the risk of change implicit in argument. Such tension is necessary to any human being who wishes to transcend the horizons of his immediate experience and inhabit a world.

The person who listens to argument is not the only one to take a risk. I have already suggested what risk is taken by the arguer. The arguer risks failure to control the belief or conduct of another. This risk, too, implies a tension. The arguer wants control over another but is willing to see that control limited by the negative responses of the other. That this is a genuine and precarious tension becomes obvious when we consider each of its terms to the exclusion of the other. An arguer who wants control pure and simple does not argue; he controls by nonargumentative means and avoids risk. An arguer purely and simply willing to be limited by the responses of the other does not argue, either; in his subservient passivity he abdicates from argument. To argue, a person must maintain the tension between control and what limits control. This tension may be characterized as tolerance, intellectual generosity, or respect. It is isomorphic with the tension I have already characterized as open-mindedness, the terms of which are self-maintenance and change. The tolerant person must find the limits of control in the act of controlling, and he must control in terms of these limits. The open-minded person must maintain himself through change, and change by maintaining himself.

I have written so far as if one could make a final distinction between the arguer and his respondent. Of course one cannot. For the respondent can also be an arguer. When this is the case, the negative responses that limit the control of the arguer will themselves be arguments, and he will submit to this limit in the role of a respondent. In other words, open-mindedness will have become a condition for tolerance. In the dialogue between two or more arguers, tolerance and open-mindedness simply become different ways of characterizing the same basic willingness to maintain the argument and follow it wherever it leads.

The arguer and the respondent may also be the same person, as in deliberation. In this situation it is the same person who seeks control and submits to control, who imposes limits and accepts limits. The tension that must be maintained here is extremely precarious, and readily collapses into habit, impulse, or panic. Deliberation eventuating in a change or reaffirmation of belief is probably capable of existing in a purer form than is deliberation eventuating in conduct because our habits and impulses constitute unargued lures to possible action in a way in which they do not necessarily constitute lures to possible belief. What I am constitutionally capable of doing will cast a stronger spell over my arguments to action than it will over my arguments to belief.

The standard view of argument is that it is a transaction that has no essential bearing on the characters of those who engage in it. The arguer attempts to persuade the listener. If he succeeds, well and good; if he fails, he may either resort to nonargumentative techniques or else give up the effort. But the argument is in no way definitive of either the arguer or the listener. It is simply a kind of communication among minds that already exist and already inhabit the world—a device that they may or may not choose to employ. And one can always choose argument without simultaneously choosing himself.

My own position is that argument is in fact essential to those who engage in it—a person who chooses argument does in fact choose himself. For the tension between conservation and change which is felt by the interlocutors is precisely what enables them to inhabit the world. Immediate experience makes no claims and raises no questions; it is transparent. It is only when action and belief become subject to argument that an opacity is introduced into experience—the opacity which is the self. There is no self for immediate experience. There is a self only when there is risk. I do not want to claim that argument provides the only sort of relevant risk. But when people argue, they take risks that raise them above the level of immediate experience and put them on the map. And unless they take risks of one kind or another they are not people. So argument does seem to me to be constitutive of those who participate in it.

Nonargumentative forms of control do not establish the self. Instead, they bypass it. They proceed on the assumption that the self is not present to interfere with their effective administration. The command, the subliminal suggestion, the hypnotic pass, avoid the risk of dealing with the self. The cajoler, the advertiser, and the hypnotist not only operate on the basis that "nobody is at home" in the body of the interlocutor but also that they are not even "at home" themselves. One who wheedles instead of arguing does not himself quite deserve to be treated as a person, and neither does one who secures the assent of another when the latter has his guard down or is looking the other way. When a man is given to using nonargumentative means of control we have no compunctions about using nonargumentative means against *him*, on the grounds that he has not shown himself to be a person.

Shall we say, then, that argumentation is a device for avoiding the need to resort to violence? That when we assume that another is "at home" and argue with him, our conduct is a *substitute* for nonargumentative forms of control including the use of force? This is the common-sense account of argument. According to it, men argue only by virtue of a prior agreement, either explicit or implicit, to substitute the conference table for the battlefield. But this fragile agreement may collapse at any time, and when it does, the first man to return to the battlefield will have the advantage. This is a cynical view of human nature, since it regards man's capacity for argument as no more than the product of a transient enlightenment—an unstable victory over the irrational forces that define him—and it regards argument itself as no more than an expedient. If argument is in fact a mere expedient to avoid violence,

6

then we ought to consider as most successful that argument which has the greatest soporific effect. More fundamentally, the standard view is in direct contradiction to the history of human hostility. Throughout recorded time, men have always based their conflicts upon arguments. Every war has been preceded by the search for an excuse for fighting. To find examples of violence not based upon argument, we must look to the annals of psychopathology. This fact shows that normal human violence already presupposes argument. Indeed, if the capacity to argue is not present from the outset, how is it possible to reach any agreement, whether explicit or implicit, to suspend hostilities in favor of argument?

The common-sense account of argumentation hardly does justice to the human need for rhetoric, advertising, and propaganda. It presents rhetorical technique as mere poses or postures that can be taken by the arguer. For every rhetorical posture, there is another that can be used to counteract it, so that human controversy appears as sequences of meaningless gestures. They are meaningless because the arguer himself can stand altogether outside them. As devices at his command, they express no feature of his ego. The arguer's ego can remain inscrutable throughout his argumentation, according to this traditional view of the role of argument in human life. It is only necessary for the arguer to *appear* to be committed to his argument. Indeed, only a fool would really be committed to his own argument, because for every argument there is an equally effective counterargument. This, too, is a cynical interpretation of human nature.

My own interpretation does not require me to deny that for every argument there is an equally effective counterargument. It merely derives a new conclusion from this premise. Instead of concluding that no one should be so foolish as to become committed to his own argument, I conclude that argument is a defining feature of the human situation. A being not capable of arguing or of listening to argument would simply not be human. Such a being would lack a self. Any reflective arguer knows, of course, that all of his arguments can be met by counterarguments. But to condemn all argument on the basis of this reflection is completely to miss the point of argument. The point of argument is not to provide effective control over others, as might be the case if there were some arguments that could not be met by counterarguments. It is rather to introduce the arguer into a situation of risk in which open-mindedness and tolerance are possible. This is the human milieu which the arguer supports through his fervent commitment to his own arguments. If he were not committed, his arguments could have no more than a strategic function, and the milieu would collapse into a game in which open-mindedness and tolerance would no longer be possibilities.

An arguer can both be fervently committed to his arguments and know that all of them can be met by counterarguments. This is possible because the reflection with regard to the counterarguments represents a momentary disengagement from the milieu in which the arguer lives. Similarly, a thinker can disengage himself from manners and mores and pronounce that they are all equally arbitrary. This pronouncement would have a point if it had ever been claimed that they were *not* equally arbitrary. But in the absence of this claim, it misses the point that a human milieu is sustained by manners and mores in much the same may as it is sustained by argument.

I have just been considering the standard view that the existence of a counterargument for every argument is evidence of the futility of argument. Sometimes it is the alleged datum of futility that makes those who share this view feel that for every argument there must be a counterargument. The history of philosophy is an alleged datum of this kind: since no philosopher has ever been known to have secured general assent to his position by means of arguments, it follows that for every philosophical argument there is a counterargument. Now if general assent were in fact a desideratum or alleged achievement of the philosophical enterprise, there would be some point in being concerned with the possibility of a philosophical argument admitting no counterargument. The layman attributes this goal to philosophy, and there are some philosophers who join him in doing so. But most philosophers are not interested in securing general assent to their views—some, indeed, would feel that such assent could only be the result of a colossal error or misunderstanding on the part of the public. Thus to most philosophers the observation that general assent has never been attained would simply seem to miss the point of the philosophical enterprise. The point of it is not to get everyone to agree but to argue for conclusions to which general agreement would be irrelevant. What could such conclusions be? Evidently they cannot be concerned with facts. In a broad sense they are indeed concerned with values. A philosophical argument may deal with such values as knowledge and morality. These are values because they enable man to transcend the horizons of immediate experience and hence to inhabit a world. Other philosophical arguments deal with other ways of moving beyond the immediate. Since it is argument *sans phrase* in the first place that opens the world to us, philosophical argument deals with the fruits of argument *sans phrase*. Argument *sans phrase* may well aim to secure general agreement. It can do this because general agreement is one of the possibilities of the world it opens up. We can escape from immediate experience into general agreement just as we can escape from it into knowledge or morality. But philosophical argument is not an escape from immediate experience. It is only an attempt to expand and consolidate the world into which the escape has been made. Therefore, it may examine the concept of general agreement as well as those of knowledge, morality, and so on. But general agreement with regard to the results of the expansion and consolidation achieved by philosophy would be beside the point.

What I am trying to say can be put more positively. I have said that argument reveals the self by confronting it with risk. Philosophy makes clear the structure of the risks faced by a person who argues or listens to argument. It articulates a world of people and of things. It tells the self who it is and where it stands. Thus philosophy may be said to serve the emerging self by contributing to its morale. Philosophical arguments, then, have a morale function rather than an information function. If we expect general agreement regarding their conclusions, we simply do not understand them correctly. Philosophical argumentation will continue with unabated force as long as there are selves confronted with a world in which they must take a stance.

My conclusion is that neither the existence of a counterargument for every argument nor the alleged futility of philosophical arguments is, if rightly interpreted, a reason for adopting a cynical view of man's argumentative nature. Indeed, without that nature he could not be man.

MAURICE NATANSON

THE CLAIMS OF IMMEDIACY

Whatever else he is, man is also the creature who argues. That argument is a constant in the history of human variables may be granted without argument, for should it be subjected to argument there would be more than a hint of circularity. What is less obvious, perhaps, is that the creature who argues is seldom concerned with argument as such; still less is he concerned with the nature of argumentation in general. His passion is arguments, but his possibility is to become aware of argument and of argumentation. The dialectical advance at issue in this listing requires specification. In its simplest aspect, an argument consists of at least two propositions, one of them being held to follow from the other. Such are the skeletal minima of "an" argument. Argument as such, however, transcends any given argument; its concern is with what transpires structurally when there are arguments advanced and pursued. Who moves from an argument to the logical form of arguments of that type turns from an argument to argument as such. Argumentation, we may suggest, goes a considerable step further: there is the total range of involvement of arguments—argument as such—and the arguers participating in such proceedings are subjected to a theoretical order of scrutiny which seeks to arrive at a rationale for the entire enterprise. In these terms, an argument is a naive content of daily life; argument as such is the theme for a disciplined inquiry which must stand outside of common-sense affairs; and theory of argumentation is a distinctively philosophical entertainment. To speak of "an" argument will ultimately mean to speak of philosophy. Now the locus of arguments, argument, and argumentation must be clarified.

Since arguments don't argue themselves, the arguer—that distinctively human agency—must be located. Where is he situated? Most simply, in the midst of an argument, i.e., in the presence of company. It is the *alter ego* who makes an argument possible. We shall set aside the question of deliberation and what is sometimes termed an interior dialogue. Unless one is willing to undertake an investigation of the nature of the deliberative self, the reflective ego, it is not possible to examine the reasons for the suggestion that I may truly pursue an argument with myself. For present purposes we shall bracket that dimension of the problem. Clearly, the paradigm case for the location of the arguer is our finding him in the process of arguing with another person. In immediate contrast, it may be noted, the locus of argument as such and of the theory of argumentation is not social but solipsistic: although I may discuss problems of argument and argumentation with a fellow man, I neither am compelled to such socialization nor do the rigor and authority of my analysis of the issues depend on such discussion. But to argue, I am indeed compelled to seek out my interlocutor. The arguer assumes his role in at least a dyadic situation. The notion of "situation" is central here and must be explored cautiously.

If a broker presents arguments to a client as to why he should make a basic change in his portfolio of holdings, we would say that the "situation" at issue is defined by the broker-client relationship. What is relevant to such a professional activity is the state of the market, in turn the state of the economy, etc. Even where "personal" elements may enter the picture, they are subordinated to the professional schema. Argument and counterargument in this case are bound within the frame of the established situation, which in turn might be analyzed into certain role-structures and societal functions. Although both broker and client are involved in the argument, they can hardly be said to be *personally* involved. The concrete existence of each member of this dyad is precisely excluded from the argument. Whatever the "risks" of the stock market, there is certainly no risk of the subjectivities arguing stocks and bonds in the office. Indeed, this example of an argument is defined by the lack of personal risk. Judgment, not subjectivity, is at issue. Shall we call this an argument then? Instead of answering directly, we will distinguish between two functions of an argument: to convince and to persuade. In this language, the broker is trying to convince his client to follow his advice. For persuasion we must turn to a different example.

Striking up acquaintances with fellow men in the course of our travels is supposed to be one of the far-from-home-ly joys of the wayfarer. On a recent trip such a boon companion initiated the conversation by asking where I was from. When I told him I lived in North Carolina, he said, "The niggers are certainly taking over the South, aren't they?" Now where does one begin his answer? Is this to be a vignette for the *Reader's Digest* in which I plant a few friendly ideas in the raw soil of my friend's mind, those spanking new fresh seeds which his local library will water, those sudden inspirational shoots to be nurtured by a subscription to the Anti-Defamation League biweekly newsletter? Is it to be a "Let's define our terms" approach? Or is it not the case that an immense weariness in-

11

forms the scene, an old and burdened haunting of bad faith which makes it practically impossible to have an argument at all. The difficulty is not in finding arguments, lines of argument, etc. Rather, it is the pointlessness of such procedures that makes for weariness here. One knows that a style of mind is already in operation and will never be stopped. That there are numerous exceptions makes no difference, unless one wants to argue for the possibility of exceptional cases. For the unexceptional mass, there is no meaningful exchange of views possible. The situation of the man in question permits no openness, and the situation defines the possibility of argument. It is conceivable that one of us might convince the other of some limited aspect of the total problem, but such convincing would be limited precisely because the basic self, the person involved, would be really not at issue. To persuade the Other in this case would mean to force the presence of the self, the risking of the self. And that is what those hard, darting eyes tell me will never be granted, for it's too late in a sense in which we might say that a perpetually renewed choice of being too late is maintained. Whatever I might convince him of I can never persuade him of.

Arguments, then, do not automatically involve the risking of the self. Indeed, they rarely do. It becomes necessary to introduce such locutions as "in all genuine arguments" the self is risked. But then we have introduced what we needed in a devious manner: this is "risk" by contraband. Before we accept it we should note a few further difficulties. Arguments can serve to close the mind instead of opening it. Again, the question is one of the situation of the arguers. Imagine—we won't detail it this time—a young man growing into radically new conceptions, discovering in himself an upheaval of values traditional to his family and background. In arguing for his new world he may be cautioned by his family, warned gently or harshly, urged and prayed with and over, and, finally, argued with directly. The result may be the close of what began to open, the return to stolidity and approval at home, the proving of his "true mettle," etc. The risking of the self, even in genuine cases of willingness to risk, by no means assures the liberation of the self. What is constitutive of liberation derives from a much more primordial stratum of argumentation. Before we arrive at it, however, we should pause long enough to examine the second term of discourse in this context—argument as such.

To turn to argument is not necessarily to be involved in an argument. Instead, the concern with argument is a movement toward discipline, the discipline of logic in broadest terms. What is presupposed here is a reflexive movement from instances to the forms which underlie those instances. The anatomy of an argument is studied by the logician, but there is a broader range of interest in the very movement from example to form which is also shared by the sociologist or the social scientist generally. I am speaking of the securing of a perspective in terms of which something previously taken for granted appears *as* being something of a structured sort. The new terrain achieved may be of political or social significance in the cases where the movement is from arguments typical of certain classes or groups within a particular social order to the new awareness that such *kinds* of arguments are indeed typical. In simple terms, a knowledge of propaganda techniques, an understanding of material fallacies, a grasp of essential forms of inference may lead to a freedom from the individual's being "used" by those instrumentalities toward his being able to use them to his own purpose and satisfaction. To the extent that he is able to "see" his arguments as exemplars of argument types or forms he is liberated somewhat from their dominion over him. And to this extent he is opened and liberated. But it should be noted that the freedom achieved here results not from risking the self in arguments but through risking the self in an essentially solitary willingness to learn, an openness to knowledge. Such openness may then reflect itself in later arguments in which that person participates, but already we have moved from arguments in the initial sense in which that term was employed. Argument, then, has advanced us in some measure toward the dialectical end of argumentation which promises to spring the philosophical prize from its trap.

Without trying to bind ourselves to labels, it may nevertheless be valuable to suggest that just as argument is the province of the logician, so argumentation is the concern of the philosopher. The full range of problems implicit in the dyadic relationship described earlier becomes explicit in the theory of argumentation, for it is there that we can approach the nature of the selves who argue, the situation underlying their arguments, and the significance of the very activity they engage in by arguing. In fine, theory of argumentation is a distinctively philosophical discipline because the essential terms at issue are problematic: speaker, listener, intention, self, interpretation, persuasion, and action. It is a part of the philosopher's craft to explore such terms and to attempt to liberate them from their ordinary placement in a mundane world which presupposes their meaning and so obscures that meaning. But once again it must be remembered that work in theory of argumentation is fundamentally isolated activity, not to be confused with the holding of arguments or discussions. Although there is nothing to hinder the philosopher from talking with others about problems in this domain or from publishing his results so that other philosophers can learn what he has to report, such social advances are extradisciplinary to the field of theory of argumentation; they are by no means to be understood as necessary accompaniments to the work of the philosopher. When *challenged* the philosopher must be prepared to state his case, to argue his case, but it is not incumbent upon him to invite a challenge. He can keep his solip-sistic peace if he wishes to. However, the involvement in the problems of theory of argumentation does affect the philosopher and, in turn, the student who interests himself in such matters.

In becoming aware that there *is* such a field as theory of argumenta-tion, in learning that it is possible to examine the taken-for-granted elements of the situations in which men argue with each other, the pro-fessional or novice advances not only in his theoretical understanding but also in a more nearly existential manner: he begins to recognize that just as the logic of argument gives the logician (or student of logic) a fresh perspective from which to view arguments, so theory of argumentation gives the initiate in that sphere a radically new vantage point from which to view men in argument. I am speaking of a kind of perspectival libera-tion, but there is certainly nothing automatic or necessary about what follows from such pursuits. It is important to try to get at what does occur when liberation is achieved, and in order to do that we must look closely at theory of argumentation, especially at the connection between the situ-ation of the self and the weight of arguments. Or to express it somewhat differently, we must look to the relationship between the subjectivity which argues and the claims of argument.

Whether the self elects to open itself up genuinely in an argument, i.e., whether it chooses to risk itself in arguing with a fellow man, hinges on the explicit or implicit, the avowed or intuitive realization that the meaning of the very activity to be pursued and supported through an argument transcends that argument and is instead part of the fabric of argumentation. More directly put: I risk myself in an argument when I know or sense that the very nature of the activity I'm engaging in has its own rationale within which what I am and who I am must be determined. When I risk myself in an argument, what I am risking is acquaintance with the problems and possibilities of theory of argumentation. To say this is, of course, already to be committed to a final dialectical step in the progression and to suggest that such commitment is the condition for the location of philosophy and the adventure of the philosphical self. For the moment, however, the initial relationship between self and argumen-tation is of prime interest. What, precisely, is it about the self which encourages risk, and what exactly is it which is risked?

I propose to follow a rather simple procedure at first: to utilize a cer-tain example of progressive movement in argument generally. In these terms, my opponent in an argument may suggest supporting reasons for a proposition which I disagree with, which I may even find rather offen-sive, and yet his argument may not reach me in any decisive personal way. I am not at issue in my counterargument any more than I was at issue in his initial argument. To use a distinction suggested earlier, we may call this an instance of argument with the intent to convince. My opponent may succeed or fail to convince me without my subjective being, my personal reality being at issue. Anyone utilizing certain argumentative strategies and anyone countering with other gambits and dodges could take the place I and my opponent had in the argument, just as any expert bridge player could take over the hand of another player and so make use of certain possibilities. The bidding of North or West around the bridge table would then be equivalent to the techniques of argument pursued by essentially uninvolved persons in an argument. In argument with intent to persuade, however, we have a different story. Here the person is being addressed and the person is addressing his alter ego; person speaks to person. In these terms, to persuade is not simply to secure power over the other, to make him do my bidding. Instead, persuasion is a primordial mode (with noncognitive analogues) of bringing self and alter ego to risk themselves by discovering the theoretic ground that undergirds an argument, i.e., by coming into awareness of the nature of argumentation. The phrase "genuine argument" may now be explained, for what is "genuine" is nothing more than the commitment of the self to the full implications of a philosophical dialectic, a saying, in effect, "if you argue you choose to open yourself to the risk of discovering that argument has a fundamental structure that has, in turn, profound implications for your own being." Risk, then, is not really the condition of serious or genuine argument; risk is rather the dialectical possibility of argument with intent to persuade. The point goes still deeper.

Arguments are traditionally said to consist of declarative sentences, propositions interrelated in cunning ways and arranged to show, demonstrate, establish some cognitive rather than affective truth. Understood in this way, there can be argument over beliefs and evaluations but not over immediately felt or experienced contents. My immediate perceptions and feelings are essentially fugitive to argument; it is said that they simply *are*. Immediacy, then, makes no claims. The force of my own argument leads me to attempt a refutation of this entire line of analysis. I wish to vindicate the claims of immediacy. The essential point can be established at the outset and then adumbrated as we proceed. What is at issue, really, in the risking of the self in genuine argument is the immediacy of the self's world of feeling, attitude, and the total subtle range of its affective and conative sensibility. To be perfectly blunt: when I truly risk myself in arguing I open myself to the viable possibility that the consequence of an argument may be to make me *see* something of the structure of my immediate world. To say that argument is constitutive of a world is right, but it is precisely the meaning of "world" that such an assertion calls into question. I am suggesting that "world" is in the first place the personal and immediate domain of individual experience. When an argument hurts me, cuts me, or cleanses and liberates me it is not because a particular stratum or segment of my world view is shaken up or jarred free but because *I* am wounded or enlivened—*I* in my particularity, and that means in my existential immediacy: feelings, pride, love, and sullenness, the world of my actuality as I live it.

Not merely can the claims of immediacy be argued; if they indeed could not be argued risk would be excluded from the entire dialectic of the development of the self, and that would mean that the dialectic would be abortive. Freedom would be alien to argumentation. That it is not is the mark of immediacy. In order to see the nexus between risk and immediacy, however, we must turn to a more careful description of the nature of immediacy. It might appear that the difficulty is verbal; I take it to be substantive but not devastating. The trouble with dichotomizing affection and cognition, feeling and thought, is that the structural features of both are darkened, as though feeling and thinking operated in different locales to be known as the private and the public. The point is that feeling is a way of meaning as much as thinking is a way of formulating. Privacy is a means of establishing a world, and what genuine argument to persuade does is to publicize that privacy. The metaphor leads us to suggest that risking the self in argument is inviting a stranger to the interior familiarity of our home, not merely the living room of the floor plan but the living space of a private sphere, home as it is meant by the one for whom it is home. When that interior is reached the nature of risk shows itself directly, for then the real shape of the argument shines through its disguises. This is the opening up of the self.

If the claims of immediacy are to the privacy of a world, then it may be said that genuine argument with intent to persuade is immanently directed to the risking of privacy itself: an argument may be taken as a condensed world. And to proceed in this way is in effect to turn to theory of argumentation as one aspect of or expression of a broader conception of ideology. A highly unusual convergence of disciplines manifests itself here: theory of argumentation and sociology of knowledge are joined as committed to the examination of immediacy in terms of a grounding dialectic. When it is said of a man "You can't argue with him; he's closed on that subject," the point at issue is not the location of rhetorical techniques but the meaning of closure. When I refuse to commit myself to genuine argument involving persuasion, I in effect make a refusal of philosophy itself; I will not risk myself and I will not risk my world. Basically, I am refusing to allow for a dialectical relationship between myself and my world. In Sartrean language, this is one of the modalities of "Bad Faith," the intrinsic attempt of consciousness to banish any distance between itself and the possibilities of the self.

The dialectic from arguments to argument as such to theory of argumentation is a way of understanding how the risking of the self is fundamentally a philosophical achievement in which traditionally noncognitive aspects of mind are really constitutive of the self. The self is not risked through arguments or even through willingness to argue seriously; only when the full range and depth of the affective life is shocked into openness is a true risk attempted. Risk, in effect, is a possibility and an achievement, not a function of willingness to argue or even of ordinary sincerity and seriousness in listening to others. The bond between the affective and the cognitive life is that of argumentation itself, the awareness that arguments and argument as such are undergirded by a theoretic matrix in terms of which they can be grasped and essentially explicated. It is in this sense that philosophy is the visitor who announces himself through the calling card of argumentation. Whether invited or not, he is in waiting for us if we venture to pass beyond an argument to what it means to engage in argumentation.

It should be evident by now that certain terms have been given a special placement: self, risk, immediacy. Perhaps it might be helpful to add "belief" and "conduct" as well, for they require special attention. Just as the bifurcation between the affective and the cognitive had to be rejected, so is it necessary to refuse to dichotomize belief and conduct. Rather, we shall say that belief is a mode of conduct. Having a belief is a way of organizing a world and a means of participating in a world. Clearly, conduct is not to be held any closer to action than is thought or attitude. If one is to speak of a world as the plenum of human concerns and possibilities, then the constitution of a world is the foundation of all action, a foundation which is itself a mode of action. Now it is possible to see that opening oneself to arguments or battling one's way through a seriously contested argument is insufficient to reach the meaning of the self and incapable as well of establishing risk with respect to that self. Arguments are already placed in the framework of a world, the individual arguer's world. Counterarguments do not throw that world into question; they merely harry the defenses of the speaker. A telling blow in argumentative warfare is equivalent to forcing the speaker to acknowledge that he cannot defend his original position in terms of his original arguments. There need be nothing more admitted. It is only when the world of the speaker is encountered that he is encountered. The question turns on how we are to understand the meaning of "world." To argue that risk is established through arguments and that through risk the self is constituted is to assume what needs to be brought to clarity: the very meaning of self, world, and the existential situation of risk. Finally, all of these terms are functional aspects of the larger problem of the meaning of communication. We are thrust into the terrain of these issues by turning back once again to our distinction between arguments to convince and arguments to persuade.

There is a rhetoric of convincing and a rhetoric of persuading, strange as that formulation may sound to ears used to hearing rhetoric spoken of as the art of persuasion. What we mean by the distinction is this: the understanding of techniques involved in attempting to control others, to convince them of this or that, is at a distance from any concern with risking the self of either speaker or listener. The issue is one of manipulation. In the case of persuasion, technique is bound to the very meaning of the self, and rhetoric becomes the inquiry into the structure of communication—the art of philosophically locating the speaker and listener and speaking and listening as features of a world. Rhetoric in this sense is the branch of philosophical inquiry whose chief object is the illumination of the relationship between theory of argumentation and the nature of the self. The dialectic of fulfillment involving the movement from an argument to argumentation finds its statement in rhetoric, conceived as a philosophical art. This raises some final questions regarding the nature of philosophical argumentation.

Let us agree that philosophical argumentation is not over matters of fact, that it differs in principle from scientific argumentation, that ultimate settlements or resolutions of basic metaphysical and epistemological issues are not to be spoken of in the language of "possibility" and "impossibility" but are rather to be comprehended as "transpossible" and "transimpossible." Philosophical work involves a kind of beginning that turns upon the inquirer; we may speak of philosophical risk as the commitment of the inquirer to reconstruct his world. Philosophical argumentation is then indeed *ad hominem*, but the "hominem" is the mystery. *Is* it the case that in arguing with a fellow philosopher I am risking myself and asking him to risk himself? *Is* the self really at issue in serious philosophical disputation? To say that the answer is "no" is to recommend that much philosophical argumentation is intended to convince and not to persuade, but that is a serious admission if true. The point is that philosophical argumentation, if our distinctions between arguments, argument, and argumentation are to hold, must in its very nature bear a reflexive dimension which leads to the true constitution of the self, that philosophical argumentation is defined by the establishment of existential risk on the part of the participants. In brief, philosophical argumentation can be itself only when the very world of the philosophers is risked and so rendered possible. The conclusion suggests itself that when philosophers agree, or when one philosopher defeats another, or when a philosopher claims to have resolved a great issue, philosophical argumentation is missing from the scene. Agreement can at best be a momentary stage in philosophical dialectic, not a state of being. Disagreement, most often, is not a matter of disputes over particular propositions but a stylistic disparity. Disagreement is a way of discovering your interlocutor's style of mind, of recognizing the geography of his world. At the same time, it is the means through which your own freedom is discovered. Philosophical argumentation that stops short of the affective world of the participants is a rhetorical failure precisely because it is a philosophical failure.

The mystery of the "hominem" remains. Let us say that it is the function of philosophical argumentation to probe that mystery and to attempt to illuminate its transcendental horizon. For the philosopher inquiring into inquiry is man investigating man. The reflexive character of the movement at issue cannot be caught at an empirical level; that is why I speak of a transcendental horizon here. The philosopher in dialogue about the meaning of philosophical dialogue is indeed paradoxically situated: *his* arguments are meaningful only in the frame of his argumentation, and that argumentation is the issue in question. But this is a transcendental paradox, not a circle. If man is the creature who argues, so is he also the being capable of exploring his arguments and of inquiring into the activity of argumentation itself. Man, then, is the being who philosophizes or, more cautiously put, he is the being capable of philosophizing. When I address an argument to a fellow philosopher I am speaking to him as that being concerned with reflexive acts, i.e., that being who may take my argument as a signal to look to argumentation, and that means to look to himself. In the act of addressing the Other, I risk the dialectic of not merely his reply through arguments but his insistence that I look beneath and through my arguments to argumentation. It is the implicit force of philosophical argumentation, then, that it poses the mystery of those who utilize its office and find themselves entrapped as well as liberated in its transcendental machinery.

It is time to terminate the discussion. I have suggested that arguments, however seriously pursued or sincerely projected, are not in themselves constitutive of the self, that they do not in themselves assure the true risking of subjectivity. Rather, I believe that argument must be transcended by argumentation in order for the self to be located and its world brought to life. Risk is established when the affective world of the person is existentially disrupted, and this disruption means that his immediate life of feeling and sensibility is challenged and made open to challenge. Argumentation involves the constitution of that total world of which the formation of arguments is but a surface part. To transcend arguments in order to locate the person is to recognize the claims of immediacy and respond to them in dialectical reciprocity. The philosophical act which liberates the self is the same act which acknowledges the mystery of dialogue by engaging in the rhetoric of risk. I conclude that philosophical argumentation is the counterexamination of the claims of immediacy.

HOYT H. HUDSON

THE FIELD OF
RHETORIC

When Bishop Whately published his *Elements of Rhetoric,* he con-
fessed in his preface that he had hesitated to use the word "rhetoric" in
his title, because, he said, it is "apt to suggest to many minds an associated idea of empty declamation, or of dishonest artifice; or at best, a
mere dissertation on Tropes and Figures of speech." We can appreciate
the good bishop's hesitancy. For "rhetoric" is one of those words which
has been so unfortunate as to lose most of its good connections and to be
known by the bad company it has sometimes kept. There are five or six
meanings given for "rhetoric" in the dictionary; but we are prone to think
of only one, and that is "artificial elegance of language, or declamation
without conviction or earnest feeling." Thus we are likely to speak of
certain pieces of writing or speaking as "mere rhetoric"; or of a writer or
speaker as "indulging in meaningless displays of rhetoric." It suggests an
inflation of style to cover weakness of thought, or, in our American phrasing, something spread-eagle or highfaluting—and, as I have suggested,
only for display.

Yet some respectable connotations have managed to cling to "rhetoric" through the centuries. Walking along a city street not long ago, I
passed a building marked "School of Expression," with a sort of menu-
card posted by the door showing the subjects that were taught in this
school. Very lowest on the list, which included two or three kinds of
dancing, elocution, dramatics, public speaking, and oratory, there was
offered "rhetoric." I was reminded of Charles Lamb's answer to the saying
that a pun is the lowest form of wit: it is the lowest, Lamb insists, only
because it is the foundation of all. And if this school of expression had
included in its list courses in salesmanship and personal efficiency, as do
some similar schools, it would be very much like the schools of the
sophists in ancient Athens, wherein rhetoric was the foundation for a
training in all the accomplishments and graces necessary to business and
social success.

We are more familiar with the word "rhetoric" in the titles of textbooks on writing, of which many published within the past two or three decades have been named "Composition and Rhetoric"; though I am tempted to believe that if you asked the authors of some of these books to tell you which pages were composition and which were rhetoric, they would be at a loss. Some books named "Rhetoric" alone strikingly resemble others named "Composition and Rhetoric" or still others named "Composition" alone. Yet careful writers have maintained a distinction here, one which will throw light on what I have to say a little later about rhetoric in ancient times. Turning to one of the best secondary school texts I know of, Clippinger's *Composition and Rhetoric*, I find these sentences:

> Rhetoric and composition are not always distinguished, because they are usually studied together; however the difference between them should be understood. Composition *produces* discourse; rhetoric *analyzes* discourse to determine its structure.

In other words, speaking roughly, a distinction is here being made between the pure science (rhetoric) and the applied science (composition); or, if we prefer, between the science of discourse (rhetoric) and the art of discourse (composition). A product of composition might be an essay; a product of rhetoric, in this sense, would be an outline or analysis of an essay, perhaps with a list of forms of arrangement and figures of speech employed in it. A similar distinction must have been in the minds of those who used to teach rhetoric and oratory; rhetoric was the theory, oratory was the practice. And yet there have been some, and the author of the definition in the *New International Dictionary* is among them, who have overlooked this distinction and have made rhetoric mean "the art of discourse"—the theory and the practice. It is all very confusing; and I trust you are ready to turn back, with me, to another meaning of the word "rhetoric," one which, with whatever incrustations of additional meanings it may have gathered, the word has held for some students and writers and speakers in every generation for nearly twenty-five centuries.

Wherever we approach the subject of rhetoric, or the subject of oratory or eloquence, we do not go far without meeting finger-posts that point us to the work of Aristotle. Welldon, the translator of Aristotle, refers to his *Rhetoric* as being "perhaps the solitary instance of a book which not only begins a science, but completes it." Welldon says a little too much. A better statement is that of Hugh Blair, the Scottish preacher whose lectures on rhetoric formed the standard textbook both in England and America for fifty years. Blair wrote in 1759:

> Aristotle laid the foundation for all that was afterwards written on the subject. That amazing and comprehensive genius . . . has investigated the principles of rhetoric with great penetration. Aristotle appears to have been the

first who took rhetoric out of the hands of the sophists, and introduced reasoning and good sense into the art. Some of the profoundest things that have been written on the passions and manners of men, are to be found in his Treatise on Rhetoric.

Sears includes in his *History of Oratory* a chapter on "Aristotle, the Rhetorician," from which I shall quote two sentences:

> He must be recognized as the father of rhetorical science, and as the man who in an age of orators compassed the whole scale of their practice. It has been observed that in the most perfect example of persuasive oratory on record —the creation of the greatest genius among the English-speaking race—Shakespeare's speech of Mark Antony—the rationale of it all had been set forth by the great Greek scientist eighteen centuries before.

In Henry Peacham's *Compleat Gentleman*, a popular work on polite accomplishments which was first published in 1622, Aristotle's *Rhetoric* is said to have been deemed by some as "being sufficient . . . to make both a Scholler and an honest man." The study of rhetoric, it is needless to say, has not always been credited with such effects.

At any rate, we do well to begin with Aristotle in building up our concept of rhetoric. With him rhetoric is a useful art, the art of persuasion, based upon a pure science. It is a useful art, because it supplements rather than imitates nature; it supplements nature, in that it helps truth and justice maintain their natural superiority. In his book Aristotle begins with the subject as a science, for he defines rhetoric not as the art of persuasion, but as "the faculty of finding, in any subject, all the available means of persuasion." That is, he makes the rhetorician a sort of diagnostician and leaves it to others to be the practitioners; the rhetorician is the strategist of persuasion, and other men execute his plans and do the fighting. In practice, however, and in any study of the subject, this distinction can hardly be maintained, since the person who determines the available means of persuasion in regard to a given subject must also be, in most cases, the one to apply those means in persuasive speech and writing. In passing I might suggest, however, that if anywhere, either in the profession of law or in advertising or in any sort of publicity work, you know a person who spends his time in analyzing subjects given him and deciding how they can best be presented, what appeals can be based upon them, yet who does not himself present the subjects or make the appeals, there you come near to having the pure rhetorician, in the narrow Aristotelian sense.

But in ancient as in modern times (as we have noted in the case of "Composition and Rhetoric") it was found impossible to divorce theory from practice. The rhetorician and the orator were one; and if not in Aristotle himself, at least in the Aristotelian school and tradition, rhetoric is the whole art of persuasion. It does not satisfy itself alone with the finding of means of persuasion; it also includes the persuasive arrangement and presentation of the speaker's material. A product of rhetoric, in this sense, then, is neither an analysis of some speech already made, with a list of figures and tropes, nor an analysis of a subject upon which a speech is to be made, showing what means of persuasion can be employed. Rather it is a speech, or some piece of persuasive discourse, persuasively presented.

I know of no statement of this meaning more simple than the earliest one to be found in any English publication: it is taken from Caxton's translation of *The Mirrour of the World*, published by himself in 1481. Caxton worded it thus: "Rhethoryke is a scyence to cause another man by speche or by wrytynge to beleue or to do that thynge whyche thou woldest haue hym for to do." This identification of rhetoric with persuasion is frequently met with in English literature throughout the sixteenth and seventeenth centuries. Thus Samuel Daniel has a line,

> Sweet, silent rhetoric of persuading eyes.

Nowadays we have a proverb, "Money talks," meaning usually, "Money is the most powerful means of persuasion." A seventeenth century writer of epigrams wrote a couplet embodying the same idea; he called his epigram, "New Rhetorique," and it runs,

> Good arguments without coyn, will not stick;
> To pay and not to say's best Rhetorick.

Obviously, such an epigram would be understandable only among readers who were accustomed to think of rhetoric as persuasion. In this sense, plainly, the man who speaks most persuasively uses the most, or certainly the best, rhetoric; and the man whom we censure for inflation of style and strained effects is suffering not from too much rhetoric, but from a lack of it.

Let us proceed with this meaning in mind. We recognize that in ancient times persuasion was carried on almost entirely by the spoken word. We know the great place held by public speaking in Greece and Rome, at least in their democratic phases. We know also of the place of preaching in the early church: "How shall they believe in him of whom they have not heard?" asks St. Paul. "And how shall they hear without a preacher?" After the invention of the printing-press we find persuasion carried on more and more by writing, through the pamphlet and the journal, until in our own day if we run over the principal manifestations of the persuasive art we find as many of them in type as in the spoken word. Editorial writing, pamphleteering, the immense business of advertising and the still more immense business of propaganda—these are occupations which modern rhetoricians may follow. Yet there are also open to them the occupations calling for public speech, those of preaching, of law, of politics, the lecture and chautauqua platform, business and culture clubs. In commerce, corresponding to advertising, there is the great field of salesmanship, carried on for the most part by speaking. We expect of our publicist that he shall both write and speak.

Yet in spite of our habit of thinking of writing and speaking as separate processes, the practice of persuasion is essentially one, in that the same principles apply everywhere in the field. A writer on public speaking at the present time would hesitate to call his work "Rhetoric," because the word is now usually applied to written discourse. But less than a hundred years ago the case was exactly reversed. Bishop Whately, in the preface already cited, gives as another reason against the use of the title, "Rhetoric," that "it is rather the more commonly employed with reference to public speaking alone." E. L. Godkin, the great American editor, wrote ninety years ago: "The art of rhetoric differs from some others in having arrived long ago at perfection. The rules are the same today as they were in the days of Quintilian and Demosthenes. The art, however, has now two distinct branches, writing and oratory." A writer in "The Nation," reviewing Donelly's The Art of Interesting, has said: The author "is a sound classical scholar. He has done us the service of showing conclusively that the underlying principles of classical rhetoric are fundamentally valid today—that Aristotle, Cicero, and Quintilian knew not only how to make speeches, but how to preach sermons, write editorials, and sell groceries."

Then, too, in spite of the great bulk of printed material in the modern world, public speaking and eloquence have by no means lost their potency; and to consider the subject of persuasion apart from speech would be indeed to play Hamlet with the prince left out. The printed word can be passed by or laid aside; the persuasive speaker wins willing and continuous attention. "What is read is accepted inertly, or, if questioned for authenticity, affords no easy measures for resolving doubt. When man listens to speaking, however, he has a definite guide for his reaction: he can look the speaker in the eye, study his face, watch his actions and bearing, analyze his voice, penetrate into the man himself, and then know whether or not he finds him worthy of credence. This is the reason why, when men really care, when an issue is deeply at stake, when the crisis impends, they resort not so much to the writer as to the speaker." [1] We may say further that speaking is still the *norm* of writing; the writer tests his article by reading it aloud "to see how it sounds," and the would-be persuasive writer can do no better than to write as a good speaker would speak.

[1] Charles Henry Woolbert, *The Fundamentals of Speech*, pp. 1-2.

We might now glance over the field historically, with a view to estimating the body of tradition which has grown up in the study of rhetoric. Greek rhetoric is a large field in itself, too large to be plotted here. Besides Aristotle the other great master of rhetorical theory in Greece was Isocrates, a successful teacher, who gave to his work a more immediately practical turn than Aristotle; the pupils of Isocrates were the great orators, generals, and statesmen of their time. It seems that Isocrates not only taught the form and means of persuasion, but also offered a certain content or body of doctrine which was to provide the subject-matter of his pupils' persuasive efforts. I suppose that when, at the present time, we combine work in Americanization or studies in patriotism with Public Speaking, preparing students to speak on principles of Americanism, we are doing somewhat as Isocrates did in his time. In Rome, Cicero and Quintilian are the great names, though by no means the only ones.[2] St. Augustine was a teacher of rhetoric, and it was as a connoisseur going to hear a great artist that Augustine went to listen to the preaching of St. Ambrose, whose persuasion led to his conversion. Rhetoric was one of the seven liberal arts of the mediaeval curriculum—and in that statement we are summing up many centuries of rhetorical pedagogy and practice, with some changes which we shall note later. Among the Humanists we find Melanchthon writing a treatise on rhetoric, while Erasmus wrote widely in rhetorical subjects; the *De Copia Verborum* of Erasmus was used as a school text in rhetoric for many years. Coxe and Wilson, two of the English Humanists, wrote the first works on rhetoric in our language.

It is interesting to find how many men who became eminent for other reasons made, at some time in their lives, researches in the field of rhetoric. Sir Francis Bacon tried to recall scholars in his day to the classical view of the subject, and also found time, in the midst of his other pursuits, to become a great speaker—in the opinion of Ben Jonson the best speaker of his generation. One of the works of Thomas Hobbes is an abridgement of the *Rhetoric* of Aristotle, with an appended treatise of his own on the same subject. Isaac Barrow, Vice-Chancellor of Cambridge University and Head of Trinity College, who was famous both as a preacher and as a mathematician second only to Newton in Newton's time, was in his early days a teacher of rhetoric and gave a year's lectures on the *Rhetoric* of Aristotle. Adam Smith, author of *The Wealth of Nations,* lectured on rhetoric for several years. John Quincy Adams was the first to hold the Boylston Chair of Rhetoric and Oratory at Harvard, and his lectures form one of the principal American contributions to the

[2] Readers of Professor Shorey's article in *The Quarterly Journal of Speech Education,* VIII, 1922, already have a better view of rhetoric in the classical period than I can hope to suggest here.

tradition of the subject. Bishop Whately, great as a logician, and Alexander Bain, great as a psychologist, were the principal British writers on rhetoric in the nineteenth century.

But in addition to writers on the theory of rhetoric, the student of the subject must take into his account the practitioners—the men who have gone to the rostrum or the senate-house, to the pulpit or the hustings, and have attempted to influence men by persuasive speech. The names of the great orators comprise too long a list to be enumerated here. It should be noted, however, that the student of rhetoric investigates eloquence, not for its graces and ornaments, and not with regard to its effect upon him as he reads it; our admiration may be excited by a splendid figure in Burke or Canning; we may gain considerable pleasure from perceiving the skill with which words have been joined euphoniously and rhythmically; but such admiration and pleasure are incidental and are shared by the student of literature or the general reader. The student of rhetoric looks upon each oration as an effort in persuasion; he must learn what he can of the audience to which it was addressed; he takes note of the appeals that are made, with reference to the motives that are touched, the emotions that are aroused. He must know the character and reputation of the speaker at the time when the speech was made; for a speech otherwise persuasive may fail of effect because the speaker lacks a persuasive *ethos*; whereas at times one sentence from a man of great ethical weight is sufficient to perform a difficult task of persuasion. It is true that we must also take into account matters of style and ornament and delivery; but these, too, are to be estimated with reference to their persuasive effect. Figures and tropes, neat turns of speech, and well-drawn pictures are used to feather the arrow of argument and appeal; but they can also impede its flight.

It is true that there are passages in oratory where the orator seems to throw off the bonds of rhetoric as a useful art and to enter the realm of the fine arts. The end of persuasion is for the moment forgotten in sheer delight at beauty of conception and expression. It is as if a stone-cutter, carving out a figure for some public building, should be touched by inspiration and become a sculptor, making of his figure a statue worthy of standing alone, and more important as art than the whole of the building. Mr. Logan Pearsall Smith, whose work as an anthologist of beautiful passages of prose is well known, says in the introduction to his volume of *Selected Passages from Donne's Sermons*:

It is in the sermon, therefore, that we find some of the highest achievements of English prose—in the sermon, or in prophetic or didactic or even political eloquence written with the same high impulse and inspiration. For great prose needs a great subject-matter, needs great themes and a high spectacular point of vision, and solemn and clear and steadfast conception of life and its meaning.

Such passages we can share with the student of literature, asking him, however, to acknowledge the credit due to the rhetorical discipline and practice which brought the orator to such a measure of perfection, and also taking into account the persuasive task which provided the occasion.

For the most part the student of rhetoric is dealing with broader effects. Goldwin Smith speaks of John Pym as the "first great wielder of public opinion in England." It is the *wielder of public opinion* that the student of rhetoric is interested in. What are the secrets of his power? The rhetorical element in statesmanship is a whole field of study in itself. How many a good policy has been beaten or postponed for want of proper presentation! How many a just and able man has suffered because of an unpersuasive announcement of his purposes! The defeat of Blaine in 1884 is laid, as we know, at the door of his campaigner who untactfully launched against the Democrats the charge of "Rum, Romanism, and Rebellion" phrased with such perverse effectiveness. I shall not enlarge upon the wielding of public opinion which was carried on by Theodore Roosevelt and Woodrow Wilson in later times, by means of their powers of presentation. Enough if I have suggested that in political life a man must be something other than a pure statesman on the one hand or a literary artist on the other; he must know and use rhetoric as a technique of power.

In recent times also we have seen a unique example of the wielding of power through propaganda in the case of the Russian Revolution. I recall from John Reed's *Ten Days that Shook the World* a story of how in the first days of the Bolshevik revolution, when the forces of Kerensky were within a few miles of Petrograd and threatening to retake the city, a courier from the battleline came in haste to the city for aid. "Do you want more soldiers?" he was asked. "No, we want orators!" he said. And a truckload of orators was mobilized and hurried to the scene of conflict. Many have wondered how the Bolsheviki, representing the opinion of only a small fraction of the Russian people, have been able to hold power, conduct military operations, and even extend their sovereignty over new territory. Their use of rhetoric as a technique of power helps answer the question. General C. Birdwood-Thompson of the English Army, writing in the *Manchester Guardian*, relates a conversation held with Trotsky, in which General Thompson asked about the "new form of war" carried on by Russia, in which the territory to be conquered was "leavened by political agents" and then easily occupied by a small military force. He goes on:

Trotsky's reply was curious. He said: "War by propaganda is not the invention of a Russian, but rather of an Englishman." And then by way of explanation he added: "Do you remember the story of Oliver Cromwell, who refused to punish one of his subordinates 'because,' he said, 'this man is a good preacher'?"

Some question is sure to arise concerning the relation of rhetoric, in our sense, to other fields of study. It is undeniable that rhetoric draws on other fields with considerable disregard for the airtight partitions sometimes put up between college departments. A student of architecture, whose aim is to learn to design buildings, cannot study that subject alone. Without becoming an engineer, he must draw on the special field of engineering for a knowledge of materials and construction. Without becoming a painter or sculptor he must know freehand drawing, color, and relief. He does well to learn something of surveying and landscape gardening. If he expects not only to design buildings but also to superintend their construction, there are a great many other subjects he must know; yet at the end of it all, he is an architect. The case with the rhetorician is analogous. He must learn much from the psychologist, especially with regard to the subjects of attention and emotion. From the social psychologist he draws what knowledge he can of the crowd-mind and the formation of public opinion. There are certain fundamental problems of society which a publicist is continually going to deal with, usually in relation to political questions. Aristotle, in discussing deliberative rhetoric, says that the subjects embraced are finance, war and peace, defense of the country, imports and exports, and legislation. Yet the rhetorician does not necessarily become an expert in those fields. He attempts to learn the authorities and sources of information in each, and to develop a method which he can apply to specific problems as they arise. He learns, in any given situation, what questions to ask—and to answer. The peculiar contribution of the rhetorician is the discovery and use, to the common good, of those things which move men to action—intangible, obscure, mystic, even, as these things may be; yet you and I and our communities find them intertwined with every problem of life.

The question of the relation of rhetoric to the work of the department of English is too involved for me to attempt an answer. From what we have already seen of the field of rhetoric, however, I think one or two suggestions might be drawn. The work of departments of English is already very broad, ranging from courses in Old English and Middle English to those in short-story writing, dramatic structure, biographical studies of authors, and historical studies of literary tendencies. If the department of English absorbs, in addition, the work in rhetoric, at least it should do so with complete knowledge of the breadth and importance of it, and aware of the distinction between rhetoric and other forms of literature. So far as English is the study of language, philology, it is not very closely related to rhetoric; so far as it is a study of literature it deals with a fine art; whereas we have seen that rhetoric is to be classed with the useful arts. Aristotle intended his *Poetics* to treat of discourse designed to delight; he wrote his *Rhetoric* to treat of discourse designed to persuade.

We can cite John Milton as a man great in both fields. The student of literature will be especially interested in Milton's poetry. To the student of rhetoric, however, the most important part of Milton's life is the twenty years when, after having written "Lycidas" and "Comus" and other poems, he turned to writing controversial prose for the influencing of public opinion.

The writer in pure literature has his eye on his subject; his subject has filled his mind and engaged his interest, and he must tell about it; his task is expression; his form and style are organic with his subject. The writer of rhetorical discourse has his eye upon the audience and occasion; his task is persuasion; his form and style are organic with the occasion. As for showing this distinction in our curricula, might it not be possible to put all study of exposition and argumentation into a course or group of courses together with other work in rhetoric and public speaking; while the teaching of narration and description, or of such literary forms as the short-story, the familiar essay, and the play, might be kept in closer relation to the courses in literature and in distinction from the forms of writing and speaking as a useful art. There is surely a closer kinship between writing a piece of argumentation and the delivery of an argumentative speech than between the writing of the same piece of argumentation and the reading of Tennyson's poems. Surely it is not asking too much to have this fact somehow recognized.

We may wonder, if the foregoing is a true description of the field of rhetoric, how it has come about that rhetoric usually includes, in present-day usage, only matters of style and ornament. A modern discussion of rhetoric will often consist of chapters on diction, figures of speech, and forms of arrangement, such as antithesis, periodicity, and balance. The identification of rhetoric with persuasion seems to have vanished. This has come about through a process of substituting a part for the whole or of losing sight of the end in the means. For example, in the Middle Ages, there were centuries when there was not a great deal of public speaking, and what was done was in a formal way upon certain conventional themes. At such times, the chief care of the speaker was in the phrasing of his material. His subject-matter was always old—probably dictated down to minute details by the conventions of the occasion; his skill was to be shown in his diction and embellishment. So rhetoric came to be the study of embellishment, and is so defined in some mediaeval and Renaissance rhetorics. At such times, the identification of rhetoric with display is quite warranted; and we can see the ground for the prevalent meaning we noted at the beginning of the essay.

This degradation of rhetoric can be traced quite clearly. The Roman rhetoricians divided the subject into five parts; to quote Cicero's statement, the orator "ought first to find what he should say (*inventio*), next to dispose and arrange his matter, not only in a certain order, but with a sort of power and judgment (*dispositio*), then to clothe and deck his thought with language (*elocutio*); then to secure them in his memory (*memoria*); and lastly to deliver them with dignity and grace (*pronuntiatio*)." Aristotle devotes practically all of his first two books to the subject of invention; in the third he treats of disposition, elocution or style, and very briefly of delivery, omitting the subject of memorizing. But it is plain that in any period when subject-matter was conventionalized, the consideration of invention would be neglected. Disposition would require only the slightest attention, whereas stylistic embellishment, memorizing, and delivery would constitute the orator's task. Some teachers of rhetoric, indeed, by the plan of having students use only the works of others, reduce the study entirely to that of the last two of the five parts—memorizing and delivery.

As we are aware, not in the Middle Ages alone has rhetoric thus been narrowed. In any and all times the tendency is present—the tendency to depend upon tradition or convention for material and devote oneself wholly to style in writing and delivery in speaking; so that rhetoric becomes a study of how to vary a phrase, how to turn a compliment, write certain kinds of letters and formal addresses, how to declaim great orations, or how to deliver a set speech suitable to a certain occasion. Order of words, with regard to emphasis and balance, beauty of figures, dignity and sonorousness become the matters of highest concern. Rhetoric is then an affair of the court and the chamber—or the parlor; and is brought back to its true self only when some divisive issue, a revolution or a great national danger, calls men to sterner tasks of discussion and persuasion. In these times of stress, oratorical power grows out of the subject-matter, eloquence is organic and not an embellishment or flourish added from without. Such eloquence, imbued with great earnestness of persuasive effort, has a simplicity of diction and style which, like poetry in its great periods, lies very close to the common speech of men, and yet at the same time exercises an exalting and purifying influence upon the language. Might it not be possible that in matters of purity and strength of speech the orators, the speaking men—such as Bunyan, Jeremy Taylor, Pitt, Fox, Burke, and Lincoln—have exerted as great an influence upon the language as the poets and essayists? Yet the speakers are too often overlooked when investigations are made upon these points.

But it occurs to me, as I glance back, that my subject is too large to cover even in a study of such inordinate length as this one is about to assume. I shall attempt no formal summary, hoping that as we have travelled about this field, some of its contours have become clearer and its boundary-lines more definite. I have tried to show that in the field of persuasive discourse, which traditionally and still to a great extent practically

is to be identified with oratory and public address, we have a rather definite body of theory and practice, with an honorable history and an excellent academic pedigree. I have mentioned some distinctions that set off
rhetorical discourses from all other forms, whether oral or written; notably,
that in rhetoric a study of the audience is fundamental; and the essence
of it is adaptation to the end of influencing hearers. Rhetoric does not
include all the work done by our present departments of public speaking:
it does not include the oral interpretation of literature, nor dramatics, nor
studies designed to improve the pronunciation and diction of ordinary
conversation. But estimated historically and by its influence upon the
affairs of the world, rhetorical discourse seems the most important subject
with which we have to do. In addition to all we inherit from the past,
with modern researches in psychology to draw upon, with modern wielders
of publicity to observe, and with the increasing use of a method for send-
ing human speech broadcast, so that a speaker may address thousands
where he once addressed scores, the significance of persuasive discourse is
continually being enhanced. Surely it would be a mistake to overlook this
significance, and in proportioning our emphasis I do not see how we can
give any but a central position to rhetorical study.

DONALD C. BRYANT

RHETORIC: ITS FUNCTIONS AND ITS SCOPE

When a certain not always ingenuous radio spokesman for one of our large industrial concerns some years ago sought to reassure his audience on the troublesome matter of propaganda, his comfort ran thus: Propaganda, after all, is only a word for anything one says for or against anything. Either everything, therefore, is propaganda, or nothing is propaganda; so why worry?

The more seriously I take this assignment from the Editor to re-explore for the *Quarterly Journal of Speech* (1953), the ground surveyed by Hudson and Wichelns thirty years ago, and since crossed and recrossed by many another, including myself,[1] the nearer I come to a position like our friend's conclusion on propaganda. When I remember Quintilian's *Institutes* at one extreme of time and lose myself in Kenneth Burke's "new rhetoric" at the other, I am almost forced to the position that whatever we do or say or write, or even think, in explanation of anything, or in support, or in extenuation, or in despite of anything, evinces rhetorical symptoms. Hence, either everything worth mentioning is rhetorical, or nothing is; so let's talk about something encompassable—say logic, or semantics, or persuasion, or linguistics, or scientific method, or poetics, or social psychology, or advertising, or salesmanship, or public relations, or pedagogy, or politics, or psychiatry, or symbolics—or propaganda.

But that is not the assignment. Others have dealt with those subjects, and have given us such illuminating definitive essays as "Speech as a Science" by Clarence Simon,[2] "The Spoken Word and the Great Unsaid"

---

[1] Hoyt H. Hudson, "The Field of Rhetoric," reprinted as Chapter 1 of this volume; Herbert A. Wichelns, "The Literary Criticism of Oratory," *Studies in Rhetoric and Public Speaking in Honor of James Albert Winans*, pp. 181-216; Donald C. Bryant, "Some Problems of Scope and Method in Rhetorical Scholarship," *Quarterly Journal of Speech*, XXIII, 1937, pp. 182-188; and "Aspects of the Rhetorical Tradition," *ibid.*, XXXVI, 1950, pp. 169-176, 326-332.

[2] *Quarterly Journal of Speech*, XXXVII, 1951, pp. 281-298.

by Wendell Johnson,[3] "General Semantics[1952]" by Irving Lee,[4] and many other interpretive essays and *apologiae* for the various branches of our curricula and for the multiform captions in our departmental catalogues and organization charts. Among these, "Rhetoric and Public Address" can hardly be thought neglected over the years, at least in the *Quarterly Journal of Speech* and *Speech Monographs*. But perhaps we have assumed too quickly that rhetoric is now at last well understood. On the other hand, Hudson's "The Field of Rhetoric" may be inaccessible or out of date, and Burke's "new rhetoric" too cumbersome or recondite in statement, even after Marie Hochmuth's admirable exposition of it.[5] Even if all this be true, however, one can hardly hope to clarify here what may remain obscure in the work of thirty years—or twenty centuries; but in proper humility, no doubt one can try. At least, common practice seems to presume a restatement of most complex ideas about once in a generation.

I shall not undertake to summarize Hudson's or Wichelns' pioneer essays, relevant as they are to the central problem. They and certain others like Hunt's "Plato and Aristotle on Rhetoric"[6] are by now woven into the fabric of our scholarship. Nor shall I try to duplicate the coverage of my two papers on "Aspects of the Rhetorical Tradition." They can be easily reread by anyone interested.

One further limitation upon the scope of this essay seems necessary: I shall not try to present a digest of rhetoric or even an explanation of the main principles of rhetorical method. Those are also easily available, from Aristotle's *Rhetoric* to the newest textbook in persuasion. Furthermore, I intend to discuss no particular system of rhetoric, but the functions and scope which any system will embrace.

CONFUSION IN MEANING OF "RHETORIC"

Very bothersome problems arise as soon as one attempts to define rhetoric, problems that lead so quickly to hairsplitting on the one hand or cosmic inclusiveness on the other, and to ethical or moral controversy, that the attempt usually ends in trifling with logomachies, gloss on Aristotle, or flat frustration. *Rhetoric* is a word in common parlance, as well as in technical use in the Speech Association of America and the Chicago school of literary critics. Hence we may presume it to have meanings which must be reckoned with, however vague, various, and disparate; for

[3] *Ibid.*, pp. 419-429.
[4] *Ibid.*, XXXVIII, 1952, pp. 1-12.
[5] *Ibid.*, pp. 133-144.
[6] *Studies . . . in Honor of James Albert Winans*, pp. 3-60.

a word means what responsible users make it mean. Various as the meanings are, however, one occasionally encounters uses which seem little short of perverse, in persons who ought to know better. Not long since, a doctoral candidate in the classics, who had written as his dissertation a "rhetorical" analysis of one of St. Paul's sermons, was asked how Aristotle had defined rhetoric. Though the question, it would appear, was relevant, the candidate was unable to answer satisfactorily. Whereupon the questioner was taken firmly to task by one of his fellow examiners and was told that after all rhetoric could be adequately defined as a *way of saying something*. Now of course rhetoric may be so defined, as poetic may be defined as a way of making something; but there is little intellectual profit in either definition.

Rhetoric also enjoys several other meanings which, though more common and less perverse, serve to make analysis of it difficult. In general these are the same meanings which Hudson reviewed thirty years ago: bombast; high-sounding words without content; oratorical falsification to hide meaning; sophistry; ornamentation and the study of figures of speech; most commonly among academic folk, Freshman English; and finally, least commonly of all, the whole art of spoken discourse, especially persuasive discourse. This last meaning has gained somewhat in currency in thirty years, especially among scholars in speech and renaissance literature.[7] During the same period the use of the term *rhetoric* (or the combinations *composition and rhetoric* and *grammar and rhetoric*) to label courses and textbooks in Freshman English has somewhat declined, and simultaneously the "rhetorical" content of them has declined also. The tendency now is to prefer just *Composition* or *English Composition,* or to resort to such loaded names as *Basic Writing, Effective Writing, Problems in Writing, Writing with a Purpose,* or *Communication and Analysis.*

In one of his early speeches, President Eisenhower declared that we want action from the Russians, not rhetoric, as evidence of their desire for peaceful settlement. Here is the common use of *rhetoric* to mean empty language, or language used to deceive, without honest intention behind it. Without question this use is in harmony with the current climate of meaning where what our opponents say is rhetoric, and what we say is something else. Hence our attempt to define rhetoric leads almost at once into questions of morals and ethics.

Rhetoric as figures of speech or artificial elegance of language is also a healthy perennial, nurtured in literary scholarship and criticism as well

---

[7] In his *The Ethics of Rhetoric,* the first chapter of which is reprinted as Chapter 3 of this volume, Richard M. Weaver of the College at the University of Chicago makes an interesting and useful effort to restore rhetoric to a central and respectable position among the arts of language and to assign it the function of giving effectiveness to truth.

34

as lay comment. Hence the second of the two meanings of *rhetorical* in *Webster's New Collegiate Dictionary* is "emphasizing style, often at the expense of thought." Here we encounter a second obscuring or limiting factor in our attempt at definition. We are to describe rhetoric in terms of those *elements* of a verbal composition for which it is to be held responsible. This mode of procedure has always been attractive. It can produce interesting and plausible conclusions, and it can be defended as schematically satisfying and pedagogically convenient. Thus it proved in the *trivium* of the Middle Ages and the Renaissance. If grammar has charge of the correctness of discourse, and if logic has charge of the intellectual content, then it is natural to assign to rhetoric the management of the language of discourse (or the *elocutio*); and, if we do not include poetic in our system, the imaginative and emotional content also.

Another definition in the *New Collegiate Dictionary* points to the identification of rhetoric not with the elements of verbal composition but with the *forms* or *genres*: "The art of expressive speech or of discourse, orig. of oratory, now esp. of literary composition; esp., the art of writing well in prose, as disting. from versification and elocution." This approach is promising and on the whole the most popular through the ages. "Originally of oratory, now especially the art of writing well in prose—" this phrase does well enough as a general description of the scope of rhetoric in ancient Greece, as Baldwin has pointed out, when prose itself was virtually defined as oratory and history, and when even history was composed largely in the spirit of oratory. That is, rhetoric could be the art of prose when prose was predominantly concerned with the intentional, directional energizing of truth, of finding in any given situation all the available means of persuasion, and of using as many of them as good sense dictated.

Even then, however, the weakness of genres as the basis for constructing theories or writing handbooks was evident. What is the art of Plato's dialogues, which are in prose? or of Sappho's compositions, which are poems? Neither poetic nor rhetoric is adequate to either. The difficulty multiplies as variety in the kinds of compositions increases in Roman, renaissance, and modern times, and as print supplements—and often supplants—speech as the medium of verbal communication. As *poetic*, the art of imitation in language, became crystallized in Roman and renaissance learning as the theory and practice of the drama (especially tragedy) and the epic; so *rhetoric*, in Quintilian's and Cicero's theory the whole operative philosophy of civil leadership, showed in practice as the art of making winning speeches in the law courts, or later in public exhibitions. The very doctrine in rhetoric of the epideictic or ceremonial speech, as I shall show later, is excellent evidence of the weakness of the types or *genres* as the basis for definition.

All these meanings of rhetoric, in spite of their limitations, contribute something to the exposition of our subject, and the pursuit of each has yielded lucrative insights into the subject, or at least into the problem. Some of them, especially rhetoric as bombast, as excessive ornamentation, and as deceit, are evidence of the falling off of rhetoricians from time to time from the broad philosophy of the art which they inherited from the founders. For a redefinition, therefore, I know no better way of beginning than to return to that broad philosophy.

WORKING DEFINITION OF RHETORIC

First of all and primarily, therefore, I take rhetoric to be the *rationale of informative and suasory discourse*. All its other meanings are partial or morally colored derivatives from that primary meaning. This rhetoric has been, at least since Aristotle; and at least since Aristotle there has existed a comprehensive, fundamental codification of its principles. It would be idolatrous to suggest that Aristotle uttered the first and last authentic words on rhetoric, or that his system is still adequate, or that it was completely satisfactory even for the Greeks of his day. Like his poetic theory, however, it enjoys unequalled scientific eminence in its field though it has sustained many additions and modifications through the centuries. Its limitations are historical rather than philosophical. Like the limitations of his poetic, the limitations of his rhetoric derive mainly from his failure to consider phenomena which had not yet occurred and to make use of learnings which had not yet been developed.

Now as then, therefore, what Aristotle said of the nature and principles of public address, of the discovery of all the available means of persuasion in any given case, must stand as the broad background for any sensible rhetorical system. Much of Aristotle's formulation, even in detail, survives ungainsaid and can only be rearranged and paraphrased by subsequent writers. Again to cite a parallel with his poetic: though the relative importance of plot in drama has shifted radically since Aristotle, when good plots are made their excellences will still be best discovered by the application of Aristotle's criteria. Similarly, though modern psychology is very different from that of the Greeks, and doubtless more scientific, modern enlightenment has produced no new method of analyzing an audience which can replace Aristotle's.

Aristotle, however, identified rhetoric with persuasion. His chief interests lay in the speaking to popular audiences in the law court and to the legislative assembly, and his system of classification and analysis obviously was framed with those types of speaking as its principal object. Some means of persuasion, however, in spite of Aristotle's comprehensive definition, are not within the scope of rhetoric. Gold and guns, for example, are certainly persuasive, and the basic motives which make them persuasive, profit and self-preservation, may enter the field of rhetoric;

but applied directly to the persons to be persuaded, guns and gold belong to commerce or coercion, not to rhetoric.

No more shall we admit the persuasive use of all symbols as belonging to rhetoric. Undoubtedly the persuasive force of pictures, colors, designs, nonlanguage sounds such as fog horns and fire alarms, and all such devices of symbolic significance is great and useful. Traffic lights, however, are not normally agents of rhetorical influence. No more, in themselves, are elephants, donkeys, lions, illuminated bottles of whiskey, or animated packs of cigarettes. Their use has a kinship to rhetoric, and when they are organized in a matrix of verbal discourse, they become what Aristotle called the extrinsic or nonartistic means of persuasion. They are instruments of the wielder of public opinion, and they are staples of two techniques which must be recognized as strongly rhetorical—advertising and propaganda. Unless we are to claim practically all interhuman activity as the field of rhetoric, however, some limits must be admitted, even within the field of persuasion. True, in the "new rhetoric" of Kenneth Burke, where the utmost extension rather than practical limit-setting is the aim, any manifestation of "identification," conscious or unconscious, is within rhetoric. Though the classic limitations of rhetoric are too narrow, others are too broad. Therefore I am assuming the traditional limitation to discourse.

Let us look now at Aristotle's apparent failure to include exposition as well as persuasion within rhetoric. Ancillary to persuasion, of course, exposition is clearly included. The idea of *demonstration*, the characteristic result of the logical mode, implies the most perfect exposition for audiences susceptible of reasoned instruction. Furthermore, another aspect of Aristotle's system admits exposition to independent status. At the expense of a slight venture into heresy (though I believe only a benign heresy) I suggest that any systematic construction of human phenomena, even Aristotle's, will either leave out something important and significant, or will include a category, however named, which is, in effect, "miscellaneous." That I think Aristotle did in discussing the rhetoric of the ceremonial or epideictic speech. The success of his categories, even so, is remarkable. The extension and effective application to the ceremonial speech in general of the principles of the persuasive speech whose end is active decision, provide very plausible coverage of that somewhat anomalous form. The threefold, tripartite classification of speeches was too nearly perfect to abandon:

Forensic (time, past; ends, justice and injustice; means, accusation and defense.)

Epideictic (time, present; ends, honor and dishonor; means, praise and blame.)

Deliberative (time, future; ends, the expedient and inexpedient; means, exhortation and dehortation.)

When the problems of what to do with time-present in the system, and with Pericles' funeral oration among the observed phenomena had to be solved, the coincidence was too attractive to be resisted. It provided for a piece of practical realism which no system should be allowed to defeat. Through that adjustment Aristotle admitted within the scope of rhetoric the predominantly literary performance on the one hand and gave an opening on the other for the primarily informative and instructional as well as the demonstative and exhibitionistic. Through this third category rhetoric embraces, in a persuasion-centered system, the *docere* and *delectare*, the teach and delight, of the Roman and renaissance rhetoric-poetic and permits them an independent status outside their strictly ancillary or instrumental functions in persuasion.

Aristotle's system, therefore, and his rationale of effective speaking comprehend with very little violence the art of the good man skilled in speaking of Cicero and Quintilian, or Baldwin's equation of rhetoric to the art of prose whose end is giving effectiveness to truth [8]—effectiveness considered in terms of what happens to an audience, usually a popular or lay audience as distinguished from the specialized or technical audience of the scientific or dialectical demonstration. This distinction, strictly speaking, is a practical rather than a logical limitation, a limitation of degree rather than kind. No matter what the audience, when the speaker evinces skill in getting into their minds, he evinces rhetorical skill.

If the breadth of scope which I have assigned to rhetoric is implicit in Aristotle's system, the basic delimitation of that scope finds early and explicit statement there. Rhetoric is not confined in application to any specific subjects which are exclusively its own. Rhetoric is method, not subject. But if it has no special subjects, neither are all subjects within its province. In its suasory phase, at least, rhetoric is concerned, said Aristotle, only with those questions about which men dispute, that is, with the contingent—that which is dependent in part upon factors which cannot be known for certain, that which can be otherwise. Men do not dispute about what is known or certainly knowable by them. Hence the characteristic concern of rhetoric is broadly with questions of justice and injustice, of the expedient and the inexpedient (of the desirable and undesirable, of the good and the bad), of praise and blame, or honor and dishonor.

To questions such as these and their almost infinite subsidiary questions, vital and perennial as they are in the practical operation of human society, the best answers can never be certain but only more or less probable. In reasoning about them, men at best must usually proceed from probable premise to probable conclusion, seldom from universal to uni-

[8] *Ancient Rhetoric and Poetic,* p. 5.

versal. Hence Aristotle described the basic instrument of rhetoric, the enthymeme, as a kind of syllogism based on probabilities and signs.

Rhetoric, therefore, is distinguished from the other instrumental studies in its preoccupation with informed opinion rather than with scientific demonstration. It is the counterpart, said Aristotle, of dialectic. Strictly speaking, dialectic also may be said to attain only probability, not scientific certainty, like physics (and, perhaps, theology). The methodology, however, is the methodology of formal logic and it deals in universals. Hence it arrives at a very high degree of probability, for it admits the debatable only in the assumption of its premises. Rhetoric, however, because it normally deals with matters of uncertainty for the benefit of popular audiences, must admit probability not only in its premises but in its method also. This is the ground upon which Plato first, and hundreds of critics since, have attacked rhetoric—that it deals with opinion rather than knowledge. This is the ground also from which certain scholars have argued,[9] after some of the mediaeval fathers, that rhetoric really deals, characteristically, not with genuine probability but only with adumbration and suggestion. It is, they say, distinguished from dialectic in *degree* of probability—dialectic very high, and rhetoric very low.

The epistemological question is interesting, and in a world of philosophers where only certain knowledge was ever called upon to decide questions of human behavior, it would be the central question. Rhetoric exists, however, because a world of certainty is not the world of human affairs. It exists because the world of human affairs is a world where there must be an alternative to certain knowledge on the one hand and pure chance or whimsey on the other. The alternative is informed opinion, the nearest approach to knowledge which the circumstances of decision in any given case will permit. The art, science, or method whose realm this is, is rhetoric. Rhetoric, therefore, is the method, the strategy, the organon of the principles for deciding best the undecidable questions, for arriving at solutions of the unsolvable problems, for instituting method in those vital phases of human activity where no method is inherent in the total subject-matter of decision. The resolving of such problems is the province of the "Good man skilled in speaking." It always has been, and it is still. Of that there can be little question. And the comprehensive rationale of the functioning of that good man so far as he is skilled in speaking, so far as he is a wielder of public opinion, is rhetoric.

[9] For example, Craig La Drière, "Rhetoric as 'Merely Verbal' Art," *English Institute Essays—1948*, edited by D. A. Robertson, Jr., pp. 123-152.

THE PROBLEMS OF VOCABULARY IN THIS ESSAY

Traditionally *rhetoric* and *oratory* have been the standard terms for the theory and the product. The *rhetor* was the speaker, the addressor of the public, or the teacher of speaking; the *rhetorician,* the teacher of rhetoric or the formulator of the principles of rhetoric. Hence the special bias of the terms as I use them has been and probably still is oral. That is a practical bias and is not carelessly to be thrown away. From the beginning of publication in writing, however, essentially rhetorical performances, whether already spoken or to be spoken, have been committed to paper and circulated to be read rather than heard—from Isocrates' *Panathenaicus* or Christ's *Sermon on the Mount* to Eisenhower's message on the state of the nation. Furthermore, for centuries now, especially since the invention and cheapening of the art of printing, the agitator, the teacher, the preacher, the wielder of public opinion has used the press quite independently of the platform. Hence, obviously, rhetoric must be understood to be the rationale of informative and suasory discourse both spoken and written: of Milton's *Aeropagitica* as well as Cromwell's Address to the Rump Parliament; of John Wilkes' *North Briton* as well as Chatham's speech on the repeal of the Stamp Act; of Tom Paine's *Common Sense* as much as Patrick Henry's Address to the Virginia Assembly; of Swift's pamphlet on the *Conduct of the Allies* as well as Dr. Sacheverell's sermon on passive obedience; of George Sokolsky's syndicated columns in the press equally with Edward R. Murrow's radio commentaries or Kenneth McFarland's appearances before conventions of the Chambers of Commerce. I will use *rhetoric* and *rhetorical* with that breadth of scope.

Furthermore, the terms *orator* and *oratory* have taken on, like *rhetoric* itself, rather limited or distorted meanings, not entirely undeserved perhaps, which make them no longer suitable for the designation of even the normal *oral* rhetorical performance. *Practitioner of public address,* or some such hyphenated monstrosity as *speaker-writer,* might be used as a generic term for the product of rhetoric, but the disadvantages of such manipulations of vocabulary are obvious. I am using the terms *speech* and *speaker* for both written and oral performance and written and oral performer, unless the particular circumstances obviously imply one or the other. Likewise, in place of such a formula as *listener-reader,* I shall use *audience,* a usage not uncommon anyway.

One must face still another problem of vocabulary, that of the term *rhetoric* in the three distinguishable senses in which I use it: (1) as the rationale of informative and suasory discourse, a body of principle and precept for the creation and analysis of speeches; (2) as a quality which characterizes that kind of discourse and distinguishes it from other kinds; (3) as a study of the phenomenon of informative and suasory discourse in the social context. Similarly, I fear, the term *rhetorician* will sometimes mean the formulator and philosopher of rhetorical theory; sometimes the teacher of the technique of discourse; sometimes the speaker with rhetorical intention; and finally the student or scholar whose concern is the literary or social or behavioral study of rhetoric. I have been tempted to invent terms to avoid certain of these ambiguities, such as *logology*, or even *rhetoristic* (parallel with *sophistic*), but the game would probably not be worth the candle.

In summary, rhetoric is the rationale of informative and suasory discourse, it operates chiefly in the areas of the contingent, its aim is the attainment of maximum probability as a basis for public decision, it is the organizing and animating principle of all subject-matters which have a relevant bearing on that decision. Now let us turn to the question of the subject-matters in which rhetoric most characteristically functions and of the relations it bears to special subject-matters.

SUBJECTS OF RHETORICAL DISCOURSE

Wrote Aristotle, "The most important subjects of general deliberation . . . are practically five, viz. finance, war and peace, the defense of the country, imports and exports, and legislation." This is still the basic list, though legislation now would be far more generally inclusive than it was to the Athenian assembly. In addition, within the scope of rhetorical discourse fall the subjects of forensic address—crime and its punishment and all the concerns of justice and injustice. Furthermore, the concerns of teaching, preaching—moral, intellectual, practical, and spiritual instruction and exhortation—and commercial exploitation, wherever the problems of adaptation of idea and information to the group mind are concerned, depend upon rhetorical skill for their fruition. Thus we are brought again to the position that the rhetorical factor is pervasive in the operative aspects of society.

Does this mean that the speaker must be a specialist in all subjects, as well as in rhetorical method? Cicero seemed willing to carry the demands thus far, at least in establishing his ideal orator; and this implication has been ridiculed from Plato onwards for the purpose of discrediting first the claims of the sophists and then all men "skilled in speaking." Plainly, in practice and in plausible human situations, the suggestion is absurd. Does the public speaker or the columnist or the agitator have to be a military specialist in order rightly to urge peace or war? Does the citizen have to be a dentist and a chemist and a pathologist intelligently to advocate the use of fluorine in the municipal water supply? He does not become a specialist in these fields, of course, any more than the head of an industrial plant is the technical master of the specialties of all the men who serve under him. "He attempts to learn the authorities and

41

sources of information in each, and to develop a method which he can apply to specific problems as they arise. He learns, in any given situation, what questions to ask and to answer. The peculiar contribution of the rhetorician is the discovery and use, to the common good, of those things which move men to [understanding and] action." [10] Looked at another way, the relation of rhetoric to the subject-matters of economics, or public health, or theology, or chemistry, or agriculture is like the relation of hydraulic engineering to water, under the specific circumstances in which the engineer is to construct his dam or his pumping station or his sewage system, and in view of the specific results he is to obtain. He develops a method for determining what questions to ask and answer from all that which can be known about water. If he is a good hydraulics engineer, he will see to it that his relevant knowledge is sound, as the good speaker will see to it that his relevant knowledge of hydraulic engineering is the best obtainable if he is to urge or oppose the building of a dam in the St. Lawrence River. If either is ignorant, or careless, or dishonest, he is culpable as a man and as a rhetorician or hydraulics engineer.

It was not the scientific chronologist, the astronomer Lord Macclesfield, who secured the adoption in England of the Gregorian calendar, thoroughly as he understood the subject in all its mathematical, astronomical, and chronometrical aspects. It was the Earl of Chesterfield, learning from the chronologist all that was essential to the particular situation, and knowing rhetoric and the British Parliament, who was able to impress upon his fellows not necessarily the validity of the calculations but the desirability and the feasibility of making a change. If the truth of scientific knowledge had been left to its own inherent force with Parliament, we would doubtless be many more days out of phase with the sun than England was in 1751. As Aristotle observed in his brief and basic justification of rhetoric, truth itself has a tendency to prevail over error; but in competition with error, where skillful men have an interest in making error prevail, truth needs the help of as attractive and revealing a setting as possible. In the Kingdom of Heaven, truth may be its own sole advocate, but it needs mighty help if it is to survive in health among the nations on earth. As Fielding wrote of prudence in *Tom Jones:* "It is not enough that your designs, nay, that your actions, are intrinsically good; you must take care that they shall appear so. If your inside be never so beautiful, you must preserve a fair outside also. This must be constantly looked to." [11]

In this sense even honest rhetoric is fundamentally concerned with appearances, not to the disregard of realities as Plato and his successors

[10] Hoyt H. Hudson, "The Field of Rhetoric," p. 28 in the present volume.
[11] Book III, Chapter 7, Modern Library Edition, p. 97.

have industriously charged, but to the enforcement of realities. Rhetoric at the command of honest men strives that what is desirable shall appear desirable, that what is vicious shall appear vicious. It intends that the true or probably true shall seem so, that the false or doubtful shall be vividly realized for what it is. A bridge or an automobile or a clothes-line must not only *be* strong but must *appear* to be so. This fact has been an obstacle to the use of many new structural materials. Accustomed to an older kind, we have been reluctant to accept the adequacy of a new, more fragile-seeming substance. Hence one important reason for surrounding steel columns with stone pillars is the necessity of making them seem as strong as their predecessors. Appearances, then, must be the concern of the wielder of public opinion, the rhetorician. Through ignorance or malice, to be sure, skill in establishing appearances may be applied to deceive. This is a grave peril which must be the concern of all men of good will. Knowledge of the devices of sophistry will always be acquired by those whose purposes are bad; ignorance of them will provide no defense for the rest. No great force can be used without hazard, or ignored without hazard. The force understood, rather than the force not understood, is likely to be the force controlled. That understanding is provided by rhetoric, the technique of discourse addressed to the enlightenment and persuasion of the generality of mankind—the basic instrument for the creation of informed public opinion and the consequent expedient public action.

OCCASIONS OF RHETORICAL DISCOURSE

Whether we will or no, we cannot escape rhetoric, either the doing or the being done to. We require it. As Edmund Burke wrote, "Men want reasons to reconcile their minds to what is done, as well as motives originally to act right." [12] Whether we seek advice or give it, the nature of our talk, as being "addressed," and the talk of which we are the audience, as being addressed to us, necessitates speaking the language of the audience or we had as well not speak at all. That process is the core of rhetoric. It goes on as genuinely, and is often managed as skillfully, over the frozen-meats counter of the local supermarket as in the halls of Congress; on the benches in front of the Boone County Court House on Saturday afternoon before election as below the benches of the Supreme Court the next Wednesday morning; around the table where a new labor contract is being negotiated as in the pulpit of Sainte-Marie de Chaillot where Bossuet is pronouncing the funeral oration upon Henriette d'Angleterre; in the petition from Yorkshire to King George III for redress of grievances as in the Communist Manifesto or the Declaration of Independence.

[12] *Correspondence*, I, p. 217.

As we are teachers, and as we are taught, we are involved with rhetoric. The success of the venture depends on a deliberate or instinctive adjustment of idea-through-speaker-to-audience-in-a-particular-situation. Pedagogy is the rhetoric of teaching, whether formally in the classroom or the book, or informally in the many incidental situations of our days and nights. The psychological principle, for example, that we learn through association becomes a rhetorical principle when we use it to connect one day's lesson with what has gone before. It is the same principle by which Burke attempted to establish in the minds of the House of Commons the rights of American colonists when he identified the colonists with Englishmen, whose rights were known.

As we are readers of newspapers and magazines and all such information-giving and opinion-forming publications, and as we write for them, we are receiving or initiating rhetorical discourse, bad or good, effective or ineffective. The obligations of the journalist as investigator of the facts, as thinker about the facts, as discoverer of ideas and analyst and critic of ideas, are fundamental. They demand all the knowledge and skill that the political, scientific, and technical studies can provide. The journalist's distinctive job, however, is writing for his audience the highest grade of informative and suasory discourse that the conditions of his medium will permit. Whether editorial writer, commentator, or plain news writer, reaching into his audience's mind is his problem. If the people who buy the paper miss the import, the paper might as well not be published. Call it *journalism* if you choose; it is the rhetoric of the press: "it is always public opinion that the press seeks to change, one way or another, directly or indirectly." [13] Seldom can the journalist wait for the solution of a problem before getting into the fray, whether the question be a more efficient way of handling municipal finances or independence for India. He must know the right questions to ask and the bases for answering them with greatest probability for his audience now. That is his rhetorical knowledge.

The same is true of the radio and television news reporter, news analyst, and commentator. He must have rhetorical skill to survive in his occupation, and he must have knowledge and integrity if his effect is to be beneficial rather than destructive to informed public opinion. His staple, also, whether good or bad, is rhetoric. His efforts are aimed at the public mind and are significant only as they affect the public mind. If he is an honest rhetorician, he does not imply of most things, "It is so because," but only "I believe so because"; or "I recommend so because it seems probable where I cannot be sure." If he is tempted into exploiting

[13] *The Press and Society: A Book of Readings*, edited by George L. Bird and Frederic E. Merwin, preface, p. iv.

the force of extravagant and authoritative assertion, his morals rather than his rhetoric have gone awry. Whether the use be honest or dishonest, the instrument is rhetoric.

It is obvious and commonplace that the agitator, the political speaker, the pamphleteer, the advocate, the preacher, the polemicist and apologist, the adviser of kings and princes, the teacher of statesmen, the reformer and counterreformer, the fanatic in religion, diet, or economics, the mountebank and messiah, have enhanced the stature of a noble discourse or have exploited a degraded shallow, and dishonest discourse. It matters not that we resort to exalted names for the one—eloquence, genius, philosophy, logic, discourse of reason; and for the other, labels of reproach and contempt—sophistry, glibness, demagoguery, chicanery, "rhetoric." That naming process itself is one of the most familiar techniques of rhetoric. The fact is that in their characteristic preoccupation with manipulating the public mind, they are one. They must not all be approved or emulated, but they must all be studied as highly significant social phenomena, lest we be ignorant of them, and hence powerless before them, for good or for ill.

Similarly, though they are perhaps not so easily acceptable, we must recognize as rhetoric most of what we know as advertising, salesmanship, propaganda, "public relations," and commercial, political, and national "information" services. I shall have some special consideration to give to these later. At present I merely cite them as great users of rhetoric. In this day of press, radio, and television perhaps their rhetoric is that most continuously and ubiquitously at work on the public.

RELATIONS OF RHETORIC TO OTHER LEARNINGS

These, then, are fundamental rhetorical situations. In them human beings are so organizing language as to effect a change in the knowledge, the understanding, the ideas, the attitudes, or the behavior of other human beings. Furthermore, they are so organizing that language as to make the change as agreeable, as easy, as active, and as secure as possible—as the Roman rhetoric had it, to teach, to delight, and to move (or to bend). What makes a situation rhetorical is the focus upon accomplishing something predetermined and directional with an audience. To that end many knowledges and sciences, concerning both what is external to audiences and what applies to audiences themselves, may be involved, many of which I have discussed in a previous essay.[14] These knowledges, however, have to be organized, managed, given places in strategy and tactics, set into coordinated and harmonious movement towards the lis-

[14] "Aspects of the Rhetorical Tradition," *Quarterly Journal of Speech*, XXXVI, 1950, pp. 169-176 and 326-332.

tener as the end, towards what happens to him and in him. In short, they have to be *put to use*, for, as Bacon said, studies themselves "teach not their own use; but that is a wisdom without them, and above them, won by observation." "Studies themselves do give forth directions too much at large, except they be bounded in by experience." [15] Rhetoric teaches their use towards a particular end. It is that "observation," that "experience" codified, given a rationale. Other learnings are chiefly concerned with the discovery of ideas and phenomena and of their relations to each other within more or less homogeneous and closed systems. Rhetoric is primarily concerned with the relations of ideas to the thoughts, feelings, motives, and behavior of men. Rhetoric as distinct from the learnings which it uses is dynamic; it is concerned with movement. It *does* rather than *is*. It is method rather than matter. It is chiefly involved with bringing about a condition, rather than discovering or testing a condition. Even psychology, which is more nearly the special province of rhetoric than is any other study, is descriptive of conditions, but not of the uses of those conditions.

So far as it is method, rhetoric is like the established procedures of experimental science and like logic. As the method for solving problems of human action in the areas of the contingent and the probable, however, it does not enjoy a privilege which is at the same time the great virtue and the great limitation of science and logic—it cannot choose its problems in accordance with the current capacities of its method, or defer them until method is equal to the task. Rhetoric will postpone decision as long as feasible; indeed one of its most valuable uses in the hands of good men is to prevent hasty and premature formulation of lines of conduct and decision. In this it is one with science—and good sense. But in human affairs, where the whole is usually greater than the most complete collection of the parts, decisions—makings up of the mind—cannot always wait until all the contingencies have been removed and solutions to problems have been tested in advance. Rhetoric, therefore, must take undemonstrable problems and do its best with them when decision is required. We must decide when the blockade is imposed whether to withdraw from Berlin or to undertake the air lift, not some time later when perhaps some of the contingencies may have been removed. And the making of the choice forever precludes trying out and testing the other possibilities under the circumstances which would have prevailed had we chosen differently at first. Likewise we must make a choice on the first Tuesday in November, whether we are scientifically sure or not. In each case, rhetoric, good or bad, must be the strategy of enlightening opinion for that choice.

[15] "Of Studies."

To restate our central idea still another way: rhetoric, or the rhetorical, is the function in human affairs which governs and gives direction to that creative activity, that process of critical analysis, and that branch of learning, which address themselves to the whole phenomenon of the designed use of language for the promulgation of information, ideas, and attitudes. Though rhetoric is instrumental in the discovery of ideas and information, its characteristic function is the publication, the publicizing, the humanizing, the animating of them for a realized and usually specific audience. At its best it seeks the "energizing of truth," in order to make "reason and the will of God prevail." But except in science, and no doubt theology, the promulgation of *truth*, sure or demonstrable, is out of the question. Normally the rhetorical function serves as high a degree of probability as the combination of subject, audience, speaker, and occasion admits. Rhetoric may or may not be involved (though the speaker-writer must be) in the determination of the validity of the ideas being promulgated. Such determination will be the province in any given situation of philosophy, ethics, physics, economics, politics, eugenics, medicine, hydraulics, or bucolics. To rhetoric, however, and to no other rationale, belongs the efficiency—the validity if you will—of the relations in the idea-audience-speaker situation.

FUNCTIONING OF RHETORIC

We are ready now, perhaps, if we were not ready much sooner, to proceed to the question of how rhetoric works, what it accomplishes in an audience. Speaking generally, we may say that the rhetorical function is the *function of adjusting ideas to people and people to ideas*. This process may be thought of as a continuum from the complete modification or accommodation of ideas to audiences (as is sometimes said, "telling people only what they want to hear") at the one extreme, to complete regeneration at the other (such perfect illumination that the "facts speak for themselves"). This continuum may, therefore, be said to have complete flattery (to use Plato's unflattering epithet) at one end and the Kingdom of Heaven at the other! Good rhetoric usually functions somewhere well in from the extremes. There, difficult and strange ideas have to be modified without being distorted or invalidated; and audiences have to be prepared through the mitigation of their prejudices, ignorance, and irrelevant sets of mind without being dispossessed of their judgments. The adjustment of ideas to people, for example, was being undertaken by the Earl of Chatham in his speech for the repeal of the Stamp Act, when he agreed that Parliament had legislative supremacy over the Colonies but that legislative supremacy did not include the right to tax without representation. And when Booker T. Washington assured the Southern white folk that they and the Negroes could be as separate as the

47

fingers in social affairs and as united as the hand in economic, he was adjusting people to the idea of real freedom for his race.

The moral disturbances which rhetoric and rhetorical activity seem to breed do not usually result from this process of mutual accommodation itself. Most of them arise when the speaker tries so to adjust ideas to people that the ideas are basically falsified, or when he attempts so to adjust people to ideas as to deform or anesthetize the people. Report has it that after Senator Hiram Johnson had campaigned through rural New England charging that England would have three votes to one for the United States in the League of Nations, he was taxed by a critic with misrepresenting the nature of the British Empire. One could not assume, so Johnson's critic declared, that Canada and South Africa would vote with England as a single bloc. "That may be" Johnson is said to have replied, "but New England farmers do not know the nature of the British Empire, and they do know common arithmetic." That is adjusting ideas to people so far as to falsify the basic idea. In the other direction, stimulating the "Red-menace-in-the-air-we-breathe" terror in order to adjust people to the idea of giving up their right of dissent is an effort to dispossess people of their judgments.

In terms of the old, but still convenient, faculty psychology, the terms in which rhetoric is most frequently attacked—reason, imagination, passions (emotions), judgment, will—rhetoric may still be described as the method of applying "reason to imagination for the better moving of the will." To complete our broad idea of the scope of rhetoric we should add "and the better clarification of the understanding." That is Francis Bacon's succinct statement of how rhetoric functions in the audience,[16] and it is still a good one. It establishes rhetoric squarely as an instrumental learning which manages the creative powers of the whole logical-psychological man toward a single dynamic end.

Rhetoric, therefore, has the greatest possible involvement with the logical and psychological studies. These learnings must be the core of the speaker's equipment. They are the *sine qua non* for the knowledge through which rhetoric must function. In the good rhetoric which Plato described in the *Phaedrus*, after knowledge of the truth, he saw the equipment of the rhetorically skilled man to consist in knowledge of the various possible kinds of arguments, knowledge of the various kinds of souls, and knowledge of which kinds of souls will be affected by which kinds of arguments—that is, knowledge of the rational processes and knowledge of the mutual adaptation of these processes to audiences. Furthermore, in the great counter-Platonic *Rhetoric* of Aristotle, the first Book

[16] From *The Advancement of Learning*. See Karl R. Wallace, *Francis Bacon on Communication and Rhetoric*, p. 27.

is devoted chiefly to the rational processes of rhetoric, and the next Book is the first extant comprehensive treatise on individual and group psychology. Likewise, in one of the best of the recent books on liberal education, which is, therefore, something like a basic statement on rhetoric, Hoyt Hudson sees the fundamental equipment of the liberally educated man to require three parts: the Arm of Information, the Arm of Operative Logic, and the Arm of Imagination.[17] Of these, in practical affairs, rhetoric is based on the second and third, and the first must be the starting place of the speaker in each particular situation.

Where in this pattern, then, does emotion come in, that famous roughneck who is said to spoil the rational life and vitiate the logic of behavior? As Hudson and many others have observed, and as Bacon knew well, emotion is a derivative of both reason and imagination. Love of truth and of the good life must be the results of any genuinely rational functioning, that is, of operative logic; and vivid realization of experience, which is imagination, can hardly occur without those strong emotional accompaniments which, in practice, have given rise to the identifying of emotion with imagination. This point seems hardly to need laboring over again. Hudson's book gives it adequate coverage, and I have summarized the traditional position of rhetoric and rhetoricians on it in the essay already mentioned.[18] The position is that a complete rhetoric, and that is the kind of rhetoric which we are discussing, knows the whole man and seeks to bring to bear the whole man in achieving its ends—what he is and what he thinks he is, what he believes and what he thinks he believes, what he wants and what he tells himself he wants. Towards its special ends, rhetoric recognizes the primacy of rational processes, their primacy in time as well as in importance, as Bacon's definition implies—applying reason to the imagination. Just so poetry recognizes the primacy for its purposes of the imagination. But rhetoric has always been akin to poetry—for long periods of history it has in fact annexed poetry—in its recognition of the honest and highly important power of imagination and of that emotion which does not supplant but supports reason, and sometimes even transcends it. Thus Sir Philip Sidney and most literary theorists of the Renaissance attributed to poetry the distinctly rhetorical function of using imagination to create what might be called historical fictions to give power and life to ideas. Rhetoric recognizes the strength of the fictions men live by, as well as those they live under;[19] and it aims to

---

[17] *Educating Liberally*, pp. 10 ff.

[18] Above, note 14.

[19] See the very relevant analysis of some of the fictions in the ideology of American business in C. Wright Mills, *White Collar*, Chapter 3, "The Rhetoric of Competition."

fortify the one and explode the other. Rhetoric aims at what is *worth* doing, what is *worth* trying. It is concerned with *values*, and values are established with the aid of imaginative realization, not through rational determination alone; and they gain their force through emotional animation.

We have observed that psychology, human nature, has been a staple of rhetorical learning through the ages. No doubt, therefore, scientific psychology will have more and more to contribute to modern rhetoric. The first notable attempt to ground rhetoric in a systematic modern psychology was made by George Campbell in his *Philosophy of Rhetoric* (1776), in which he stated as his purpose

to exhibit . . . a tolerable sketch of the human mind; and, aided by the lights which the poet and the orator so amply furnish, to disclose its secret movements, tracing its principal channels of perception and action, as near as possible, to their source: and, on the other hand, from the science of human nature, to ascertain with greater precision, the radical principles of that art, whose object it is, by the use of language, to operate on the soul of the hearer, in the way of informing, convincing, pleasing, moving, or persuading.[20]

That same purpose governs our contemporary writers of treatises and textbooks on public speaking, argumentation, and persuasion, and most of them include as up-to-date a statement as possible of the psychological and the rational bases of rhetoric. It is a commonplace that of the studies recently come to new and promising maturity, psychology, especially social psychology, and cultural anthropology have much to teach modern rhetoric and to correct or reinterpret in traditional rhetoric. The same may be said of the various new ventures into the study of meaning, under the general head of semantics. How language *means* is obviously important to the rationale of informative and suasory discourse. Nevertheless, in spite of I. A. Richards' book,[21] the theory of meaning is not *the* philosophy of rhetoric, any more than is the psychology of perception. Rhetoric is the organizer of all such for the wielding of public opinion.

ADVERTISING, SALESMANSHIP, AND PROPAGANDA

Now that we have sketched the rhetorical process functioning at its best for the exposition and dissemination of ideas in the wielding of public opinion, with the ethical and pathetic modes of proof in ancillary relation to the logical, with the imagination aiding and reinforcing the rational, let us turn to some of the partial, incomplete, perhaps misused, rhetorics which I have already mentioned briefly.

It is axiomatic that men do not live by reason alone or even predomi-

[20] 7th edition, pp. vii-viii.
[21] *The Philosophy of Rhetoric.*

nantly, though reason is such a highly prized commodity and stands in so high a repute even among the unreasoning and unreasonable, that men prefer to tell themselves and to be told that they make up their minds and determine their choices from reason and the facts. Intellectual activity, both learning and thinking, is so difficult that man tends to avoid it wherever possible. Hence education has almost always put its first efforts into cultivating the reasonable portion of the mind rather than the imaginative or emotional. Furthermore, the strength and accessibility of imaginative and emotional responses is so great in spite of education that though men seldom make effective reasonable decisions without the help of emotion, they often make, or appear to make, effective emotional decisions without the help of rational processes or the modification of reasonable consideration. Inevitably, therefore, the available reason in rhetorical situations will vary tremendously, and the assistance which imagination must provide towards the moving of the will must vary accordingly. Except in Swift's unexciting land of the Houyhnhnms, however, imagination will always be there.

Ever since men first began to weave the web of words to charm their fellows, they have known that some men can impose their wills on others through language in despite of reason. Almost as long, other men have deplored and feared this talent. If the talent were wholly a matter of divine gift and were wholly unexplainable, the only alternative to succumbing to the orator would be to kill him. In time it appeared, however, that this skill could be learned, in part at least, and could be analyzed. Thus if it were good, men could learn to develop it further; and if it were bad, they could be armed in some measure against it. Hence rhetoric, and hence the partial rhetoric of antireason and pseudo reason. And hence the appeal of such rhetorical eruptions as Aldous Huxley's total condemnation of oratory in *The Devils of Loudun*.[22] His indictment of public speakers is indeed skillful, and ought to be taken seriously. If the talent of his golden-voiced Grandiers be indeed magic, then we will have to agree that the fate of man before such wizards is hopeless. Rhetoric teaches, however, that the method and the power of this kind of discourse can be analyzed, at least in large part, and if its subtleties cannot be wholly *learned* by every ambitious speaker, the characteristics of its operation can be understood, and if understood, then controlled, for better or for worse.[23]

The oratory which Huxley would extirpate presents a rewarding ap-

[22] Pp. 18-19.

[23] Observe the tradition of rhetoric as a systematic study, summarized in my "Aspects of Rhetorical Tradition," *Quarterly Journal of Speech*, XXXVI, 1950, pp. 169-172.

proach to the rhetoric of advertising and propaganda, of which it is the historic prototype. In them the techniques of suggestion, reiteration, imaginative substitution, verbal irrelevance and indirection, and emotional and pseudological bullying have been developed beyond, one might hazard a guess, the fondest dreams of the sophists and the historic demagogues. This development does not represent a change in intention from them to our contemporaries, but an advance in knowledge and opportunity and media.

If you have a soap or a cigarette or a social order for quick, profitable sale, you do not neglect any method within your ethical system of making that sale. That is the paramount problem of the advertiser and the propagandist, and their solutions are very much alike. They are rhetorical solutions, at their best very carefully gauged to the mass audience, adapted to special audiences, and varying basically only as the initial sale or the permanent customer is the principal object. What advertising is in commerce, propaganda is in politics, especially international politics. Neither scorns reason or the likeness of reason, the rhetoric of information and logical argument, if the message and the audience seem to make that the best or only means to the sale. Neither, on the other hand, prefers that method to the shorter, quicker ways to unconsidered action. They concentrate—forcibly where possible, rhetorically where necessary—on the exclusion of competing ideas, on the short-circuiting or bypassing of informed judgment. By preference they do not seek to balance or overbalance alternative ideas or courses of action; they seek to obliterate them, to circumvent or subvert the rational processes which tend to make men weigh and consider. As Adlai Stevenson said, slogans, the common staple of advertising and propaganda, "are normally designed to get action without reflection."

That advertising should enjoy a happier reputation than propaganda in a competitive, commercial-industrial nation such as the United States, which is only just now learning the term *psychological warfare*, is not to be wondered at. We do not have a public service institution for the defensive analysis of advertising, like the Institute of Propaganda Analysis, which assumed that propaganda is something from which we must learn to protect ourselves. The ethical superiority of our advertising is no doubt a compliment to our dominant business code—and to our laws. Still, if one wishes to know what the ungoverned rhetoric of advertising can be, he may get a suggestion by listening to some of what is beamed to us from radio stations south of the border.

The kinship of advertising and salesmanship and their somewhat denatured relatives "public relations" and "promotion" to conventional public address, the established vehicle of rhetoric, may be embarrassing at times, but it must be acknowledged. The family resemblance is too strong to be ignored and too important to be denied. The omnipresence of the rhetoric of advertising, as I have suggested, gives it a standing which must be reckoned with, no matter what opinion the student of public address may hold of it. The rhetoric of public address, in this country at least, must function, whether or no, in a public mind which is steeped in the rhetoric of advertising, a rhetoric whose dominating principles must be recognized as adaptations of a portion of the fundamentals of any rhetoric. One need only compare a textbook or handbook of advertising methods with standard, conventional rhetorics—textbooks in public speaking and persuasion—especially in the handling of such topics as interest, suggestion, and motivation, to be convinced of the coincidence of method if not of philosophic outlook. Many times in adult evening classes in public speaking, have I heard speeches on the secrets of successful salesmanship, and as often have I found myself being offered a more or less competent parody of certain portions of our textbook, which for some reason the student had omitted to read. Not by mere chance, one must confess, does the nonacademic public take great interest in the four "miracle" courses to be found among the offerings of many universities—advertising, salesmanship, psychology, and effective speaking. Nor is it remarkable, though one may think it deplorable, that appearances of the officers of our national government before the mass audience of the citizens are characteristic products of the country's leading advertising agencies.

Likewise propaganda and its brother "information" borrow and refine upon certain portions of rhetoric. No doubt it serves a useful purpose to identify propaganda with the vicious forces in the modern world, with the German Government of World War I and with the Nazi and Soviet totalitarianisms of the present time. At the same time, however, it would be the better part of wisdom to recognize that most of the major techniques of this propaganda are long-known rhetorical techniques gone wrong, that propaganda is not a new invention which we have no ready equipment for combatting, let alone fumigating and using for our honorable ends. The understanding of propaganda will be founded in the understanding of rhetoric first of all, whatever else may be necessary.[24] Both Ross Scanlan and Kenneth Burke have demonstrated the enlightenment which can come from the application of rhetorical criticism to both the internal and external propaganda of the Nazis;[25] and two articles by Scanlan and Henry C. Youngerman in the first issue of *Today's Speech*

[24] See, for example, Everett L. Hunt, "Ancient Rhetoric and Modern Propaganda," *Quarterly Journal of Speech*, XXXVII, 1951, pp. 57-160.

[25] Burke, *The Philosophy of Literary Form*, pp. 191-220; Scanlan, "The Nazi Party Speaker System, I & II," *Speech Monographs*, XVI, 1949, pp. 82-97, XVII, 1950, pp. 134-148; "The Nazi Rhetorician," *Quarterly Journal of Speech*, XXXVII, 1951, pp. 430-440.

(April, 1953) are grounded on the assumption of a close kinship between rhetoric (or its corollary, "public address") and propaganda.[26] In fact, one of Scanlan's concluding statements indirectly makes both the identification and the basic distinction: "Today it is to be hoped that America will find means to match enemy propaganda in effectiveness without sacrificing the standards of morality and intellect that distinguish democracy from the totalitarian order."

RHETORIC AS A METHOD OF INQUIRY

More than once in the preceding pages I have in passing assigned to rhetoric a secondary function of the discovery of ideas, contributory to its prime function of the popularizing of ideas. That is the consequence of the division of *inventio*, the term applied in Roman rhetoric to the systematic investigative procedures by which rhetoric sought to turn up all the relevant arguments or considerations in any given situation. As part of *inventio*, for example, the elaborate doctrine of *status* was developed, through which by the application of analytical criteria it was possible to determine just what was the core, the central issue in any given case, just what had to be proved as a *sine qua non*, and where the lines of argument for proving it would lie if they were available. In general the division of *inventio* constituted a codification of the *topoi* or *places where arguments are to be found*; for instance, in *fact past, fact future, more and less, etc.* Rhetoric, thus, as we have said, provides scientific assistance to the speaker in discovering what questions to ask and how to go about answering them. It serves the speaker as laboratory procedures for analysis serve the chemist—by systematic inventory it enables him to determine with reasonable completeness what is present and what is absent in any given case.

We need not be surprised, therefore, that so useful a method tended to be incorporated into other arts and sciences where its original provenience was often forgotten. Historically, some of the studies to profit greatly from this borrowing from rhetoric have been the law, theology, logic, and poetic.[27] The polarizing of rhetoric, one of the characteristic phenomena of its history, accounts in large part for the splinter meanings and the distortions which we have seen as typical of its current and historic significance. It has been the fate of rhetoric, the residual term, to be

---

[26] "Two Views of Propaganda," pp. 13-14; "Propaganda and Public Address," pp. 15-17.

[27] See Richard McKeon, "Rhetoric in the Middle Ages," *Critics and Criticism, Ancient and Modern*, edited by R. S. Crane, pp. 260-296; and Marvin T. Herrick, "The Place of Rhetoric in Poetic Theory," *Quarterly Journal of Speech*, XXXIV, 1948, pp. 1-22.

applied to the less intellectual segments of itself, while its central operating division, *inventio*, has been appropriated by the studies and sciences which rhetoric serves.

The functions of a complete rhetoric, however, have usually been operative under whatever temporary auspices as the whole art of discourse, even as they were in the renaissance tripartite grammar-logic-rhetoric. This splintering may go so far towards specialism, however, that the investigative function of rhetoric, the method of *inventio*, may be diverted from that to which it most properly applies. This diversion may very well be the tendency today, where a complete rhetoric hardly exists as a formal discipline except in those classically oriented courses in public speaking, debate, group discussion, argumentation, and persuasion whose central focus is on *inventio*—the investigation and discovery of lines of argument and basic issues. Mostly rhetoric today survives, as we have seen, under other names and special applications in those specialties which contribute to it or draw upon it or appropriate selectively from its store of method— psychology, advertising, salesmanship, propaganda analysis, public opinion and social control, semantics, and that which is loosely called "research" in common parlance.

May I attempt in summary of this matter to bring rhetoric back to its essential investigative function, its function of discovery, by quoting from Isocrates, the Athenian politico-rhetorical philosopher, and from Edmund Burke, the eighteenth-century British statesman-orator? Wrote Isocrates in the *Antidosis*, "With this faculty we both contend against others on matters that are open to dispute and seek light for ourselves on things which are unknown; for the same arguments which we use in persuading others when we speak in public, we employ when we deliberate in our thoughts." [28] Twenty-two centuries later the young Burke included in his notebook digest of the topics of rhetoric, which he headed "How to Argue," the following succinct, Baconian statement about the functions of *inventio*:

To invent Arguments without a thorough knowledge of the Subject is clearly impossible. But the Art of Invention does two things—
1. It suggests to us more readily those Parts of our actual knowledge which may help towards illustrating the matter before us, &
2. It suggests to us heads of Examination which may lead, if pursued with effect into a knowledge of the Subject.
So that the Art of Invention may properly be considered as the method of calling up what we do know, & investigating that of which we are ignorant.[29]

[28] *Isocrates*, trans. George Norlin, II, p. 327.

[29] From an original manuscript among the Wentworth-Fitzwilliam papers in the Sheffield City Library, used with the kind permission of Earl Fitzwilliam and the trustees of the Fitzwilliam settled estates.

RHETORIC IN EDUCATION

If the burden of the preceding pages is not misplaced, the importance of rhetoric in the equipment of the well-educated member of society can hardly be in doubt. I am not inclined, therefore, especially in this article, to offer to demonstrate the desirability of speech as an academic study. Our conventions and our journals have been full of such demonstration for, lo, these thirty years.[30] If enlightened and responsible leaders with rhetorical knowledge and skill are not trained and nurtured, irresponsible demagogues will monopolize the power of rhetoric, will have things to themselves. If talk rather than take is to settle the course of our society, if ballots instead of bullets are to effect our choice of governors, if discourse rather than coercion is to prevail in the conduct of human affairs, it would seem like arrant folly to trust to chance that the right people shall be equipped offensively and defensively with a sound rationale of informative and suasory discourse.

In general education, especially, rhetoric would appear to deserve a place of uncommon importance. That is the burden of a recent article by Dean Hunt of Swarthmore. Rhetoric is the organon of the liberal studies, the formulation of the principles through which the educated man, the possessor of many specialties, attains effectiveness in society.[31] A complete rhetoric is a structure for the wholeness of the effective man, the aim of general education. But, as Dean Hunt concludes, the rhetorician himself must not become a technical specialist:

> He will keep his wholeness if he comes back again and again to Aristotle, but he must supplement those conceptions with what modern scientists have added to the mirror for man; he must illuminate the classical rhetoric with psychology, cultural anthropology, linguistics and semantics, special disciplines, perhaps, but disciplines in which he can lean heavily on interpreters who speak to others than their professional colleagues. Departments of speech which have emphasized training in rhetoric have a new opportunity to establish their place in general education. Their very claim to wholeness has been a source of distrust in an atmosphere of specialism. If now they can relate themselves to newer conceptions in the sciences, social sciences, and humanities, they can show that the ideal of the good man skilled in speaking is like the sea, ever changing and ever the same.[32]

So much for rhetoric in education as a study directed at the creation and at the analysis and criticism of informative and suasory discourse—at

[30] See, for example, one of the latest, W. N. Brigance, "General Education in an Industrial Free Society," *Quarterly Journal of Speech*, XXXVIII, 1952, esp. p. 181.

[31] "Rhetoric and General Education," *Quarterly Journal of Speech*, XXXV, 1949, pp. 275, 277.

[32] *Ibid.*, p. 279.

the ability, on the one hand, "to summon thought quickly and use it forcibly," [33] and on the other to listen or read critically with the maximum application of analytical judgment.

Rhetoric would appear thus to be in certain senses a literary study, or as Wichelns wrote, at least "its tools are those of literature." It is a literary study as it is involved in the creative arts of language, of informing ideas. It is a literary study also as it contributes substantially to literary scholarship. Not only have literature and literary theory been persistently rhetorical for long periods—during much of the Renaissance, for example, the seventeenth and eighteenth centuries in England, and for most of the short history of American literature—but writers and readers until fairly recently had been so generally educated in rhetoric that it provided the vocabulary and many of the concepts in terms of which much literature was both written and read. Clark's *Milton at St. Paul's School* may be cited as one conclusive demonstration of the importance of rhetoric in renaissance education and its importance in renaissance literature. This importance is now being recognized by literary scholars, and rhetoric is taking on considerable proportions in their studies, especially among those who are studying the Renaissance. Myrick's study of Sir Philip Sidney as a literary craftsman,[34] for example, demonstrates how thoroughly Sidney was schooled in rhetoric and how carefully he constructed his defense of poetry on familiar rhetorical principles. If Myrick has been in error in his construction of the specific genealogy of Sidney's rhetoric, the fact of Sidney's rhetorical system is nevertheless in no doubt.

The plain truth is that whatever the inadequacies in specific cases of the analytical method ingrained in our educated ancestors, they *had* method, the method of formal rhetoric; whereas a general characteristic of our contemporary education is that it inculcates *no* method beyond a rather uncertain grammar and a few rules of paragraphing and bibliography. Rigidity of method is doubtless a grievous obstacle to the greatest fulfillment of genius in either belles-lettres or public address; but the widespread impotence and ineptitude even of our best-educated fellows when faced with the problem of constructing or analyzing any but the most rudimentary expository or argumentative discourse, much less a complicated literary work, are surely worse. Rhetoric supplies the equipment for such practical endeavor in the promulgation of ideas, and twenty centuries have learned to use it to supplement and perfect chance and natural instinct.

[33] Herbert A. Wichelns, "Public Speaking and Dramatic Arts," in *On Going to College: A Symposium*, p. 240.

[34] Kenneth O. Myrick, *Sir Philip Sidney as a Literary Craftsman*.

That such method has at times become sterile or mechanical, that at other times it has been put to uses for which it was least adapted is amusing, perhaps lamentable, but not surprising. The remote uses to which rhetorical methods of analysis and description have been put, in the absence of a more appropriate method, are well illustrated by the following passage from Sir John Hawkins' *History of Music*, first published in the late eighteenth century:

The art of invention is made one of the heads among the precepts of rhetoric, to which music in this and sundry instances bears a near resemblance; the end of persuasion, or affecting the passions being common to both. This faculty consists in the enumeration of common places, which are revolved over in the mind, and requires both an ample store of knowledge in the subject upon which it is exercised, and a power of applying that knowledge as occasion may require. It differs from memory in this respect, that whereas memory does but recall to the mind the images or remembrance of things as they were first perceived, the faculty of invention divides complex ideas into those whereof they are composed, and recommends them again after different fashions, thereby creating variety of new objects and conceptions. Now, the greater the fund of knowledge above spoken of is, the greater is the source from whence the invention of the artist or composer is supplied; and the benefits thereof are seen in new combinations and phrases, capable of variety and permutation without end.[35]

From its lapses and wanderings, however, rhetoric when needed has almost always recovered its vitality and comprehensive scope, by reference to its classic sources. But that it should be ignored seems, as Dean Hunt suggests, hardly a compliment to education.

Rhetoric as a serious scholarly study I have treated in my former essay, and I shall not go over the same ground again. That there is a body of philosophy and principle worth scholarly effort in discovery, enlargement, and reinterpretation is beyond question, and fortunately more competent scholars each year are working at it. Rhetorical criticism and the study of rhetoric as a revealing social and cultural phenomenon are also gaining ground. New and interesting directions for research in these areas are being explored, or at least marked out; they are based on newly developed techniques and hitherto neglected kinds of data. One might mention, for example, those new approaches listed by Maloney: [36] the quantitative content analysis as developed by Lasswell; the qualitative content analysis as used by Lowenthal and Guterman; figurative analysis such as applied to Shakespeare by Caroline Spurgeon; and intonational analysis. Extensive and provocative suggestions are to be found in quantity in the text and bibliography of Brembeck and Howell's *Persuasion: A Means of Social Control*, especially in Part VI. Lucrative also are the new attempts at the analysis of the rhetoric of historical movements, such as Griffin's

---

[35] I, p. xxv.

[36] "Some New Directions in Rhetorical Criticism," *Central States Speech Journal*, IV, 1953, pp. 1-5.

study of the rhetoric of the anti-masonic movement and others under way within the Speech Association of America. Thonssen's review of recent rhetorical studies illustrates amply both the new and the traditional in rhetorical scholarship; and the section on rhetoric in the annual Haberman bibliography is convincing evidence of the vitality of current enterprise.[37]

Though new avenues, new techniques, new materials such as the foregoing are inviting to the increasing numbers of scholars whose interests and abilities—to say nothing of their necessities—lie in rhetorical research, especially those new directions which lead to rhetoric as a cultural, a sociological, a social-psychiatric phenomenon, the older literary-historical-political studies are still neither too complete nor too good. In any event, each new generation probably needs to interpret afresh much of the relevant history of thought, especially the thought of the people as distinguished from what is commonly considered the history of ideas. For this the scholarship of rhetoric seems particularly adapted. Towards this purpose, I find no need to relocate the field of rhetorical scholarship as envisioned by Hudson and Wichelns, nor to recant from the considerations which I outlined in the *Quarterly Journal of Speech* in 1937.[38] One may find it reassuring to observe, however, that much which was asked for in those essays has since then been undertaken and often accomplished with considerable success. Especially is this true of the study of public address in its bulk and day-to-day manifestations: in the movement studies, the "case" studies, the sectional and regional studies, the studies of "debates" and "campaigns" such as the debates on the League of Nations and the campaigns for conservation.

There remains much to do, nevertheless, and much to re-do in the more familiar and conventional areas of research and interpretation. The editing and translation of rhetorical texts is still far from complete or adequate. The canon of ancient rhetoric is, to be sure, in very good shape, and when Caplan's translation of the *Ad Herennium* is published in the Loeb Library there will hardly be a major deficiency. In post-classical, mediaeval, and renaissance rhetoric the situation is not so good, though it is improving. There are still too few works like Howell's *Rhetoric of Alcuin and Charlemagne* and Sister Therese Sullivan's commentary on and translation of the fourth book of St. Augustine's *De Doctrina*. Halm's *Rhetores Minores*, for example, is substantially unmolested so far.

English and continental rhetoric of the sixteenth, seventeenth, and

---

[37] Lester Thonssen, "Recent Literature in Rhetoric," *Quarterly Journal of Speech*, XXXIX, 1953, pp. 501-505; "A Bibliography of Rhetoric and Public Address," edited by F. W. Haberman, formerly appearing in the *Quarterly Journal of Speech*, latterly in *Speech Monographs*.

[38] See above, note 1.

eighteenth centuries is slowly appearing in modern editions by scholars who know rhetoric as the theory of public address. Our bibliographies show increasing numbers of these as doctoral dissertations, most of which, alas, seem to be abandoned almost as soon as finished. Only a few works of the sort, like Howell's *Fénelon*, represent mature, published work.

In the history and historical analysis of rhetoric, nothing of adequate range and scope yet exists. Thonssen and Baird's *Speech Criticism*, ambitious as it is, is only a beginning. The general history of rhetoric, and even most of the special histories, have yet to be written. Works now under way by Donald L. Clark and Wilbur S. Howell will make substantial contributions, but rhetoric from Corax to Whately needs far fuller and better treatment than it gets in the series of histories of criticism by the late J. W. H. Atkins.

Towards the study of the rhetorical principles and practice of individual speakers and writers the major part of our scholarly effort seems to have been directed. The convenience of this kind of study is beyond question and is hard to resist, either in public address or in literature. And this is as it should be. The tendency to write biographies of speakers, however, rather than rhetorico-critical studies of them, must be kept in check, or at least in proportion. Again for reasons of convenience, if not also of scholarly nationalism, the studies of American speakers are proportionately too numerous. British and foreign public address is still far too scantily noticed by competent rhetorical scholars.

RHETORIC AND POETIC

This would not be the place, I think, for a survey of rhetorical scholarship. The preceding paragraphs are intended only as a token of decent respect to accomplishment and progress in a discrete and important branch of humane scholarship. A further area where rhetorical scholarship may be very profitably pursued, however, perhaps deserves some special consideration.

Even if it were not for the contributions of Kenneth Burke, the study of rhetoric in literature and of the relation of the theory of rhetoric to the theory of poetic would be taking on renewed importance at the present time. The lively revival of rhetorical study in renaissance scholarship which I have mentioned is only one phase of the problem. A renewed or increased interest in satire, deriving in part, perhaps, from the excellent work which of late has been done on Swift, leads directly to rhetoric. The rhetorical mode is obviously at the center of satire, and any fundamental analysis of satire must depend upon the equipment of rhetorical analysis. Likewise a complete dramatic criticism must draw upon rhetoric, both practically and philosophically. The internal rhetoric of the drama was specifically recognized by Aristotle when he referred readers of the *Poetics* to the *Rhetoric* for coverage of the element of *dianoia,* for the analysis of speeches in which agents try to convince or persuade each other. What, however, is the external rhetoric of the drama? What is the drama intended to do to an audience? Herein lies the question of the province of poetic as opposed to the province of rhetoric. When Antony addresses the Roman citizens in *Julius Caesar,* the existence of an internal rhetoric in the play is clear enough; the relation between Antony and his stage audience is unmistakably rhetorical. But what of the relation between Antony and the audience in the pit, or the Antony-stage-audience combination and the audience in the pit? The more we speculate about the effect of a play or any literary work on an audience, the more we become involved in metaphysical questions in which rhetoric must be involved.

Much contemporary poetry or pseudo poetry in any generation is rhetorical in the most obvious sense—in the same sense as the epideictic oration. It "pleases" largely by rhetorical means or methods. It "reminds" us of experience instead of "organizing" or "creating" experience. It appeals to our satisfaction with what we are used to; it convinces us that what *was* still may be as it was, that old formulas are pleasantest if not best. It is not so much concerned with pointing up the old elements in the new, even, as establishing the identity of the old and the contemporary. "What oft was thought, but ne'er so well expressed" is a distinctly rhetorical attainment, and it would not have occurred to Pope to suppose that the poetic and the rhetorical were antithetical, if indeed they were separable. Though sporadically the effort of critics and theorists has been to keep *rhetoric* and *poetic* apart, the two rationales have had an irresistible tendency to come together, and their similarities may well be more important than their differences. When the forming of attitude is admitted into the province of rhetoric, then, to Kenneth Burke, rhetoric becomes a method for the analysis of even lyric poetry. Hence a frequent term in certain kinds of literary analysis now is *poetic-rhetoric,* as for example in the first two sentences in Ruth Wallerstein's analysis of two elegies: "I want this paper to consider two poems, John Donne's elegy on Prince Henry and Milton's *Lycidas,* in the light that is shed on them by seventeenth-century rhetoric-poetic as I understand it. Both the significance of that rhetoric and the test of my view of it will reside in its power to illuminate the poems." [39]

Undoubtedly there are basic differences between *poetic* and *rhetoric,* both practical and philosophical, and probably these differences lie both in the kind of method which is the proper concern of each and the kind

[39] "Rhetoric in the English Renaissance: Two Elegies," *English Institute Essays, 1948,* p. 153.

61

of effect on audiences to the study of which each is devoted. The purely poetic seeks the creation or organization of imaginative experience, probably providing for reader or audience some kind of satisfying spiritual or emotional therapy. The rhetorical seeks a predetermined channeling of the audience's understanding or attitude. Poetry works by representation; rhetoric by instigation. The poetic is fulfilled in creation, the rhetorical in illumination. "An image," wrote Longinus, "has one purpose with the orators and another with the poets; . . . the design of the poetic image is enthralment; of the rhetorical, vivid description. Both, however, seek to stir the passions and the emotions. . . . In oratorical imagery its best feature is always reality and truth." [40] Poetry, declared Sir Philip Sidney, cannot lie because it affirms nothing; it merely presents. Rhetoric not only presents but affirms. That is its characteristic. Both poetic and rhetoric attain their effects through language. If the poet's highest skill lies in his power to make language do what it has never done before, to force from words and the conjunction of words meanings which are new and unique, perhaps it is the highest skill of the speaker to use words in their accepted senses in such a way as to make them carry their traditional meanings with a vividness and effectiveness which they have never known before.

SUMMARY

In brief we may assign to rhetoric a fourfold status. So far as it is concerned with the management of discourse in specific situations for practical purposes it is an instrumental discipline. It is a literary study, involving linguistics, critical theory, and semantics as it touches the art of informing ideas and the functioning of language. It is a philosophical study so far as it is concerned with a method of investigation or inquiry. And finally, as it is akin to politics, drawing upon psychology and sociology, rhetoric is a social study, the study of a major force in the behavior of men in society.

[40] Translated by Rhys Roberts, sec. 15.

RICHARD M. WEAVER

THE PHAEDRUS AND THE
NATURE OF RHETORIC

Our subject begins with the threshold difficulty of defining the question which Plato's *Phaedrus* was meant to answer. Students of this justly celebrated dialogue have felt uncertain of its unity of theme, and the tendency has been to designate it broadly as a discussion of the ethical and the beautiful. The explicit topics of the dialogue are, in order: love, the soul, speechmaking, and the spoken and written word, or what is generally termed by us "composition." The development looks random, and some of the most interesting passages appear *jeux d'esprit*. The richness of the literary art diverts attention from the substance of the argument.

But a work of art which touches on many profound problems justifies more than one kind of reading. Our difficulty with the *Phaedrus* may be that our interpretation has been too literal and too topical. If we will bring to the reading of it even a portion of that imagination which Plato habitually exercised, we should perceive surely enough that it is consistently, and from beginning to end, about one thing, which is the nature of rhetoric.[1] Again, that point may have been missed because most readers conceive rhetoric to be a system of artifice rather than an idea,[2] and the *Phaedrus*, for all its apparent divagation, keeps very close to a single idea. A study of its rhetorical structure, especially, may give us the insight which has been withheld, while making us feel anew that Plato possessed the deepest divining rod among the ancients.

For the imaginative interpretation which we shall now undertake, we have both general and specific warrant. First, it scarcely needs pointing out that a Socratic dialogue is in itself an example of transcendence. Beginning with something simple and topical, it passes to more general levels of application; and not infrequently, it must make the leap into

[1] Cf. A. E. Taylor, *Plato: the Man and his Works*, p. 300.
[2] Cf. P. Albert Duhamel, "The Concept of Rhetoric as Effective Expression," reprinted as Chapter 4 of this volume, *passim*.

allegory for the final utterance. This means, of course, that a Socratic dialogue may be about its subject implicitly as well as explicitly. The implicit rendering is usually through some kind of figuration because it is the nature of this meaning to be ineffable in any other way. It is necessary, therefore, to be alert for what takes place through the analogical mode.

Second, it is a matter of curious interest that a warning against literal reading occurs at an early stage of the *Phaedrus*. Here in the opening pages, appearing as if to set the key of the theme, comes an allusion to the myth of Boreas and Oreithyia. On the very spot where the dialogue begins, Boreas is said to have carried off the maiden. Does Socrates believe that this tale is really true? Or is he in favor of a scientific explanation of what the myth alleges? Athens had scientific experts, and the scientific explanation was that the north wind had pushed her off some rocks where she was playing with a companion. In this way the poetical story is provided with a factual basis. The answer of Socrates is that many tales are open to this kind of rationalization, but that the result is tedious and actually irrelevant. It is irrelevant because our chief concern is with the nature of the man, and it is beside the point to probe into such matters while we are yet ignorant of ourselves. The scientific criticism of Greek mythology, which may be likened to the scientific criticism of the myths of the Bible in our own day, produces at best "a boorish sort of wisdom (ἀγροίκῳ τινὶ σοφίᾳ)." It is a limitation to suppose that the truth of the story lies in its historicity. The "boorish sort of wisdom" seeks to supplant poetic allegation with fact, just as an archaeologist might look for the foundations of the Garden of Eden. But while this sort of search goes on the truth flies off, on wings of imagination, and is not recoverable until the searcher attains a higher level of pursuit. Socrates is satisfied with the parable, and we infer from numerous other passages that he believed that some things are best told by parable and some perhaps discoverable only by parable. Real investigation goes forward with the help of analogy. "Freud without Sophocles is unthinkable," a modern writer has said.[3]

With these precepts in mind, we turn to that part of the *Phaedrus* which has proved most puzzling: why is so much said about the absurd relationship of the lover and the nonlover? Socrates encounters Phaedrus outside the city wall. The latter has just come from hearing a discourse by Lysias which enchanted him with its eloquence. He is prevailed upon to repeat this discourse, and the two seek out a shady spot on the banks of the Ilissus. Now the discourse is remarkable because although it was "in a way, a love speech," its argument was that people should grant favors to nonlovers rather than to lovers. "This is just the clever thing

[3] James Blish, "Rituals on Ezra Pound," *Sewanee Review*, LVIII, 1950, p. 223.

about it," Phaedrus remarks. People are in the habit of preferring their lovers, but it is much more intelligent, as the argument of Lysias runs, to prefer a nonlover. Accordingly, the first major topic of the dialogue is a eulogy of the nonlover. The speech provides good subject matter for jesting on the part of Socrates, and looks like another exhibition of the childlike ingeniousness which gives the Greeks their charm. Is it merely a piece of literary trifling? Rather, it is Plato's dramatistic presentation of a major thesis. Beneath the surface of repartee and mock seriousness, he is asking whether we ought to prefer a neuter form of speech to the kind which is ever getting us aroused over things and provoking an expense of spirit.

Sophistications of theory cannot obscure the truth that there are but three ways for language to affect us. It can move us toward what is good; it can move us toward what is evil; or it can, in hypothetical third place, fail to move us at all.[4] Of course there are numberless degrees of effect under the first two heads, and the third, as will be shown, is an approximate rather than an absolute zero of effect. But any utterance is a major assumption of responsibility, and the assumption that one can avoid that responsibility by doing something to language itself is one of the chief considerations of the *Phaedrus*, just as it is of contemporary semantic theory. What Plato has succeeded in doing in this dialogue, whether by a remarkably effaced design, or unconsciously through the formal pressure of his conception, is to give us embodiments of the three types of discourse. These are respectively the nonlover, the evil lover, and the noble lover. We shall take up these figures in their sequence and show their relevance to the problem of language.

The eulogy of the nonlover in the speech of Lysias, as we hear it repeated to Socrates, stresses the fact that the nonlover follows a policy of enlightened self-interest. First of all, the nonlover does not neglect his affairs or commit extreme acts under the influence of passion. Since he acts from calculation, he never has occasion for remorse. No one ever says of him that he is not in his right mind, because all of his acts are within prudential bounds. The first point is, in sum, that the nonlover never sacrifices himself and therefore never feels the vexation which overtakes lovers when they recover from their passion and try to balance their pains with their profit. And the nonlover is constant whereas the lover is inconstant. The first argument then is that the nonlover demonstrates his superiority through prudence and objectivity. The second point of superiority found in nonlovers is that there are many more of them. If one is limited in one's choice to one's lovers, the range is small; but as there are

---

[4] The various aesthetic approaches to language offer refinements of perception, but all of them can be finally subsumed under the first head above.

always more nonlovers than lovers, one has a better chance in choosing among many of finding something worthy of one's affection. A third point of superiority is that association with the nonlover does not excite public comment. If one is seen going about with the object of one's love, one is likely to provoke gossip; but when one is seen conversing with the non-lover, people merely realize that "everybody must converse with some-body." Therefore this kind of relationship does not affect one's public standing, and one is not disturbed by what the neighbors are saying. Finally, nonlovers are not jealous of one's associates. Accordingly they do not try to keep one from companions of intellect or wealth for fear that they may be outshone themselves. The lover, by contrast, tries to draw his beloved away from such companionship and so deprives him of im-proving associations. The argument is concluded with a generalization that one ought to grant favors not to the needy or the importunate, but to those who are able to repay. Such is the favorable account of the nonlover given by Lysias.

We must now observe how these points of superiority correspond to those of "semantically purified" speech. By "semantically purified speech" we mean the kind of speech approaching pure notation in the respect that it communicates abstract intelligence without impulsion. It is a simple instrumentality, showing no affection for the object of its symbolizing and incapable of inducing bias in the hearer. In its ideal conception, it would have less power to move than $2 + 2 = 4$, since it is generally ad-mitted that mathematical equations may have the beauty of elegance and, hence, are not above suspicion where beauty is suspect. But this neuter language will be an unqualified medium of transmission of meanings from mind to mind, and by virtue of it minds can remain in an unprejudiced relationship to the world and also to other minds.

Since the characteristic of this language is absence of anything like affection, it exhibits toward the thing being represented merely a sober fidelity, like that of the nonlover toward his companion. Instead of pas-sion, it offers the serviceability of objectivity. Its "enlightened self-inter-est" takes the form of an unvarying accuracy and regularity in its symbolic references, most, if not all, of which will be to verifiable data in the extra-mental world. Like a thrifty burgher, it has no romanticism about it; and it distrusts any departure from the literal and prosaic. The burgher has his feet on the ground; and similarly the language of pure notation has its point-by-point contact with objective reality. As Stuart Chase, one of its modern proponents, says in *The Tyranny of Words*: "*If we wish to understand the world and ourselves, it follows that we should use a lan-guage whose structure corresponds to physical structure*" [5] (italics his). So

---

[5] *The Tyranny of Words*, p. 80. T. H. Huxley in *Lay Sermons*, p. 112, outlined a noticeably similar ideal of scientific communication: "Therefore, the great

66

this language is married to the world, and its marital fidelity contrasts with the extravagances of other languages.

In second place, this language is far more "available." Whereas rhetorical language, or language which would persuade, must always be particularized to suit the occasion, drawing its effectiveness from many small nuances, a "utility" language is very general and one has no difficulty putting his meaning into it if he is satisfied with a paraphrase of that meaning. The 850 words recommended for Basic English, for example, are highly available in the sense that all native users of English have them instantly ready and learners of English can quickly acquire them. It soon becomes apparent, however, that the availability is a heavy tax upon all other qualities. Most of what we admire as energy and fullness tends to disappear when mere verbal counters are used. The conventional or public aspect of language can encroach upon the suggestive or symbolical aspect, until the naming is vague or blurred. In proportion as the medium is conventional in the widest sense and avoids all individualizing, personalizing, and heightening terms, it is common, and the commonness constitutes the negative virtue ascribed to the nonlover.

Finally, with reference to the third qualification of the nonlover, it is true that neuter language does not excite public opinion. This fact follows from its character outlined above. Rhetorical language on the other hand, for whatever purpose used, excites interest and with it either pleasure or alarm. People listen instinctively to the man whose speech betrays inclination. It does not matter what the inclination is toward, but we may say that the greater the degree of inclination, the greater the curiosity or response. Hence a "style" in speech always causes one to be a marked man, and the public may not be so much impressed—at least initially—by what the man is for or against as by the fact that he has a style. The way therefore to avoid public comment is to avoid the speech of affection and to use that of business, since, to echo the original proposition of Lysias, everybody knows that one must do business with others. From another standpoint, then, this is the language of prudence. These are the features which give neuter discourse an appeal to those who expect a scientific solution of human problems.

In summing up the trend of meaning, we note that Lysias has been praising a disinterested kind of relationship which avoids all excesses and irrationalities, all the dementia of love. It is a circumspect kind of relationship, which is preferred by all men who wish to do well in the world

business of the scientific teacher is, to imprint the fundamental, irrefragable facts of his science, not only by words upon the mind, but by sensible impressions upon the eye, and ear, and touch of the student in so complete a manner, that every term used, or law enunciated should afterwards call up vivid images of the particular structural, or other, facts which furnished the demonstration of the law, or illustration of the term."

and avoid tempestuous courses. We have compared its detachment with the kind of abstraction to be found in scientific notation. But as an earnest of what is to come let us note, in taking leave of this part, that Phaedrus expresses admiration for the eloquence, especially of diction, with which the suit of the nonlover has been urged. This is our warning of the dilemma of the nonlover.

Now we turn to the second major speech of the dialogue, which is made by Socrates. Notwithstanding Phaedrus' enthusiastic praise, Socrates is dissatisfied with the speech of the nonlover. He remembers having heard wiser things on the subject and feels that he can make a speech on the same theme "different from this and quite as good." After some playful exchange, Socrates launches upon his own abuse of love, which centers on the point that the lover is an exploiter. Love (ἔρως) is defined as the kind of desire which overcomes rational opinion and moves toward the enjoyment of personal or bodily beauty. The lover wishes to make the object of his passion as pleasing to himself as possible; but to those possessed by this frenzy, only that which is subject to their will is pleasant. Accordingly, everything which is opposed, or is equal or better, the lover views with hostility. He naturally therefore tries to make the beloved inferior to himself in every respect. He is pleased if the beloved has intellectual limitations because they have the effect of making him manageable. For a similar reason he tries to keep him away from all influences which might make a man of him, and of course the greatest of these is divine philosophy. While he is working to keep him intellectually immature, he works also to keep him weak and effeminate, with such harmful result that the beloved is unable to play a man's part in crises. The lover is, moreover, jealous of the possession of property because this gives the beloved an independence which he does not wish him to have. Thus the lover in exercising an unremitting compulsion over the beloved deprives him of all praiseworthy qualities, and this is the price the beloved pays for accepting a lover who is "necessarily without reason." In brief, the lover is not motivated by benevolence toward the beloved, but by selfish appetite; and Socrates can aptly close with the quotation: "As wolves love lambs, so lovers love their loves." The speech is on the single theme of exploitation. It is important for us to keep in mind the object of love as here described, because another kind of love with a different object is later introduced into the dialogue, and we shall discuss the counterpart of each.

As we look now for the parallel in language, we find ourselves confronting the second of the three alternatives: speech which influences us in the direction of what is evil. This we shall call base rhetoric because its end is the exploitation which Socrates has been condemning. We find that base rhetoric hates that which is opposed, or is equal or better because all such things are impediments to its will, and in the last analysis it knows only its will. Truth is the stubborn, objective restraint which this will endeavors to overcome. Base rhetoric is therefore always trying to keep its objects from the support which personal courage, noble associations, and divine philosophy provide a man.

The base rhetorician, we may say, is a man who has yielded to the wrong aspects of existence. He has allowed himself to succumb to the sights and shows, to the physical pleasures which conspire against noble life. He knows that the only way he can get a following in his pursuits (and a following seems necessary to maximum enjoyment of the pursuits) is to work against the true understanding of his followers. Consequently the things which would elevate he keeps out of sight, and the things with which he surrounds his "beloved" are those which minister immediately to desire. The beloved is thus emasculated in understanding in order that the lover may have his way. Or as Socrates expresses it, the selfish lover contrives things so that the beloved will be "most agreeable to him and most harmful to himself."

Examples of this kind of contrivance occur on every hand in the impassioned language of journalism and political pleading. In the world of affairs which these seek to influence, the many are kept in a state of pupillage so that they will be most docile to their "lovers." The techniques of the base lover, especially as exemplified in modern journalism, would make a long catalogue, but in general it is accurate to say that he seeks to keep the understanding in a passive state by never permitting an honest examination of alternatives. Nothing is more feared by him than a true dialectic, for this not only endangers his favored alternative, but also gives the "beloved"—how clearly here are these the "lambs" of Socrates' figure —some training in intellectual independence. What he does therefore is dress up one alternative in all the cheap finery of immediate hopes and fears, knowing that if he can thus prevent a masculine exercise of imagination and will, he can have his way. By discussing only one side of an issue, by mentioning cause without consequence or consequence without cause, acts without agents or agents without agency,[6] he often successfully blocks definition and cause-and-effect reasoning. In this way his choices are arrayed in such meretricious images that one can quickly infer the juvenile mind which they would attract. Of course the base rhetorician today, with his vastly augmented power of propagation, has means of deluding which no ancient rhetor in forum or market place could have imagined.

Because Socrates has now made a speech against love, representing it as an evil, the nonlover seems to survive in estimation. We observe, however, that the nonlover, instead of being celebrated, is disposed of

[6] That is, by mentioning only parts of the total situation.

dialectically. "So, in a word, I say that the nonlover possesses all the advantages that are opposed to the disadvantages we found in the lover." This is not without bearing upon the subject matter of the important third speech, to which we now turn.

At this point in the dialogue, Socrates is warned by his monitory spirit that he has been engaging in a defamation of love despite the fact that love is a divinity. "If love is, as indeed he is, a god or something divine, he can be nothing evil; but the two speeches just now said that he was evil." These discourses were then an impiety—one representing nonlove as admirable and the other attacking love as base. Socrates resolves to make amends, and the recantation which follows is one of the most elaborate developments in the Platonic system. The account of love which emerges from this new position may be summarized as follows.

Love is often censured as a form of madness, yet not all madness is evil. There is a madness which is simple degeneracy, but on the other hand there are kinds of madness which are really forms of inspiration, from which come the greatest gifts conferred on man. Prophecy is a kind of madness, and so too is poetry. "The poetry of the sane man vanishes into nothingness before that of the inspired madman." Mere sanity, which is of human origin, is inferior to that madness which is inspired by the gods and which is a condition for the highest kind of achievement. In this category goes the madness of the true lover. His is a generous state which confers blessings, ignoring the self, whereas the conduct of the nonlover displays all the selfishness of business: "the affection of the nonlover, which is alloyed with mortal prudence and follows mortal and parsimonious rules of conduct, will beget in the beloved soul the narrowness which common folk praise as virtue; it will cause the soul to be a wanderer upon the earth for nine thousand years and a fool below the earth at last." It is the vulgar who do not realize that the madness of the noble lover is an inspired madness because he has his thoughts turned toward a beauty of divine origin.

Now the attitude of the noble lover toward the beloved is in direct contrast with that of the evil lover, who, as we have seen, strives to possess and victimize the object of his affections. For once the noble lover has mastered the conflict within his own soul by conquering appetite and fixing his attention upon the intelligible and the divine, he conceives an exalted attitude toward the beloved. The noble lover now "follows the beloved in reverence and awe." So those who are filled with this kind of love "exhibit no jealousy or meanness toward the loved one, but endeavor by every means in their power to lead him to the likeness of the god whom they honor." Such is the conversion by which love turns from the exploitative to the creative.

Here it becomes necessary to bring our concepts together and to think of all speech having persuasive power as a kind of "love." [7] Thus, rhetorical speech is madness to the extent that it departs from the line which mere sanity lays down. There is always in its statement a kind of excess or deficiency which is immediately discernible when the test of simple realism is applied. Simple realism operates on a principle of equation or correspondence; one thing must match another, or, representation must tally with thing represented, like items in a tradesman's account. Any excess or deficiency on the part of the representation invokes the existence of the world of symbolism, which simple realism must deny. This explains why there is an immortal feud between men of business and the users of metaphor and metonymy, the poets and the rhetoricians.[8] The man of business, the narrow and parsimonious soul in the allusion of Socrates, desires a world which is a reliable materiality. But this the poet and rhetorician will never let him have, for each, with his own purpose, is trying to advance the borders of the imaginative world. A primrose by the river's brim will not remain that in the poet's account, but is promptly turned into something very much larger and something highly implicative. He who is accustomed to record the world with an abacus cannot follow these transfigurations; and indeed the very occurrence of them subtly undermines the premise of his business. It is the historic tendency of the tradesman, therefore, to confine passion to quite narrow channels so that it will not upset the decent business arrangements of the world. But if the poet, as the chief transformer of our picture of the world, is the peculiar enemy of this mentality, the rhetorician is also hostile when practicing the kind of love proper to him. The "passion" in his speech is revolutionary, and it has a practical end.

We have now indicated the significance of the three types of lovers; but the remainder of the *Phaedrus* has much more to say about the nature of rhetoric, and we must return to one or more points to place our subject in a wider context. The problem of rhetoric which occupied Plato persistently, not only in the *Phaedrus* but also in other dialogues where this art is reviewed, may be best stated as a question: if truth alone is not sufficient to persuade men, what else remains that can be legitimately added? In one of the exchanges with Phaedrus, Socrates puts the question in the mouth of a personified Rhetoric: "I do not compel anyone to learn to

[7] It is worth recalling that in the Christian New Testament, with its heavy Platonic influence, God is idenified both with *logos*, "word, speech" (*John* 1:1); and with *agape*, "love" (1 *John* 4:8).

[8] The users of metaphor and metonymy who are in the hire of businessmen of course constitute a special case.

71

speak without knowing the truth, but if my advice is of any value, he learns that first and then acquires me. So what I claim is this, that without my help the knowledge of the truth does not give the art of persuasion."

Now rhetoric as we have discussed it in relation to the lovers consists of truth plus its artful presentation, and for this reason it becomes necessary to say something more about the natural order of dialectic and rhetoric. In any general characterization rhetoric will include dialectic,[9] but for the study of method it is necessary to separate the two. Dialectic is a method of investigation whose object is the establishment of truth about doubtful propositions. Aristotle in the *Topics* gives a concise statement of its nature. "A dialectical problem is a subject of inquiry that contributes either to choice or avoidance, or to truth and knowledge, and that either by itself, or as a help to the solution of some other such problem. It must, moreover, be something on which either people hold no opinion either way, or the masses hold a contrary opinion to the philosophers, or the philosophers to the masses, or each of them among themselves." [10] Plato is not perfectly clear about the distinction between positive and dialectical terms. In one passage [11] he contrasts the "positive" terms "iron" and "silver" with the "dialectical" terms "justice" and "goodness"; yet in other passages his "dialectical" terms seem to include categorizations of the external world. Thus Socrates indicates that distinguishing the horse from the ass is a dialectical operation; [12] and he tells us later that a good dialectician is able to divide things by classes "where the natural joints are" and will avoid breaking any part "after the manner of a bad carver." [13] Such, perhaps, is Aristotle's dialectic which contributes to truth and knowledge.

But there is a branch of dialectic which contributes to "choice or avoidance," and it is with this that rhetoric is regularly found joined. Generally speaking, this is a rhetoric involving questions of policy, and the dialectic which precedes it will determine not the application of positive terms but that of terms which are subject to the contingency of evalua-

---

[9] Cf. 277 B: "A man must know the truth about all the particular things of which he speaks or writes, and must be able to define everything separately; then when he has defined them, he must know how to divide them by classes until further division is impossible; and in the same way he must understand the nature of the soul, must find out the class of speech adapted to each nature, and must arrange and adorn his discourse accordingly, offering to the complex soul elaborate and harmonious discourses, and simple talks to the simple soul."

[10] 104b.

[11] 263 A.

[12] 260 B.

[13] 265 A.

tion. Here dialectical inquiry will concern itself not with what is "iron" but with what is "good." It seeks to establish what belongs in the category of the "just" rather than what belongs in the genus *Canis*. As a general rule, simple object words such as "iron" and "house" have no connotations of policy, although it is frequently possible to give them these through speech situations in which there is added to their referential function a kind of impulse. We should have to interpret in this way "Fire!" or "Gold!" because these terms acquire something through intonation and relationship which places them in the class of evaluative expressions.

Any piece of persuasion, therefore, will contain as its first process a dialectic establishing terms which have to do with policy. Now a term of policy is essentially a term of motion, and here begins the congruence of rhetoric with the soul which underlies the speculation of the *Phaedrus*. In his myth of the charioteer, Socrates declares that every soul is immortal because "that which is ever moving is immortal." Motion, it would appear from this definition, is part of the soul's essence. And just because the soul is ever tending, positive or indifferent terms cannot partake of this congruence. But terms of tendency—goodness, justice, divinity, and the like—are terms of motion and therefore may be said to comport with the soul's essence. The soul's perception of goodness, justice, and divinity will depend upon its proper tendency, while at the same time contacts with these in discourse confirm and direct that tendency. The education of the soul is not a process of bringing it into correspondence with a physical structure like the external world, but rather a process of rightly affecting its motion. By this conception, a soul which is rightly affected calls that good which is good; but a soul which is wrongly turned calls that good which is evil. What Plato has prepared us to see is that the virtuous rhetorician, who is a lover of truth, has a soul of such movement that its dialectical perceptions are consonant with those of a divine mind. Or, in the language of more technical philosophy, this soul is aware of axiological systems which have ontic status. The good soul, consequently, will not urge a perversion of justice as justice in order to impose upon the commonwealth. Insofar as the soul has its impulse in the right direction, its definitions will agree with the true nature of intelligible things.

There is, then, no true rhetoric without dialectic, for the dialectic provides that basis of "high speculation about nature" without which rhetoric in the narrower sense has nothing to work upon. Yet, when the disputed terms have been established, we are at the limit of dialectic. How does the noble rhetorician proceed from this point on? That the clearest demonstration in terms of logical inclusion and exclusion often fails to win assent we hardly need state; therefore, to what does the rhetorician resort at this critical passage? It is the stage at which he passes from the logical to the analogical, or it is where figuration comes into rhetoric.

To look at this for a moment through a practical illustration, let us suppose that a speaker has convinced his listeners that his position is "true" as far as dialectical inquiry may be pushed. Now he sets about moving the listeners toward that position, but there is no way to move them except through the operation of analogy. The analogy proceeds by showing that the position being urged resembles or partakes of something greater and finer. It will be represented, in sum, as one of the steps leading toward ultimate good. Let us further suppose our speaker to be arguing for the payment of a just debt. The payment of the just debt is not itself justice, but the payment of this particular debt is one of the many things which would have to be done before this could be a completely just world. It is just, then, because it partakes of the ideal justice, or it is a small analogue of all justice (in practice it will be found that the rhetorician makes extensive use of synecdoche, whereby the small part is used as a vivid suggestion of the grandeur of the whole). It is by bringing out these resemblances that the good rhetorician leads those who listen in the direction of what is good. In effect, he performs a cure of souls by giving impulse, chiefly through figuration, toward an ideal good.

We now see the true rhetorician as a noble lover of the good, who works through dialectic and through poetic or analogical association. However he is compelled to modulate by the peculiar features of an occasion. This is his method.

It may not be superfluous to draw attention to the fact that what we have here outlined is the method of the *Phaedrus* itself. The dialectic appears in the dispute about love. The current thesis that love is praiseworthy is countered by the antithesis that love is blameworthy. This position is fully developed in the speech of Lysias and in the first speech of Socrates. But this position is countered by a new thesis that after all love is praiseworthy because it is a divine thing. Of course, this is love on a higher level, or love redefined. This is the regular process of transcendence which we have noted before. Now, having rescued love from the imputation of evil by excluding certain things from its definition, what does Socrates do? Quite in accordance with our analysis, he turns rhetorician. He tries to make this love as attractive as possible by bringing in the splendid figure of the charioteer.[14] In the narrower conception of this art, the allegory is the rhetoric, for it excites and fills us with desire for this kind of love, depicted with many terms having tendency toward the good. But in the broader conception the art must include also the dialectic,

[14] In the passage extending from 246 A to 256 D.

which succeeded in placing love in the category of divine things before filling our imaginations with attributes of divinity.[15] It is so regularly the method of Plato to follow a subtle analysis with a striking myth that it is not unreasonable to call him the master rhetorician. This goes far to explain why those who reject his philosophy sometimes remark his literary art with mingled admiration and annoyance.

The objection sometimes made that rhetoric cannot be used by a lover of truth because it indulges in "exaggerations" can be answered as follows. There is an exaggeration which is mere wantonness, and with this the true rhetorician has nothing to do. Such exaggeration is purely impressionistic in aim. Like caricature, whose only object is to amuse, it seizes upon any trait or aspect which could produce titillation and exploits this without conscience. If all rhetoric were like this, we should have to grant that rhetoricians are persons of very low responsibility and their art a disreputable one. But the rhetorician we have now defined is not interested in sensationalism.

The exaggeration which this rhetorician employs is not caricature but prophecy; and it would be a fair formulation to say that true rhetoric is concerned with the potency of things. The literalist, like the antipoet described earlier, is troubled by its failure to conform to a present reality. What he fails to appreciate is that potentiality is a mode of existence, and that all prophecy is about the tendency of things. The discourse of the noble rhetorician, accordingly, will be about real potentiality or possible actuality, whereas that of the mere exaggerator is about unreal potentiality. Naturally this distinction rests upon a supposal that the rhetorician has insight, and we could not defend him in the absence of that condition. But given insight, he has the duty to represent to us the as yet unactualized future. It would be, for example, a misrepresentation of current facts but not of potential ones to talk about the joys of peace in a time of war. During the Second World War, at the depth of Britain's political and military disaster, Winston Churchill likened the future of Europe to "broad sunlit uplands." Now if one had regard only for the hour, this was a piece of mendacity such as the worst charlatans are found committing; but if one took Churchill's premises and then considered the potentiality, the picture was within bounds of actualization. His "exaggeration" was that the defeat of the enemy would place Europe in a position for long and peaceful progress. At the time the surface trends ran the other way; the actuality was a valley of humiliation. Yet the hope which transfigured this to "broad sunlit uplands" was not irresponsible, and we conclude by saying that the rhetorician talks about both what

[15] Cf. 263 D ff.

exists simply and what exists by favor of human imagination and effort.[16]

This interest in actualization is a further distinction between pure dialectic and rhetoric. With its forecast of the actual possibility, rhetoric passes from mere scientific demonstration of an idea to its relation to prudential conduct. A dialectic must take place *in vacuo*, and the fact alone that it contains contraries leaves it an intellectual thing. Rhetoric, on the other hand, always espouses one of the contraries. This espousal is followed by some attempt at impingement upon actuality. That is why rhetoric, with its passion for the actual, is more complete than mere dialectic with its dry understanding. It is more complete on the premise that man is a creature of passion who must live out that passion in the world. Pure contemplation does not suffice for this end. As Jacques Maritain has expressed it: "love . . . is not directed at possibilities or pure essences; it is directed at what exists; one does not love possibilities, one loves that which exists or is destined to exist." [17] The complete man, then, is the "lover" added to the scientist; the rhetorician to the dialectician. Understanding followed by actualization seems to be the order of creation, and there is no need for the role of rhetoric to be misconceived.

The pure dialectician is left in the theoretical position of the nonlover, who can attain understanding but who cannot add impulse to truth. We are compelled to say "theoretical position" because it is by no means certain that in the world of actual speech the nonlover has more than a putative existence. We have seen previously that his speech would consist of strictly referential words which would serve only as designata. Now the question arises: at what point is motive to come into such language? Kenneth Burke in *A Grammar of Motives* has pointed to "the pattern of embarrassment behind the contemporary ideal of a language that will best promote good action by entirely eliminating the element of exhortation or command. Insofar as such a project succeeded, its terms would involve a narrowing of circumference to a point where the principle of personal

[16] Indeed, in this particular rhetorical duel we see the two types of lovers opposed as clearly as illustration could desire. More than this, we see the third type, the nonlover, committing his ignominious failure. Britain and France had come to prefer as leaders the rhetoricless businessman type. And while they had thus emasculated themselves, there appeared an evil lover to whom Europe all but succumbed before the mistake was seen and rectified. For while the world must move, evil rhetoric is of more force than no rhetoric at all; and Herr Hitler, employing images which rested on no true dialectic, had persuaded multitudes that his order was the "new order," *i.e.*, the true potentiality. Britain was losing and could only lose until, reaching back in her traditional past, she found a voice which could match his accents with a truer grasp of the potentiality of things. Thus two men conspicuous for passion fought a contest for souls, which the nobler won. But the contest could have been lost by default.

[17] "Action: the Perfection of Human Life," *Sewanee Review*, LVI, 1948, p. 3.

action is eliminated from language, so that an act would follow from it only as a nonsequitur, a kind of humanitarian after-thought." [18]

The fault of this conception of language is that scientific intention turns out to be enclosed in artistic intention and not *vice versa*. Let us test this by taking as an example one of those "fact-finding committees" so favored by modern representative governments. A language in which all else is suppressed in favor of nuclear meanings would be an ideal instrumentality for the report of such a committee. But this committee, if it lived up to the ideal of its conception, would have to be followed by an "attitude-finding committee" to tell us what its explorations really mean. In real practice the fact-finding committee understands well enough that it is also an attitude-finding committee, and where it cannot show inclination through language of tendency, it usually manages to do so through selection and arrangement of the otherwise inarticulate facts. To recur here to the original situation in the dialogue, we recall that the eloquent Lysias, posing as a nonlover, had concealed designs upon Phaedrus, so that his fine speech was really a sheep's clothing. Socrates discerned in him a "peculiar craftiness." One must suspect the same today of many who ask us to place our faith in the neutrality of their discourse. We cannot deny that there are degrees of objectivity in the reference of speech. But this is not the same as an assurance that a vocabulary of reduced meanings will solve the problems of mankind. Many of those problems will have to be handled, as Socrates well knew, by the student of souls, who must primarily make use of the language of tendency. The soul is impulse, not simply cognition; and finally one's interest in rhetoric depends on how much poignancy one senses in existence.[19]

Rhetoric moves the soul with a movement which cannot finally be justified logically. It can only be valued analogically with reference to some supreme image. Therefore when the rhetorician encounters some soul "sinking beneath the double load of forgetfulness and vice" he seeks to reanimate it by holding up to its sight the order of presumptive goods. This order is necessarily a hierarchy leading up to the ultimate good. All

---

[18] *A Grammar of Motives*, p. 90.

[19] Without rhetoric there seems no possibility of tragedy, and in turn, without the sense of tragedy, no possibility of taking an elevated view of life. The role of tragedy is to keep the human lot from being rendered as history. The cultivation of tragedy and a deep interest in the value-conferring power of language always occur together. The *Phaedrus*, the *Gorgias*, and the *Cratylus*, not to mention the works of many teachers of rhetoric, appear at the close of the great age of Greek tragedy. The Elizabethan age teemed with treatises on the use of language. The essentially tragic Christian view of life begins the long tradition of homiletics. Tragedy and the practice of rhetoric seem to find common sustenance in preoccupation with value, and then rhetoric follows as an analyzed art.

of the terms in a rhetorical vocabulary are like links in a chain stretching up to some master link which transmits its influence down through the linkages. It is impossible to talk about rhetoric as effective expression without having as a term giving intelligibility to the whole discourse, the Good. Of course, inferior concepts of the Good may be and often are placed in this ultimate position; and there is nothing to keep a base lover from inverting the proper order and saying, "Evil, be thou my good." Yet the fact remains that in any piece of rhetorical discourse, one rhetorical term overcomes another rhetorical term only by being nearer to the term which stands ultimate. There is some ground for calling a rhetorical education necessarily an aristocratic education in that the rhetorician has to deal with an aristocracy of notions, to say nothing of supplementing his logical and pathetic proofs with an ethical proof.

All things considered, rhetoric, noble or base, is a great power in the world; and we note accordingly that at the center of the public life of every people there is a fierce struggle over who shall control the means of rhetorical propagation. Today we set up "offices of information," which like the sly lover in the dialogue, pose as nonlovers while pushing their suits. But there is no reason to despair over the fact that men will never give up seeking to influence one another. We would not desire it to be otherwise; neuter discourse is a false idol, to worship which is to commit the very offense for which Socrates made expiation in his second speech.

Since we want not emancipation from impulse but clarification of impulse, the duty of rhetoric is to bring together action and understanding into a whole that is greater than scientific perception.[20] The realization that just as no action is really indifferent, so no utterance is without its responsibility introduces, it is true, a certain strenuosity into life, produced by a consciousness that "nothing is lost." Yet this is preferable to that desolation which proceeds from an infinite dispersion or feeling of unaccountability. Even so, the choice between them is hardly ours to make; we did not create the order of things, but being accountable for our impulses, we wish these to be just.

Thus when we finally divest rhetoric of all the notions of artifice

---

[20] Cf. Maritain, op. cit., pp. 3-4: "The truth of practical intellect is understood not as conformity to an extramental being but as conformity to a right desire; the end is no longer to know what is, but to bring into existence that which is not yet; further, the act of moral choice is so individualized, both by the singularity of the person from which it proceeds and the context of the contingent circumstances in which it takes place, that the practical judgment in which it is expressed and by which I declare to myself: this is what I must do, can be right only if, hic et nunc, the dynamism of my will is right, and tends towards the true goods of human life.

That is why practical wisdom, prudentia, is a virtue indivisibly moral and intellectual at the same time, and why, like the judgment of the conscience itself, it cannot be replaced by any sort of theoretical knowledge or science."

which have grown up around it, we are left with something very much like Spinoza's "intellectual love of God." This is its essence and the *fons et origo* of its power. It is "intellectual" because, as we have previously seen, there is no honest rhetoric without a preceding dialectic. The kind of rhetoric which is justly condemned is utterance in support of a position before that position has been adjudicated with reference to the whole universe of discourse—[21] and of such the world always produces more than enough. It is "love" because it is something in addition to bare theoretical truth. That element in addition is a desire to bring truth into a kind of existence, or to give it an actuality to which theory is indifferent. Now what is to be said about our last expression, "of God"? Echoes of theological warfare will cause many to desire a substitute for this, and we should not object. As long as we have in ultimate place the highest good man can intuit, the relationship is made perfect. We shall be content with "intellectual love of the Good." It is still the intellectual love of good which causes the noble lover to desire not to devour his beloved but to shape him according to the gods as far as mortal power allows. So rhetoric at its truest seeks to perfect men by showing them better versions of themselves, links in that chain extending up toward the ideal, which only the intellect can apprehend and only the soul have affection for. This is the justified affection of which no one can be ashamed, and he who feels no influence of it is truly outside the communion of minds. Rhetoric appears, finally, as a means by which the impulse of the soul to be ever moving is redeemed.

It may be granted that in this essay we have gone some distance from the banks of the Ilissus. What began as a simple account of passion becomes by transcendence an allegory of all speech. No one would think of suggesting that Plato had in mind every application which has here been made, but that need not arise as an issue. The structure of the dialogue, the way in which the judgments about speech concentre, and especially the close association of the true, the beautiful, and the good, constitute a unity of implication. The central idea is that all speech, which is the means the gods have given man to express his soul, is a form of eros, in the proper interpretation of the word. With that truth the rhetorician will always be brought face to face as soon as he ventures beyond the consideration of mere artifice and device.

[21] Socrates' criticism of the speech of Lysias (263 D ff.) is that the latter defended a position without having submitted it to the discipline of dialectic.

P. ALBERT DUHAMEL

THE FUNCTION OF RHETORIC
AS EFFECTIVE EXPRESSION

The recent increase in the critical literature concerned with rhetoric, whether of the Renaissance, Mediaeval, or Classical Periods, calls for a re-examination of the assumptions of past histories of rhetoric and a definition of the fundamental relations existing between rhetoric and other branches of knowledge which future studies must consider. There is a sufficiency of monographs occupied with the determination of the influence of particular rhetoric books on selected authors, or of histories supplying chronological lists of the contents of successive manuals. It is high time that a study of rhetoric, which, even with the limitations of past studies, has long been recognized as fruitful, be established on firm ground. This can come about only through recognizing that rhetoric occupies a peculiar position among the arts and that it cannot be adequately interpreted apart from the ideological context in which it occurs. Consequently this essay does not attempt to rewrite the history of rhetoric during any period of its history, but it does propose to consider some questions of method which must be taken into consideration in any discussion of rhetoric. This purpose can best be accomplished by an evaluation of the methods and assumptions of some past histories of rhetoric and the illustration of the proposed method by reference to the problems to be encountered in some periods of rhetorical history. The rhetoric of Greece and Rome as presented by its better known theorists affords excellent working material for determining the principles which should guide any examination of rhetoric, and, further, the rhetoricians of the Classical Period must be most carefully studied for they established the art and the direction it was to take for a long time afterwards.

Rhetoric is better thought of as an idea, the concept of effective expression, than as a set or collection of principles with an abiding purpose. The content and purpose of rhetoric books differ from author to author, and the assumption that techniques and devices in any books are commensurable is unfounded. Terms and purposes are meaningful only within the context of the author's system taken as a whole. All rhetoricians have had one object: the teaching of effective expression. That object can be considered as the "least common denominator" of mental notes which undergo accretion and modification in accordance with an author's conception of what constitutes eloquence. The idea or concept of effective expression is not simple but complex, for it contains more than one element and is invested with several relations. In its simplest form the idea may be said to be undetermined. It is determined by influences external to itself, its relations, which constitute the more basic elements of the rhetoricians's philosophy.

The content of the idea "rhetoric," or of the conception of what constitutes effective expression, is dependent upon the epistemology, psychology, and metaphysic of the system in which it occurs. The rhetorical is determined by the epistemological. The rhetorician's conception of the value of argument, the process of invention by which arguments are to be discovered, the extent to which the devices of elocution are to be employed, is the result of his evaluation of the reliability of the intellect, the nature and availability of truth, and the existence of certitude. Thus Aristotle's idea of rhetoric, or of what constitutes effective expression, differs from Plato's mainly because he conceived of probable truth as valuable in se and frequently the best human intelligence can expect. The Middle Ages evidenced some scientific curiosity in their attempt to assimilate Aristotelian science but had a tendency to eschew systems which sought only the probable, for the conviction that all necessary truth was present in revelation underlay most of their thought. Thus Aristotle was preoccupied with the erection of a system of rhetoric which would discover and express probabilities; Plato valued only the Absolute. The arts of probability and practicality occupied a relatively low position in the mediaeval scheme of values. Interest was focussed upon the expression of ideas for which the highest type of certitude was already present, divine testimony. Thus the systems of invention which had been essential in some classical rhetorics for the discovery of arguments disappear as such from the mediaeval rhetorics and are transferred to mediaeval logics where they appear as means of discovering the sense in which terms are to be understood. In place of the traditional inventio are extensive considerations of the devices of ornamentation traditionally discussed under elocution. This is easily explained, for the later period merely sought to express more effectively the truth already possessed; Aristotle sought, in his Rhetoric, to discover and organize arguments about doubtful matters. Under such different philosophical circumstances the idea of effective expression undergoes extensive modifications, and ars bene dicendi cannot mean the same thing to Aristotle and Hrabanus Maurus.

Further, the content of the idea "rhetoric" when realized in a manual or reduced to practice has an influence upon an orator or stylis Cicero's style was influenced by his rhetoric. He sought to speak effec tively, and his expression mirrors his conception of rhetoric. If he had conceived of effective speech as synonymous with the widespread application of the devices usually considered under *elocutio* to the exclusion of valid arguments, his style would undoubtedly have been more Asiatic. The excessive amount of ornamentation in the expression of an age or author is usually correlated to a rhetorical conception which either lacks, or treats very lightly, a system for the discovery of arguments, because it is convinced that truth either is safely within its grasp or not worth worrying about. The conviction of the Middle Ages and the degeneration of later Stoicism may be taken as ready illustrations. The rhetorical theory may come before or after the expression, as a rationalization *post factum* or as a working hypothesis, but in all instances it aids in the explanation of the manner of expression.

If future histories of rhetoric are to avoid such criticism as that of Mr. Richard P. McKeon, that they are but the "monotonous enumeration of doctrines, or preferably sentences, repeated from Cicero, or commentators on Cicero," they must avoid assumptions such as those made in the past, which have always been implicit determinations or limitations of the idea of effective expression to preconceived or accepted definitions.[1] Such historians of rhetoric have been treating rhetoric in some particular sense, defining a concept which must be kept fluid, if histories of rhetoric are not to be negative or deprecatory.[2] If histories of rhetoric are to be written after first postulating a definition of the concept and then re-examining the history of the assumed concept, the resulting inquiry would be the history not of rhetoric but of one conception of rhetoric. If the definition of the concept postulated be that of Aristotle, the history of rhetoric would reveal a tremendous gap between the decline of the Roman Empire and the writings of Francis Bacon.[3] If the definition assumed were that of Martianus Capella or Isidore of Seville, rhetoric would not begin till the Middle Ages, nor would it survive the Renaissance. The varying subject matter attributed to rhetoric by individual theorists, the changing conceptions of the purpose and value of rhetoric, are reflections of more basic changes in the broad spheres of in-

[1] Richard P. McKeon, "Rhetoric in the Middle Ages," *Speculum*, XVII, 1942, p. 1.

[2] *Ibid.*, p. 2.

[3] On this point, see Karl R. Wallace, *Francis Bacon on Communication and Rhetoric*, pp. 172-173 and 76 and 147.

dividual ideology. The determination of the concept of effective expression to any complete definition as an assumption of a projected history forestalls the recognition of the relations of the concept and deprives the study, which should be the study of an idea and its interrelations, of its most fruitful potentialities. A re-evaluation of the conception of rhetoric, therefore, requires a recognition of the relation of effective speech to truth and to style. An adequate study of rhetoric implies a consideration of the assumed content of the rhetoric itself and of the ideas which have determined that content. Such a study may also look to the concrete results, in the styles of various writers or speakers, to evaluate the end product.

Even within the limits of Greek thought it is possible to find changes in the conception of effective expression resulting from alterations in the definition of truth and man. As long as the Greeks defined areté, or excellence, in terms of physical prowess and considered it hereditary, democracy was obviously impossible. Democracy became a reality and culture concerned itself with nonphysical and nonhereditary elements when political virtues were admitted to some validity.[4] Obviously this change, which can be seen in the overthrow of Achilles as the ideal Greek by Odysseus, represents a change in the conception of man. It represents the development of the concept of justice and the value of deliberation in arriving at a practical course of action. The articulation of this limited idea of humanity was the work of the Sophists. They continuously thought of man as a social animal and of his nature as adequately fulfilled by assuming a share in the government of the *polis*. Thus their system of education became a preparation for political effectiveness. Since any person might speak in the city state, "eloquence, then, was the point from which any attempt to educate a man for political leadership was bound to start." [5] Rhetoric thus became the chief instrument of their teaching.

Sophistic rhetoric is usually criticized because of its preoccupation with devices of ornamentation, its tendency to treat logic lightly, and its emphasis on form.[6] This criticism of the Sophists is based mostly upon indirect evidence, for our knowledge of their techniques and purposes is derived mainly from the dialogues, like the *Gorgias* and the *Phaedrus*, wherein Plato has the Sophists examine their method and content. Essen-

---

[4] Werner Jaeger, *Paideia*, I, pp. 286-287.

[5] *Ibid.*, pp. 285 and 287.

[6] See the standard treatment of Heinrich Gomperz, *Sophistik und Rhetorik, das Bildungsideal des* εὖ λέγειν; also E. M. Cope, "On the Sophistical Rhetoric," *Journal of Classical and Sacred Philosophy*, III, 1856, pp. 147 ff., and *ibid.*, III, 1858, pp. 35-80, 253-288.

tially, the Sophists were humanists attempting to educate to a limited aim dictated by the pragmatic nature of the society in which they lived and taught. The seriousness with which they took up the challenge of changing conditions and the sincerity with which they tried to perpetuate their ideal could not preserve them from an attack accusing them of not meeting problems which, within the limits of their definition of "humanism," they could not feel as problems. Plato, and later Aristotle, directed their attack against the Sophists on two levels: on a very simple level Plato, in particular, expressed his distaste for what their oratorical style had become and, on a more fundamental level, both Aristotle and Plato criticized their estimate of human nature and man's relation to the universe. As humanists the Sophists failed because they could not answer Socrates' challenging concept of the soul; as rhetoricians they failed because of the degeneration of their style. The stylistic failure was intimately linked to their failure as humanists, for their formalism resulted from an inability to provide substantiating material as the vehicle of their figures. The matter could have been produced by a logical system of investigation, which they lacked, for they lacked the λόγος.

The statement of Protagoras that man is the measure of all things gives a good insight into the basic principles of the Sophists.[7] For Plato, God was much more the measure of things than man.[8] The criterion of educational measure thus changes and the previous anthropocentric nature of Greek thought is temporarily suspended as Plato's orientation becomes completely transcendental. The evaluation of an educational system or of an element in an educational system proceeded on vastly different grounds for Plato than it had for the Sophists. A thing was no longer valuable because it improved the political life of the individual, but only in so far as it contributed to the knowledge of transcendentals. Truth was no longer to be determined by political expediency; it was something withdrawn and abstract, apart from time and place. Rhetoric could be expected, a priori, to fall from its former important position unless it could demonstrate an ability to reach truth or enable man to acquire the Good.

In the very earliest of his works Plato foreshadowed the aim of his educational activity— "how men can acquire the knowledge of the Idea of the Good." [9] Since rhetoric remains content with emotional persuasion

---

[7] Herman Diels, Die Fragmente der Vorsokratiker, Zweite Auflage, zweiter Band, erste Hälfte, p. 536. Protagoras, Frg. 1.

[8] Plato, Laws, 716 C. ὁ δὴ θεὸς ἡμῖν πάντων χρημάτων μέτρον ἂν εἴη μάλιστα καὶ πολὺ μᾶλλον ἢ πού τις ὥς φασιν ἄνθρωπος.

[9] Werner Jaeger, Paideia, II, p. 96.

and does not instruct in the matter of right and wrong,[10] it can only be classed with cookery and other skills.[11] The orator thus becomes a mountebank peddling gaudy trifles.[12] Plato, however, like every other theorist, considered some forms of expression better than others. His idea of what constituted effective expression can be inferred from Socrates' second speech in the *Phaedrus*, which is characterized by a plainness of delivery, a following of the natural movements of the mind, and an insistence upon logical definition.[13] In Socrates' opinion, it is the matter and organization of a speech which are worthy of praise; added ornamentation is vain and superfluous.[14] Socrates clearly expected the Sophist, Lysias, to produce finely turned expression, embroidered trivialities, and trite epigrams, for it was against these tendencies of the Sophists that he had been in continual opposition.[15] He criticizes Lysias' speech for its disorderly arrangement of the topics and an absence of logical sequence.[16] Plato's conception of effective speech, or rhetoric, is thus revealed as insistent upon basic wisdom and a knowledge of the truth. The speech should not be amorphous, but then again it should not be shaped to conform to an artificial pattern. The essentials are the search and discovery of the truth, its expression in unvarnished terms, and the avoidance of all that does not aid in a clearer perception of the ultimate realities which alone are desirable.

The difference between the Platonic and Aristotelian rhetoric is intelligible ultimately only in terms of the profound difference between their two attitudes. Aristotle's view of the world "was essentially pagan because it saw things from the point of view of things themselves," and thus "it is no marvel if Aristotle's philosophy has succeeded in the interpretation of the things of nature: from the first moment it was turned toward the earth and organized for its conquest." Plato's philosophy, on the other hand, "was in the very first intention a philosophy of what is beyond, placing the reason of things outside the things themselves. . . . It was, then, a philosophy of the insufficiency of things and the knowledge we possess of them." [17] Plato constantly sought the Truth, whereas Aristotle

[10] Plato, *Phaedrus*, 260-262 C. Also 272-273 A.

[11] Plato, *Gorgias*, 463.

[12] *Ibid.*, 459 C.

[13] Plato, *Phaedrus*, 244-257 B.

[14] *Ibid.*, 236 A-C.

[15] *Ibid.*, 234 E.

[16] *Ibid.*, 264 B.

[17] Etienne Gilson, *The Philosophy of St. Bonaventure*, p. 96.

was willing to admit the inadequacy of our knowledge of some things and to establish an art with probability as its ultimate goal. Aristotle admitted the certitude of certain basic principles in science, but probability was the very basis and foundation of the Aristotelian system of rhetoric.[18]

Aristotelian rhetoric is to be primarily concerned with the deliberation of things in which two alternatives are possible.[19] Those things which are certain, whether of past, present, or future, do not fall into the province of rhetoric, for no one deliberates about them. As for those things which are metaphysically certain, there is so overwhelmingly obvious evidence present that the mind immediately concedes assent. Aristotle distinguishes himself from the previous compilers of arts of rhetoric who have "provided us with only a small portion of this art, for proofs are the only thing in it that come within the province of the art; everything else is merely an accessory. And yet they say nothing about enthymemes which are the body of proof, but chiefly devoted their attention to matters outside the subject; for the arousing of prejudice, compassion, anger, and similar emotions . . ." [20] Here he is obviously taking the advice of the *Phaedrus* and repudiating the shallow sophistical view which had seen rhetoric as an instrument for the agitation of the passions.[21]

After this brief criticism of the Sophists, Aristotle begins to develop his own position and to connect rhetoric with dialectic, which was to remain the distinguishing mark of his system.[22] His arguments for uniting the two are mainly psychological: the true and that which resembles it come under the same faculty, and he who divines well in regard to the truth will divine well in regard to probabilities.[23]

The war between philosophy and rhetoric did not end in Greece; it

---

[18] Everett Lee Hunt, "Plato and Aristotle on Rhetoric and Rhetoricians," *Studies in Rhetoric and Public Speaking in Honor of James Albert Winans,* pp. 28 and 49; also E. M. Cope, *An Introduction to Aristotle's Rhetoric,* p. 7. See also Thomas De Quincey's remarks in his *Collected Writings,* edited by David Masson, X, pp. 90-91.

[19] Aristotle, *Rhetoric,* 1357ᵃ. βουλευόμεθα δὲ περὶ τῶν φαινομένων ἐνδέχεσθαι ἀμφοτέρως ἔχειν.

[20] John Henry Freese, editor and translator, *Aristotle's "The Art of Rhetoric,"* p. 5.

[21] Cf. G. L. Hendrickson, "Origin and Meaning of the Characters of Style," *American Journal of Philology,* XXVI, 1905, pp. 248-290; also by the same author, "The Peripatetic Mean of Style and the Three Stylistic Characters," *ibid.,* XXV, 1904, pp. 125-146. Also E. M. Cope, "On Sophistical Rhetoric," pp. 158-159.

[22] Cf. Cope, *Introduction to Aristotle's Rhetoric,* p. 6.

[23] J. H. Freese, *op. cit.,* p. 11.

was continued in Rome. The battle was always joined between those who maintained the relative superiority of philosophy to rhetoric and those who claimed that effective speaking was a question of formal arrangement and that no other substantiation was needed. With the disappearance of the Roman Republic and the advent of the Empire, Roman rhetoric underwent a profound change. Deliberative and forensic oratory assumed a new tone; the previous public interest in the determination of basic issues disappeared and was replaced by a resigned attitude. Justice and lawmaking had been taken over by the Emperors, and the purpose of oratory was not so much to discover as to approve the Imperial will. Cicero was conscious of this change in its earliest stages but hardly foresaw the complete degeneration of rhetoric. He felt that since the time of Socrates a division, as between soul and body, had been made in the teaching of thought and expression. This separation, really the disjunction of *inventio* and *elocutio*, was the cause of the disreputable state in which rhetoric found itself in Cicero's time.[24] His answer to the situation was simple enough; if you wish to be a great orator, like Demosthenes or Pericles, study Aristotle.[25]

Cicero thereby reveals himself as maintaining a position similar to that of Aristotle. He holds that a philosophical basis, a system of invention to provide matter, is necessary to forestall degeneration into sheer formalism. Through the many Ciceronian works it is possible to trace a conception of rhetoric and the orator which is more fully developed than the short Aristotelian notes. Even a brief review of the first two sections of the first book of Cicero's ethical treatise, *De Officiis*, is sufficient to demonstrate that he was intent upon making man more eloquent about moral ideals. The Ciceronian humanism was based upon a far deeper conception of human nature than the convenient rhetoricism of sophistry could satisfy. Cicero frequently makes his point that the orator is to be concerned with something else beyond mere form. The orator can employ the voice of a tragedian, the gestures of the greatest actors, but he requires also the acumen of the dialectician and the ethical knowledge of philosophers.[26] Also, the orator works for the good of the state and cannot rest in the flowery excursus of the pedant who acts before his students or a select group of admirers.

Again in the *Brutus*, the thoroughly Ciceronian view, which would not permit a dissociation of thought and expression or an expression

[24] Cicero, *De Oratore*, III, xix.

[25] *Loc. cit.*

[26] *De Oratore*, I, xxvii.

which was unmotivated by questions of truth, serves as a guide in the estimation of the great orators of Roman history. The orators whom he admires were not the formalists, but those who were learned as well as good speakers. Among them Demosthenes was successful because he studied Plato. In two other works, the *Partitiones Oratoriae* and the *Topica*, the relationship of rhetoric to dialectic is examined.[27] The two works are similar to Aristotle's in intention, for they insist upon argument. There is a difference, however, between the two, for Cicero chose "to preserve in a work on rhetoric the emphasis upon the nonlogical means of persuasion, and to create in the field where rhetoric assumes the burden of positive demonstration, a system of invention analogous to that used by dialectic." [28] Aristotle, on the contrary, had assumed that the system used by the dialecticians had validity in rhetoric and needed no special interpretation.[29] Aristotle placed his trust in the Organon, while Cicero had his experience with the mobs to require an adjustment of his views.

Quintilian comes at the end. His is the last synthesis within the Classical Period of a fully expressed system of rhetoric which maintains the position suggested by the *Phaedrus* and sketched by Aristotle. He considers the split between rhetoric and philosophy and the subsequent withdrawal of the teachers of each to their own fields as the source of the decay of rhetoric.[30] Here again we find a rhetorician insisting that the end of the speaker is persuasion about matter which must be expressed in a convenient form and that vain exhibition of self and glittering generalities are not the end of rhetoric. Like Cicero, he maintains that dialectic is but a concise form of oratory and that the material of the one is the material of the other.[31]

Quintilian tried to prevent what eventually happened to classical thinking about effective expression. Though his emphasis was upon the teaching of rhetoric, he also insisted that effective expression required a union of matter to a form which made the expression more effective. With his failure the Sophists and declaimers won the field. Votiemus Maximus summarizes what happened to oratory in his criticism of Seneca the Elder: "In declamation men speak to please and not to persuade; ornaments are sought for, while argument is dispensed with as being

27 *Partitiones Oratoriae*, XXXIX, 139.

28 See the interesting discussion of the relation between rhetoric and dialectic in the introduction of Wilbur Samuel Howell, *The Rhetoric of Alcuin and Charlemagne*, p. 53.

29 *Loc. cit.*

30 Quintilian, *Institutiones Oratoriae*, Bk. I, par. xiii.

31 *Ibid.*, Bk. II, par. xv.

troublesome and uninteresting; it is sufficient to please by means of sententiae and amplifications, the aim being that of personal triumph rather than the triumph of a cause." [32] What had happened can be stated in still other terms: the later rhetoricians, instead of attempting to discover new arguments to persuade about their propositions, sought to express old ideas in epigrammatic form, their sententiae. They did not seek to discover the more probable truth of an issue; they sought to delight their hearers. Preoccupation with form had captured the art of rhetoric and effective expression had become the expression in a well-turned phrase of inconsequential material.

The end of the Classical Period saw a wholesale turning to epideictic oratory or panegyric.[33] This change in the conception of rhetoric can be explained on different levels. C. S. Baldwin offers this excellent summary on purely historical grounds.

> Of the three fields of oratory distinguished by Aristotle, deliberative, forensic, and occasional, the first was restricted by political changes. It faded with democracy. So later it faded at Rome, and still later in other realms. Deliberative oratory presupposes free discussion and audiences that vote. The steady increase of government from above administered by an appointed official class hastened also the tendency of the second kind of oratory, forensic, to become technical, the special art of legal pleading. Thus the only field left free was the third, the occasional oratory, encomium or panegyric, the commemoration of persons and days, the address of welcome, and the public lecture.[34]

Of late the term "Second Sophistic" has been extended to apply to this period of Roman oratory, though it is more properly applied to the second, third, and fourth Christian centuries of Greek rhetoric.[35] The noticeably widespread distribution of panegyric within this period is fitting in an educational system which was concerned with the forms of things and lacked firmer foundation.[36] Gone were the older days of Roman rhetoric when "on ne parlait pas pour parler, on parlait pour agir." [37] "Rem tene, verba sequuntur," was no longer the guiding principle, as it had been in the days of Cato the orator.[38] More and more, Roman education became

[32] Quoted by J. W. H. Atkins, *Literary Criticism in Antiquity*, II, p. 148.

[33] Theodore C. Burgess, *Epideictic Literature*.

[34] Charles S. Baldwin, *Medieval Rhetoric and Poetic*, p. 5.

[35] *Ibid.*, p. 8.

[36] Gaston Boissier, *La Fin du Paganisme*. Cf. particularly Bk. V, Chap. II, Section 3.

[37] Gaston Boissier, "Les Écoles de Déclamation à Rome," *Revue des Deux Mondes*, XI, 1902, pp. 480-502, 482.

[38] *Ibid.*, p. 484.

an education in literary form; but form degenerates when cultivated to the exclusion of substance which should determine it.[39] Subjects were selected "in order to cultivate cleverness of expression," and they did not "bind the writer or speaker to pertinency to the matter in hand." [40] There was no longer any *inventio* or search after truth; there was only an *elocutio* or urge toward ornamentation.

A descriptive statement stops there. It is possible, however, to probe more deeply into the currents of thought at the end of the classical world to discover why these changes in the conception of effective speech radically altered its matter and purpose. What happened to rhetoric is the reflection of deeper, more significant changes in the spheres of thought, and the change in rhetoric can not be said to be thoroughly understood apart from an understanding of those underlying causes.

Plato's question in the *Protagoras*, "About what does the Sophist make man more eloquent?" [41] had been a constant reminder to Greek rhetoricians that there must be a search for truth or the art of rhetoric would degenerate into mere skill. Aristotle's answer to the problem posed by Plato had been formulated within an ideological context which differed radically from that of the Sophists. Aristotle had sought to make man more eloquent for the good of the commonwealth and the ultimate betterment of the people as a whole. The Sophists were without such an aim, for those relationships existing in the individual as a result of his rational relations were entirely foreign to the Sophist assumptions about the nature of man and the end of life. Even Isocrates, who is commonly accused of being a simple stylist, proposed the moral code of the Panhellenic ideal, about which he tried to make man more eloquent.[42] He also suggested a "union of philosophy and the earlier rhetoric . . . for to the acquiring of sound views on life he attached a prime importance." [43] Cicero's conception of eloquent wisdom is too well known to require further delineation. The rhetoric of Plato, Aristotle, Cicero, and Quintilian may be said to be founded upon a belief in the perfectibility of man, the existence of truth, and the possibility of its acquisition by the individual. The knowledge of the truth would then lead to a better and fuller life.

"The Second Sophistic should be taken to heart as a complete historic demonstration of what must become of rhetoric without the urgen-

[39] Henry Osborn Taylor, *The Classical Heritage of the Middle Ages*, p. 37.

[40] *Ibid.*, p. 35.

[41] Plato, *Protagoras*, 312.

[42] Werner Jaeger, *Paideia*, III, Chap. 2.

[43] J. W. H. Atkins, *Literary Criticism in Antiquity*, I, p. 136.

cies of matter and motive." [44] Greece was kept from that position by the presence of matter and the desire to achieve the ideal life possible in the *polis*. The Roman world did not have the matter or the motive for long. When man came to doubt, when he no longer had any hope of making anything new, then the arts relapsed into a refurbishment of the old. Not only rhetoric but "tragedy, like any other art of mankind, can live and grow only so long as men have hope of making it say something new about the significance of the world." [45] The decline of Greek tragedy seemingly coincides with the decline of Greek philosophy.[46] So also rhetoric degenerated in antiquity when there was a weakening of faith in and a loss of hope in the human intellect. Beginning in the second and developing through the immediately succeeding centuries, the feeling grew that the struggle of the mind with the problems of ethics, government, and life was fruitless. There was no need for man to attempt to find the answer to the contemporary chaos, for the Stoics considered this the best of all possible worlds. Stoicism is not unlike Sophism in its tendency to de-emphasize theoretical problems and both seemingly reached a similar position, for they both lapsed into encomium as their standard stock in trade. There was no matter or motive to their expression because there was no reason for the human mind's struggling with greater or less probability.

One of the logical implications of the Stoic position seems to have been a curtailment of the intellectual life.[47] The aim of rhetoric had been conceived as the discovery of and the persuasion to right action. The rhetorics of Aristotle and Cicero had as their ultimate aim the erection of a system which made it possible for man to discover truth and then apply it to the people that they might thereby profit and act in a more intelligent manner. With the passing of belief in a validity of reason, there disappeared any hope of finding a firm substance or basis for rhetoric. Thus to say that there was a "Classical Rhetoric" is to compound a gratuitous tag. There were as many conceptions of rhetoric in the period usually called "Classical" as there were philosophies, and the rhetoric can be understood only within the commensurable terms of the philosophy. In every observable instance the rhetoric is dependent for its content and

[44] Charles S. Baldwin, *Medieval Rhetoric and Poetic*, p. 12.

[45] Cf. the interesting introductory chapter of Willard Farnham's *Medieval Heritage of Elizabethan Tragedy*, p. 11, which correlates the growth and decline of tragedy to more fundamental ideological tendencies.

[46] *Ibid.*, p. 9.

[47] *Loc. cit.*

orientation upon the more fundamental concepts which are the burden of epistemological or metaphysical discussion. The complete understanding of a system of rhetoric not only entails a scrutiny of the underlying philosophy but the elucidation of those implications is the task of any future historian of the concept of effective expression.

MAURICE NATANSON

THE LIMITS OF RHETORIC

There are signs of a new excitement in the discipline of contemporary rhetoric; but there are also indications of basic difficulties in the discussions going on to determine the proper province of rhetoric and the possible meaning of a "philosophy of rhetoric." As a philosopher, I think that an effort to show the relationship between rhetoric and philosophy might lead to some clarification of the underlying issues. If the philosopher cannot give the answers, he can perhaps clarify the questions.

But first, what do these "difficulties" in the discussions about rhetoric consist in? Undoubtedly one vast difficulty is generated by the very term "rhetoric." As Bryant points out, rhetoric may mean ". . . bombast; high-sounding words without content; oratorical falsification to hide meanings; sophistry, ornamentation and the study of figures of speech . . . and finally, least commonly of all, the whole art of spoken discourse, especially persuasive discourse." [1] The classical Aristotelian definition of rhetoric is no longer adequate to dispel all these variant connotations, but the inadequacy of defining rhetoric as "the faculty of observing in any given case the available means of persuasion" is to be explained at a different, far deeper level. It will be here that we come to the nucleus of the difficulties regarding rhetoric.

It would appear that what characterizes the Aristotelian as well as recent definitions of rhetoric is a stress on its functional and dynamic character. As Bryant writes:

> Rhetoric is primarily concerned with the relations of ideas to the thoughts, feelings, motives, and behavior of men. Rhetoric as distinct from the learnings which it uses is dynamic; it is concerned with movement. It *does* rather than *is*. It is method rather than matter. It is chiefly involved with bringing about a condition, rather than discovering or testing a condition.[2]

[1] Donald C. Bryant, "Rhetoric: Its Functions and Its Scope," reprinted as Chapter 2 of this volume, p. 34.

[2] *Ibid.*, p. 46; cf. Hoyt H. Hudson, "The Field of Rhetoric," reprinted as Chapter 1 of this volume, where the essence of rhetoric is held to be "adaptation to the end of influencing hearers." (p. 31)

Now the emphasis on the directional and pragmatic aspect of rhetoric leads immediately to the question, Is rhetoric truly to be characterized as functional, and is the rhetorical function that of "adjusting ideas to people and . . . people to ideas?" [3] The fundamental difficulty, it seems to me, that has confused the discussion is a failure on the part of the analyst to distinguish between the theory of rhetoric and the practice of rhetoric: the former involves ultimately a philosophy of rhetoric; the latter pre-supposes that philosophy and directs its attention to the structure of rhetorical technique and methodology. But before proceeding to the analysis of these elements, I think it necessary to examine more carefully what is meant by the functional aspect of rhetoric, since my claim is that much confusion is created by assuming this interpretation of the nature of rhetoric.

It is well known that Aristotle begins his *Rhetoric* by asserting that "Rhetoric is the counterpart of Dialectic." If dialectic is the art of logical discussion, then rhetoric is the art of public speaking; but the distinction between rhetoric and dialectic is a more profound one. Dialectic, for Aristotle, has as its object the achievement of knowledge; rhetoric, persuasion. Dialectic strives for and may achieve *epistēmē*; rhetoric, *doxa*. Thus rhetoric is subordinate in the hierarchy of knowledge to dialectic as belief is subordinate to knowledge. Now if we consider the relationship between the Aristotelian rhetoric and the Platonic critique of rhetoric, it becomes evident that Aristotle has articulated a division between rhetoric and dialectic for definite reasons: essentially, for the rescue of "good" rhetoric from "bad," i. e., from sophistic rhetoric. Good rhetoric, as Plato pointed out in *Phaedrus*, presupposes dialectic: persuasion presupposes truth. The division of rhetoric and dialectic warns us against confounding truth with its artful presentation and at the same time shows that they are separate facets of a single universe of discourse: the intelligible world.[4] But what really separates knowledge from belief, dialectic from rhetoric? It is here that we come to the problem of function.

It is certainly the case that Aristotle, after distinguishing between rhetoric and dialectic, proceeds to analyze the applicative uses of rhetoric. His discussions of the modes of persuasion stress the functional character of rhetorical method. Thus the subject matter of rhetoric becomes evidenced in the problems of speaker and audience, political oratory and its devices, etc. And it is precisely here that the subsequent tradition of rhetoric takes it point of departure and so abandons the awareness of the intimate nexus between rhetoric and dialectic; and it is here that confusions begin to germinate.

[3] Bryant, *op. cit.*, p. 47.
[4] Cf. E. M. Cope, *An Introduction to Aristotle's Rhetoric*, p. 6.

For Plato, rhetoric—good rhetoric, that is—aspired to be (but was not) *technē*, i.e., art involving knowledge.[5] While dialectic alone could achieve the status of *theōria*, rhetoric nevertheless had a powerful bond which tied it to knowledge. Though Aristotle's division of rhetoric and dialectic preserves the original intention of that bond, his stress on the subject matter of rhetoric (the modes of persuasion) lends itself to a misleading emphasis on rhetorical technique and to a lack of emphasis on the theoretical aspects of rhetoric. In other words, instead of a philosophy of rhetoric, we have drawn from Aristotle a manual of oratorical technique and a debater's guide. The ultimate import of this attitude towards rhetoric is an interpretation of the nature of rhetoric which holds it to be functional in character, directed toward practical problems of convincing and persuading, and so aimed at a pragmatic, instigative goal: rhetoric is conceived of in terms of men in action.

Now it is the thesis of this essay that this stress on the functional, pragmatic character of rhetoric is the origin of the confusion regarding the role and province of rhetoric today and, further, that the confusion consists precisely in the fact that the Platonic and Aristotelian emphasis on the link between dialectic and rhetoric has been ignored in favor of the pragmatic subject matter, with the result that the theoretical nature of rhetoric is obscured. It is my contention that a reapproach to the nature of rhetoric is possible through a philosophical examination of its foundations in dialectic.

The need for re-examination of the nature and scope of rhetoric is voiced in many and diverse quarters today, but the stress on the relationship of philosophy to rhetoric is not a recent development. As a matter of fact, it is Bishop Whately who makes the point in connection with a criticism of Cicero as rhetorician:

> Cicero is hardly to be reckoned among the number [of rhetoricians]; for he delighted so much more in the practice than in the theory of his art, that he is perpetually drawn off from the rigid philosophical analysis of its principles, into discursive declamations, always eloquent indeed, and often interesting, but adverse to regularity of system, and frequently as unsatisfactory to the practical student as to the philosopher.[6]

The rhetorician, then, according to Whately, must attend seriously to the philosophical problems which are at the root of his discipline. With regard to logic, Whately writes: "Rhetoric being in truth an offshoot of Logic, that Rhetorician must labor under great disadvantages who is not only ill acquainted with that system, but also utterly unconscious of his

[5] See Werner Jaeger, *Paideia*, III, Ch. 8.
[6] Richard Whately, *Elements of Rhetoric*, p. 24.

deficiency." [7] Unfortunately, as I. A. Richards points out,[8] Whately does not follow his own advice, with the result that instead of taking "a broad philosophical view of the principles of the Art," Whately gives us "a very ably arranged and discussed collection of prudential Rules about the best sorts of things to say in various argumentative situations, the order in which to bring out your propositions and proofs and examples. . . ." [9] Just as Richards correctly states Whately's failure to follow his own directive, so we must also add that Richards fails to carry out a sustained inquiry into the philosophy of rhetoric, though he does develop one subsidiary line of approach, that of the analysis of linguistic structure and meaning. The philosophy of rhetoric remains then an unexamined realm; and it is especially interesting that a volume published in 1953 takes as its theme the relationship between philosophy and rhetoric and seeks a radical reapproach to the ancient dualism of rhetoric and dialectic. We shall take Richard Weaver's *Ethics and Rhetoric* as a point of departure in analyzing the problem before us.

Weaver begins his study of rhetoric by calling us back to the original Aristotelian distinction between rhetoric and dialectic. As we indicated before, rhetoric is concerned with persuasion, dialectic with truth. However, it is necessary to remember that for Aristotle, *both* rhetoric and dialectic are concerned with the world of probability, both begin with the common-sense reality of contingency, not with the realm of apodeictic logic. Aristotle's distinction between scientific knowledge (which includes the organon of deductive logic) and argumentative inquiry (which includes both rhetoric and dialectic) makes clear the difference between the formal deductive syllogism which begins with stipulated premises and arrives then at necessary conclusions and, on the other hand, rhetoric and dialectic, which inquire into the empirical grounds of propositions in an effort to establish the truth and then make clear the available means of its artful presentation.[10] For Aristotle, deductive logic cannot provide any proof of its ultimate premises: such proof is the task of dialectic.[11] The ultimate foundations of science and formal logic, then, rest on dialectic: logic is concerned with validity, dialectic with truth. Thus Weaver writes:

[7] *Ibid.*, p. 26.

[8] I. A. Richards, *The Philosophy of Rhetoric*, p. 7.

[9] *Ibid.*, p. 7.

[10] Cf. James H. McBurney, "The Place of the Enthymeme in Rhetorical Theory," *Speech Monographs*, III, 1936, p. 52

[11] Cf. W. Windelband, A *History of Philosophy*, p. 137; also P. Albert Duhamel, "The Function of Rhetoric as Effective Expression," reprinted as Chapter 4 of the present volume, p. 81.

"Dialectic is a method of investigation whose object is the establishment of truth about doubtful propositions." [12]

Now it would appear that there are different fields of study dialectic may pursue: the scientific method of induction in the field of botany is quite different from the endeavor to establish the truth in matters of politics or ethics. Which field of dialectic will rhetoric concern itself with? Weaver holds:

There is a branch of dialectic which contributes to "choice or avoidance" and it is with this that rhetoric is regularly found joined. Generally speaking, this is a rhetoric involving questions of policy, and the dialectic which precedes it will determine not the application of positive terms but that of terms which are subject to the contingency of evaluation.[13]

The dialectic which seeks to establish terms having to do with policy is in an intimate relationship with rhetoric, for rhetoric is meaningful only if dialectic is presupposed. As Weaver says, "there is . . . no true rhetoric without dialectic, for the dialectic provides that basis of 'high speculation about nature' without which rhetoric in the narrower sense has nothing to work upon." [14] It is this internal connection, rooted in the very nature of rhetoric, that provides Weaver with his *rapprochement* between rhetoric and philosophy.

Weaver's original contribution to the problem is expressed in a particular characterization of dialectic. Turning to a more nearly Platonic than Aristotelian conception of dialectic (though the Neo-Aristotelian overtones are obvious), Weaver interprets dialectic as a distinguishable stage in argumentation: "Dialectic is that stage which defines the subject satisfactorily with regard to the *logos*, or the set of propositions making up some coherent universe of discourse; and we can therefore say that a dialectical position is established when its relation to an opposite has been made clear and it is thus rationally rather than empirically sustained." [15] This view of dialectic as purely conceptual leads to a notion of rhetoric as applicative or practical. Thus for Weaver "the urgency of facts is never a dialectical concern;" [16] "what a successful dialectic secures . . . is not actuality but possibility; and what rhetoric thereafter accomplishes is to take any dialectically secured position . . . and show its relationship

---

[12] Richard M. Weaver, "The *Phaedrus* and the Nature of Rhetoric," reprinted as Chapter 3 of this volume, p. 72.

[13] *Ibid.*, pp. 72-73.

[14] *Ibid.*, p. 73.

[15] Richard M. Weaver, *The Ethics of Rhetoric*, p. 27.

[16] *Loc. cit.*

to the world of prudential conduct." [17] The relationship between dialectic and rhetoric may now be stated as Weaver understands it.

Rhetoric in the wider sense includes dialectic,[18] in so far as dialectic has already functioned in providing the rhetorician with the truth, or in so far as the application of a dialectically secured position is made to the real world. The action that rhetoric professes presupposes in this sense the understanding that good action always involves. This being so, Weaver's point emerges: the duty of rhetoric in the widest sense is "to bring together action and understanding into a whole that is greater than scientific perception." [19] By itself, then, rhetoric is blind, for it has not truth; concomitantly, an isolated dialectic is empty, for it never engages the issues of the empirical world. Combined, dialectic and rhetoric constitute an instrument for reapproaching the multiple problems of politics, ethics, linguistics, and literary criticism. But in what sense does this union of rhetoric and dialectic provide us with a *rapprochement* between rhetoric and philosophy? At this point we must return to the original problem and see where the argument has led us.

We began, it may be recalled, with the functional stress which is placed on rhetoric today and suggested that much of the confusion regarding the nature and province of rhetoric is due to the divorce between rhetoric and dialectic. Our thesis here converges with that of Weaver, for it is precisely Weaver's point, as we have just seen, that rhetoric must go with dialectic if it is to be meaningful. Now the union of rhetoric with dialectic means, in Weaver's terms, a return of rhetoric to a dialectic understood not as the "art of logical discussion" but in the much broader sense of the conceptual ordering of propositions into coherent structures of an *a priori* nature. Dialectic in this sense is no longer "argumentative inquiry" but rather, I submit, philosophical inquiry. The unification of rhetoric and dialectic is really the *rapprochement* between philosophy and rhetoric because dialectic is given a unique interpretation: dialectic constitutes the true philosophy of rhetoric.

Understood in this way, the original Platonic and Aristotelian notions of rhetoric and dialectic become clarified: the philosophy of rhetoric achieves the Platonic idea of *technē*, and the Aristotelian idea of dialectic is seen in its most challenging aspect. Rhetoric ceases to be the *technique* of persuasion and truly becomes the *art* it was originally held to be, an art, however, which sustains itself only in and through its involvement with dialectic.

[17] *Ibid.*, pp. 27-28.
[18] "The *Phaedrus* and the Nature of Rhetoric," p. 72.
[19] *Ibid.*, p. 78.

If all this is true, the question naturally arises. What, after all, is the subject matter of the philosophy of rhetoric? Granted the meaningfulness of interpreting rhetoric in this way, what is to be done with the interpretation? Have we invoked Whately's criticism of Cicero, Richards' criticism of Whately, and added our criticism of Richards, only to fall into the same trap ourselves? The unavoidable question is, What problems constitute the subject matter of the philosophy of rhetoric, and how may such a philosophy be articulated? Obviously, we can offer only a fragmentary indication here of the way in which we would approach these problems.

Let us return once again to Aristotle's concept of dialectic. As we noted, dialectic is understood by Aristotle as operating in the realm of probability, not necessity. Dialectic seeks the truth but conducts the search in the midst of the real world of contingency and doubt.[20] Now the new enriched conception of dialectic that we are offering here—dialectic understood as the philosophy of rhetoric—concerns itself not with fact but with the theoretical structure that is logically prior to fact. How is such an *a priori* system related to the contingent world? The question then is, What is the relationship of dialectical theory to rhetorical fact? Stated in still another way, the question is, What is the relationship of theory to practice? All of these questions are transpositions of our fundamental problem: the true province of rhetoric. The answer to these questions and the exploration of the fundamental problem lead necessarily to the nature of philosophy itself. To answer the question, What is the subject matter of the philosophy of rhetoric, we must investigate the foundational discipline of philosophy, which is the bedrock, the ultimate and absolute ground of all inquiry.

I propose to understand by philosophy the critique of presuppositions. Philosophy in its synthetic aspect seeks to comprehend the nature of reality by inquiring critically into the categories of reality: quantity, quality, relation, and modality, to refer to the Kantian categories. In its analytic aspect philosophy attempts to bring to clarity the meaning of terms which are basic and crucial to the conceptual structure of all special disciplines. So in history, for example, analytic philosophy investigates the meaning of such terms as "fact," "event," "cause," "effect," "consequence," etc. These are the basic terms out of which history constructs its subject matter and builds its schemata. Both the synthetic and analytic aspects of philosophy turn upon a single, though complex, focal point: the systematic and persistent exploration of elements and themes which are taken for granted in both common-sense reality and in the special disciplines. Thus, philosophy is the critique of such presuppositions as the

---

[20] The tremendous philosophical problem of the meaning of "probability" in common-sense reality is necessarily beyond the scope of this essay.

belief in the existence of an external world, of other fellow men in that world, of communication between those fellow men, etc. Philosophy does not deny the existence of these things; rather it seeks to express their meaningful structure, to bring to complete clarity the conditions which make common-sense experience possible and comprehensible. As a critique of presuppositions, philosophy is a reflexive discipline, i.e., it not only takes for investigation objects and problems external to it, but it also seeks to understand itself. Philosophy is self-problematic: it is the only discipline that begins by inquiring into its own nature and goes on to examine its own instruments of inquiry. The subject matter of philosophy, then, consists of the categories of reality and the basic terms of all particular disciplines; the ultimate goal of the critique of these elements is the reconstruction of the real in perfect self-clarity and illumination.

If this may be taken as the nature of philosophy generally, what is the province of the philosophy of rhetoric? I would suggest that the philosophy of rhetoric directs itself toward the following problems: the relationship between language and what language denotes; the relationship between mind and what mind is aware of; the relationship between knowledge and what knowledge is "of"; the relationship between consciousness and its various contents; etc. Now what differentiates these problems from their generalized setting in the theory of knowledge is the particular kind of context in which these problems arise in rhetoric. Instead of the general problem of meaning, the philosopher of rhetoric is interested in how this problem arises with regard to speaker and listener, poet and reader, playwright and audience. Instead of the epistemology of consciousness, the philosopher of rhetoric directs his attention to those states of consciousness manifest in persuasion. Instead of the generalized problem of knowledge, the philosopher of rhetoric attends to the status of that knowledge which the persuader seeks to persuade us of.

The philosophy of rhetoric, then, has as its subject matter the application of the critique of presuppositions to those presuppositions which characterize the fundamental scope of rhetoric: presuppositions in the relationship of speaker and listener, the persuader and the one persuaded, judger and the thing judged. *The specific object of inquiry here is not the technique of speaking or persuading or judging but the very meaning of these activities.* Thus rhetoric stands in relation to philosophy as science stands in relation to philosophy. In both cases, philosophy investigates what both disciplines presuppose: knowledge, existence, communication, and value. Just as the philosophy of science analyzes the meaning of such elements as "fact," "causation," and "law," so the philosophy of rhetoric studies the elements of "language," "meaning," and "persuasion." This brings us to the question of the relationship of the philosophy of rhetoric to rhetoric in the narrower sense.

The conclusion of our analysis may be expressed in a typology or hierarchical ordering of the different aspects of rhetoric. This will help to make clear precisely what is meant by rhetoric in the broader and narrower sense of the term. Going from the narrower meaning down to the broadest meaning, we have the following aspects of rhetoric: rhetorical intention in speech or writing, the technique of persuasion, the general rationale of persuasion, and finally the philosophy of rhetoric. Rhetoric in the narrower aspect involves rhetorical intention in the sense that a speaker or writer may devote his effort to persuade for some cause or object. Since much of what is commonly called "bad" rhetoric frequently is found in such efforts, the field of rhetoric understood as the technique of persuasion is systematically studied and taught. Here the teacher of rhetoric investigates the devices and modes of argument, the outline for which is to be found in Aristotle's *Rhetoric* or other classical rhetorics. Reflection of a critical order on the significance and nature of the technique of persuasion brings us to rhetoric understood as the general rationale of persuasion. This is what might be termed the "theory" of rhetoric in so far as the central principles of rhetoric are examined and ordered. The emphasis is on the general principles of rhetoric as rhetoric is intimately related to functional, pragmatically directed contexts. Finally, we come to the critique of the rationale of rhetoric which inquires into the underlying assumptions, the philosophical grounds of all the elements of rhetoric.[21] It is here that a philosophy of rhetoric finds its placement. If rhetoric is bound to and founded on dialectic, and dialectic on philosophy, then the limits of rhetoric find their expression in the matrix of philosophical inquiry.

[21] It is interesting to note that Donald C. Bryant approaches a similar typology, though he stops short of the philosophy of rhetoric as we understand it. Speaking of the rhetorician, Bryant writes, *op. cit.*, p. 41: "the term *rhetorician* will sometimes mean the formulator and philosopher of rhetorical theory; sometimes the teacher of the technique of discourse; sometimes the speaker with rhetorical intention; and finally the student or scholar whose concern is the literary or social or behavioral study of rhetoric. I have been tempted to invent terms to avoid certain of these ambiguities such as *logology*, or even *rhetoristic* (parallel with *sophistic*), but the game would probably not be worth the candle." Our point in this essay has been to show that not only is the game worth the candle, but that in a sense without the game no ultimate rhetoric is possible.

CH. PERELMAN AND
L. OLBRECHTS-TYTECA

Translated from the French by William Sacksteder

ACT AND PERSON

IN ARGUMENT

In order to specify the import of the following observations, it will be
well to indicate briefly the framework in which they are located. Man
living in society has discussions with his fellows and tries to bring them
to share some of his views and to perform certain actions. Relatively
rarely does he have recourse solely to coercion in order to do this. In general, he seeks to persuade or to convince; and to this end he reasons, in
the broadest sense of the term, and presents proofs. In those cases in
which the means of proof consist in rigorous demonstration, they are
studied by a well-defined science: logic. But to the extent that it has
developed into a purely formal science which determines the conditions
of correct deduction, it appears that a great many of the proofs utilized in
law, ethics, philosophy, political debate, and daily life cannot be considered relevant to logic in the strict sense.

All these arguments evidently might be relegated to the sphere of
mental suggestion and denied any kind of rationality. This has been, more
or less explicitly and to a greater or less extent, the viewpoint of a great
many logicians and philosophers. But the consequences of this point of
view can be quite serious, for it tends to put all kinds of informal procedures of argument on the same footing, whether those of the confidence
man or the philosopher; and, on the other hand, this point of view places
the system of logic, as well as of science, beyond all the rest of mental
life and almost without contact with it. It seems to us, on the contrary,
that it is worth while to study more closely those argumentative procedures which are of such social and philosophic importance. We have
given the name "rhetoric" to the discipline which we thus propose to
revive, in recognition of the fact that, at least in Greek antiquity and

particularly for Aristotle, the object of rhetoric was precisely the study of these techniques of nondemonstrative argument, its end being to support judgments and thereby win or reinforce the assent of other minds.[1]

It soon appeared to us that all argument presupposes that those to whom it is addressed agree on a certain number of data. This agreement may serve as a point of departure for further agreements, but it may also be questioned, in which case the discussion turns on the justification of this agreement, on the basis of other elements presumed to be accepted.

This viewpoint involves another: we will constantly need a notion correlative to agreement, that of the audience. For what is accepted by certain persons is not necessarily accepted by others; and so the audience may extend from the individual himself—in the case of deliberation with one's self, which in several respects can be considered as a special case of discussion with others—through the whole series of particular audiences to the universal audience. Of course, the universal audience never actually exists; it is an ideal audience, a mental construction of him who refers to it. We could easily show that this so-called "universal audience" varies with the epoch and with the person: each creates its own idea of the universal audience. This fact explains the interest of the sociology of knowledge.[2]

Any audience accepts a certain number of data which it will call "facts," "truths," "presumptions," or "values." A fact is important in argument because it is considered as forming the object of universal agreement: it *must* be accepted by everyone. If someone says, "I opened this book," we would doubtless see in this the statement of a fact. But at any time this status may be taken away from it by objections such as: "No, the book was opened by someone else," "The book opened itself," or even "There is no book there at all, but only loose pages," etc. What is understood by "fact" thus furnishes us the first example of an agreement always subject to revision. It likewise shows us that as long as this agreement is not questioned, it does not occur to anyone to demand a justification of it; as long as the agreement lasts, the fact can serve as a point of departure for further argument, such as "I opened the book; therefore I intend to read it." It can be seen at once how this conception of fact differs from that of the scientist or philosopher who would seek to extricate the facts which underly a theory and the immediate premises, logically or genetically prior, which serve as foundation for his conceptual system. It is true that rhetoric, as a discipline, likewise presupposes the

[1] Cf. Ch. Perelman and L. Olbrechts-Tyteca, "Logique et rhétorique," *Revue philosophique*, CXL, 1950.
[2] Cf. Ch. Perelman, "Sociologie de la connaissance et philosophie de la connaissance," *Revue internationale de philosophie*, IV, 1950.

existence of facts appropriate to it. These are audiences, arguments, and adherences. The conception of these may, moreover, always be modified. That on which we ask agreement is that there exists argument which, starting from certain given opinions, seeks to win new opinions or to reinforce other opinions already obtained.

All audiences accept values as well, whether abstract values, such as justice, or concrete values, such as one's country. These values are generally accepted only by a particular audience. Some of them are considered universal values, but it could doubtless be shown that they are so regarded only on condition that their content is not specified. Besides, it is not so much the values to which they adhere as the manner in which they arrange the values in a hierarchy, which makes it possible to describe a particular audience. Indeed, audiences accept not only facts and values but also hierarchies, constructs of reality, and connections between facts and values—in short, a totality of common beliefs, which we shall call "places," in recognition of the ancient usage of the term "commonplaces." These make it possible to argue with more or less effectiveness. An argument always introduces elements of this sort. For example, to support the fact, challenged by an interlocutor, that I opened this book, others might suggest presumptions (e.g., that an open book has been opened by someone) or values (e.g., truth, to which it is claimed I pay respect and conform my conduct). In the end, the matter might be resolved by admitting that it is indeed a fact; but it is so regarded only on condition that it is again separated from the arguments by which the agreement was obtained.

We have said that among the elements of agreement are found certain structures of reality which are considered as accepted. We may divide them into two broad categories: connections of succession, such as the relation of cause to effect, and connections of coexistence, such as the structural properties of a single body. Philosophical argument may seek to reduce some of these connections to others, which are considered more fundamental. But, from our viewpoint, any effort at systematization being at least premature, it is proper to recognize the broad types of connection which are explicitly used in discussion and are implicit at other times.

One of the connections of coexistence which may be considered as very generally accepted by all sorts of audiences and which seems to us to have a great importance is that of the relation of the person to the act which is attributed to him, a relation which is the prototype of a large number of connections of coexistence.

The makeup of the human person and its separation from his acts is tied to a distinction between what is considered important, natural, and characteristic of the being under discussion and what is regarded as a transitory and external manifestation thereof. The makeup of the person always gives us a rule, in virtue of which the essence may be distinguished from its manifestations.

Since this connection between the person and his acts does not constitute a necessary link or possess the same sort of stability as the relation between an object and its qualities, a simple repetition of an act may involve either a reconstruction of the person or a reinforced adherence to the previous makeup. The precariousness of the relation determines a constant interaction between the act and the person.

Of course, the conception of what constitutes the person may vary considerably according to the epoch and according to the metaphysics to which one connects the construction. It is very likely that the argument of primitive peoples made use of a much broader conception of the person than ours has become. They doubtless would include therein all the incidentals, such as the shadow, the totem, and detached fragments of the body. Whereas we must make use of special connections in order to join these elements to the person, primitive man would have to use disassociation in order to isolate the personality in the limited sense from this more extended personality.

The person, as we will consider it, will be that which occurs in different epochs and according to different authors, so that we will not have to ask ourselves, in this more general investigation, how the person is defined or what are the elements which, for practical purposes, enter into its makeup or which, according to the psychologists, should theoretically enter into it.

It may be useful to show by an example that phenomena of this sort may or may not be regarded as a part of the person rather than merely as a purely external manifestation, i.e., an act. A woman's beauty can be considered as a quality constitutive of the person rather than as a transitory and contingent manifestation of it. In this regard it should be noticed that the fact that such a phenomenon is attached to the makeup of the person rather than treated as an accidental manifestation, i.e., as an act, may be considered one way of placing this phenomenon in a hierarchy in relation to others. As a general rule, the more important traits are integrated into the makeup of the person. That is to say, the manner of formation of the person may be the object of the uncertain and limited agreement of a given group, although this will always be susceptible of revision.

We must emphasize a primary characteristic of the person, namely, that the person introduces an element of stability. An argument concerning the person takes advantage of this stability, since we presume it in interpreting the act as dependent upon the person, or we deplore the fact that this stability has not been respected, when someone is reproached for inconstancy or an unjustified change. A large number of arguments attempt to prove that the person has not changed, that the change is merely apparent, or that it is the circumstances which have changed, etc.[3]

But the stability of the person is never completely assured, though certain linguistic techniques help to emphasize the impression of stability. The use of proper names allows the continuity of the person to be presumed; other ways of speaking manifest a permanent trait of the person. Thus the insertion of a typical category ("your stingy father"), the use of an epithet ("Charlemagne of the flowery beard") or the hypostasis ("his generosity has contributed . . .")—each of these reinforces the impression of the stability of the whole person by emphasizing a characteristic of the person which is regarded as permanent. In this regard we may note the role in argument of what are called "figures of speech"—a role which confers on them an important place in all rhetoric aimed at achieving the adherence of minds.

The person, considered as the support underlying a series of qualities, as the author of a series of acts and judgments, and as the object of a series of evaluations, is thus this enduring being around which clusters a complete series of phenomena to which it gives coherence and significance. But, on the other hand, this person is himself known in virtue of his actions and his manifestations, for there is a deep community between the idea which we have of the person and our knowledge of the totality of his acts. Indeed, we are faced with a constant interrelationship between the act and the person.

Both moral life and legal life need these two notions, both as they are joined together and in their relative independence. Ethics and law judge the act and the agent at the same time; and neither would be satisfied to consider one of these elements alone. By the very fact that it is the individual, and not his act, which we judge, it is granted that he is linked to the acts which he committed. But, on the other hand, if we are interested in the person, it is on account of acts, which can be characterized independently of him. If the notions of responsibility, merit, and guilt emphasize the person, those of norm and rule are primarily preoccupied with the act. But this separation of the act and the person is never more than partial and unstable. The merit of a person may be seen independently of his acts, but this would be possible only in a metaphysics in which the reference to acts is given by the context. On the other hand, if the rules prescribe or forbid certain acts, their moral or legal import consists in the fact that they are addressed to persons. The terms of the relation of act and person are sufficiently independent to permit each of them

[3] Cf. the study by Nathan Leites, "The Third International on Its Changes of Policy," in the collective work edited by Harold D. Lasswell, *Language of Politics: Studies in Quantitative Semantics*.

to be used in isolation at certain times, but they are sufficiently connected that their joint interaction characterizes entire areas of social life.

The distinction between the act and the person and the interaction of these two notions are not utilized by moralists alone. They permit the introduction into all thought of distinctions which are important for argument and play an outstanding role, even if they are not explicitly invoked, as will be shown by the two examples which follow.

The first of these examples is furnished for us by a little dialogue imagined by Stevenson:

A (*speaking to C, a child*): "To neglect your piano practice is naughty."
B (*in C's hearing*): "No, no, C is very good about practicing." (*Out of C's hearing*): "It's hopeless to drive him, you know: but if you praise him, he will do a great deal." [And Stevenson adds] Here B is not opposed to the general direction of A's influence on C, but wishes to change the manner in which it is exerted.[4]

A judges the act of C and decides that C does not conform to the rule, since he neglects his piano. B forms a judgment on the person and says that he works well, hoping to see him conform to the flattering picture which is presented to him. Both seek the same result, and at first glance they seem opposed only because the first blames that which the second praises. But let us note that the two arguments are not the counterparts of each other. Actually, the blame puts the emphasis on the violated norm, and the person is involved only because of this violation; in the second case the accent is put on the person in the attempt to encourage him in spite of his action.

The second example is furnished us by a text of Chevalier de Méré,[5] in which he distinguishes two modes of expression: "Among all the servants, those who served him well were rewarded" and "Among these numerous gentlemen, those who were judged worthy were pleased by his recognition." Méré here opposes a delicate mode of expression to another which expresses the same fact. According to the second formula, the person seems to be rewarded, not his act. A merit is recognized, not a service —which seems more honorable, at least in Méré's surroundings. Moreover, the persons are placed in the esteemed class of gentlemen; and, finally, a reward is alluded to only in an indirect manner, by the appreciation of those who benefit from it. In the same way it is implied that they have the added merit of being able to appreciate the recognition of their master, i.e., a reciprocal recognition is indicated. In general, to proceed in this way ends in an evaluation of the person; the acts fall into the background.

---

4 Charles L. Stevenson, *Ethics and Language*, p. 128.
5 Chevalier de Méré, *Œuvres complètes*, III, p. 134.

After these general considerations, we will examine successively the influence of acts on the conception of the person and that of the person on his acts.

The reaction of the act on the agent is of such a nature as to modify constantly our conception of the person, whether it is a question of new acts which are attributed to him or of former actions which are referred to. Both play an analogous role in argument, although greater weight is given to the more recent acts. Except in limited cases, of which we will speak, the makeup of the person is never completed, not even by his death. However, certain makeups necessary for consistency are much more constant than others. This is the case particularly with historical personages. It is this which was well recognized by Mr. Aron, when he wrote: "Another, when he is present, reminds us constantly of his capacity to change; when he is absent, he is the prisoner of the image of him which we have formed. And if we distinguish what our friends are from what they do, this distinction fades away to the extent that they sink into the past." [6] In place of speaking of a distinction which fades away, we would rather say that the reaction of the acts on the person no longer has occasion to manifest itself. Nevertheless, this constancy is only relative: not only might new documents give rise to a revision, but, completely apart from any new fact, the evolution of the personality of the historian or a change of public opinion might modify the conception of a personage, owing to the inclusion in his makeup of acts considered unimportant until that time or by the minimization of acts formerly judged significant.

This conception, which stresses the uncertainty of the makeup of the person, is sharply opposed to a "thinglike" conception thereof, whereby each act is considered merely as a sign which reveals an unchangeable personality, which exists prior to its manifestation. Thus it happens that the person is separated from his acts, as the fire is distinguished from the smoke; but the systematic utilization of such a conception would appear rather strange to us. Witness this passage from Isocrates, which speaks of men as things: "If some sign distinguished vicious men, it would indeed be best to punish them before they had done any harm to their fellow citizens. But since people cannot recognize them before they have harmed someone, it is at least proper for everyone to hate them and regard them as an enemy when they are discovered." [7] In this way the punishment would not be proportionate to the seriousness of the offense but to the wickedness which the offense reveals. But it often happens that an act obliges us to reconstruct our conception of the person and to place a person in a category different from that to which he had been believed

[6] Raymond Aron, *Introduction à la philosophie de l'histoire*, p. 80.
[7] Isocrates, "Contre Lobbites," in *Discours*, I, No. 14.

to belong. This revision, with the transfer of value which accompanies it, is often expressed by the assertion of a qualification applying to the person.

Everyone knows the famous passage by Pascal. "There are only three sorts of persons: some who have found God and serve him; others who search for him but have not found him; and still others who neither search for him nor have found him. The first are reasonable and happy; the last are mad and unhappy; those in between are unhappy but reasonable." [8] The act serves to characterize the person, to make him a reasonable being or a madman; we should notice, however, that this characterization of the person must serve to disqualify certain behavior. It is the act which determines our conception of the agent, but the interrelation is such that, to that extent, we end up with an evaluation of the act.

The value which we attribute to an act leads us to attribute a certain value to the person, but this is not merely a higher or lower evaluation. In the case in which an act determines a transfer of value, this is correlative with a revision of our conception of the person, to whom we explicitly or implicitly attribute certain tendencies, aptitudes, instincts, or sentiments.

In the relation of act to person, we understand by "act" anything which may be considered as an emanation of the person; in addition to actions, these might be judgments, modes of expression, emotional reactions, or involuntary mannerisms. In this way, in placing value on a judgment, an evaluation is thereby accorded to its author. The manner in which he judges permits the judge to be judged, and, in the absence of accepted criteria applying to the object, it is extremely difficult to prevent the interaction of the act and the person in this area. The judgment which is applied to both is, at the same time, quite often dependent upon the idea which has been formed of the subject discussed. To call a man "frivolous" because he has treated frivolously things which are considered important constitutes a well-founded judgment only in the eyes of those who agree on the importance of what has been neglected; thanks to this mechanism, an ambiguity is introduced into the debate, whereby certain cases are prejudiced by judging the persons.

Very rarely is the effect of the act on the person limited simply to a higher or lower evaluation of the latter. More often the person serves as what might be called a steppingstone, permitting the passage from known to unknown act, from the knowledge of past acts to the anticipation of future ones. Often the argument concerns acts of the same nature, as in Calvin: "Is it plausible that we would plot to overthrow kingdoms—we, from whom a seditious word was never heard and whose life was known

---

[8] Blaise Pascal, *Œuvres complètes, Pensées*, No. 364

to be simple and peaceful, when we lived under you, Sire?" [9] Often acts of the past must render likely acts which are a little different. In his speech against Callimachus, Isocrates argues that one who had borne false witness would not hesitate to produce false witnesses in his own favor.[10] However different they may be, one always tries to make known acts and presumed acts fall into the same category.

One may base an argument on habitual acts which are sufficiently numerous to characterize a way of being; but it is also possible to use a unique act or a single judgment, the importance of which is underlined. The uniqueness of the act is no obstacle to proceeding in this way, unless use is made of techniques, of which we will speak later, which seek to separate the act sharply from the person. It is by making use of a single act that the establishment of heresy on a lone issue makes the entire doctrine of a condemned theologian suspected. Likewise, Simone Weil argues from the fact that we find a defense of slavery in the writings of Aristotle, to the condemnation not only of all Aristotelianism but also of the Thomistic movement which is inspired by it.[11]

Past acts and effects produced by them may acquire a certain firmness and form a sort of asset which their author would not wish to lose. Enjoyment of a good reputation must be taken into consideration, and Isocrates does not hesitate to invoke it in the defense of his client: "[I] would be the most unhappy of men if, having paid out a good bit of money to the state, I were said to covet that of others or to take no account of your opinion—when people see that I have been much less concerned not merely with my fortune, but even with my life, than with the good reputation which you give me." [12] Past care for the reputation becomes a guaranty that nothing would be done that would bring about its loss. Previous actions and the reputation which results from them become a sort of capital which is incorporated in the person. It becomes a sort of acquired asset which one may invoke in his own defense. We should notice in this respect that, although the rhetorical argument may never be restraining, the very fact that people affirm that it must not be overlooked and must be attended to is itself the sign of its rationality and its value for a universal audience.[13]

In the preceding pages, although we have discussed the effect of the

[9] John Calvin, Institution de la religion Chrétienne, p. 14.

[10] Isocrates, "Contre Callimakhos," par. 57, op. cit., I.

[11] Simone Weil, L'Enracinement, p. 260.

[12] Isocrates, "Contre Callimakhos," par. 63.

[13] Cf. Ch. Perelman, "La Quête du rationnel," in Études de philosophie des sciences en hommage à F. Gonseth, p. 141.

act on the agent, we have been induced to allude also to the effect of the agent on the act. But the idea which we form of the agent is itself founded on previous acts and it often happens that the idea we form of the person is the point of departure for the argument, serving to anticipate certain unknown actions, to interpret them in a certain way, or to transfer to them the judgment applied to the person.

An example is furnished us by a joke attributed to the Belgian statesman, P. H. Spaak. After a press conference, a reporter pressed him: "Is it really true, what you have just told us?" and Spaak retorted, "With a good head like mine, could I tell you something which wasn't true?" We should mention in this regard that there is a humor in argumentation which results from the application of argumentative schemas beyond their conditions of normal application. The study of this sort of joke, which need not be confused with general use of humor in persuasion, should show us certain schemas of argument. It doubtless permits us, as well, to specify their conditions of application. Mr. Spaak's joke caricatures the passage from the person to the act as it is currently practiced.

In reasoning concerning a person, as concerning things, we constantly infer his future behavior from what is known of him and his past and move to unknown cases from those which are known. But it is more interesting to declare that the behavior of persons may be predicted not merely on the basis of our past experience but on the basis of the idea of a moral impossibility, furnished by a system of beliefs, which is completely parallel to the physical impossibility furnished by a scientific system. It is thus that Pascal tells us, concerning miracles, "There is a great deal of difference between not being for Christ and saying so, and not being for Christ, though pretending to be. The first may do miracles, the second not, for the first are clearly seen to be against the truth; but not so the others, and thus miracles are more clear" [14] and "him who is a covert enemy, God would not permit to do miracles adversely." [15] Diabolical miracles are possible, because they fool nobody; but it is not possible, conversely, that God should permit hidden enemies of Christ to fool the faithful with miracles.

The interpretation of acts in terms of the image we form of the person constitutes a more specific aspect of argument in this area. The context which the person supplies and which permits better comprehension of his acts most often appears in terms of the notion of "intention."

When we pass from the knowledge of a person's previous acts to considerations concerning future ones, the role of the person stands out,

14 *Pensées*, No. 751.
15 *Pensées*, No. 753.

but it constitutes merely a sort of privileged link in the totality of facts which are invoked, whereas the notion of intention puts the emphasis much more on the permanent character of the person. The intention is, indeed, intimately tied to the agent, being the emanation of his personality or the result of his will—that is, of that which characterizes him most fully. Since the intention of others is never known directly, we simply presume it through what is known of this person and his permanent characteristics. Generally the intention is presumed in virtue of repeated and consistent acts, but there are cases in which merely the idea which we form of the agent permits his intentions to be determined. The same act, committed by someone else, would be considered as different and esteemed otherwise, because it would be believed to have been done with a different intention. So recourse to intentions constitutes the heart of the argument and subordinates the act to the agent, whose intention permits the understanding and evaluation of the act. It is thus that Calvin, recalling that the afflictions of Job could be attributed simultaneously to three authors—God, Satan, and men—finds that God has acted properly, whereas Satan and the men were to be condemned because their intentions were different.[16] But the idea we have of the intentions depends entirely on what we know about the agents.

All moral argument based on intention constitutes a morality of the agent, in opposition to a morality of the act, which is much more formalistic. The above example shows clearly the mechanism of these arguments because it brings in agents, as well, characterized as God and Satan, but there is no moral controversy which does not make use of such a mechanism. The intention of the agent and the motives which determined his action are often considered as the reality, which is hidden behind purely external manifestations. It is assumed that knowledge of them must be sought through appearances, for they alone have importance in the final analysis.

Here is another little dialogue by Stevenson, the effect of which, according to the author, is to disqualify the interlocutor and to remove all value from his advice:

A: You ought to vote for him, by all means.
B: Your motives for urging me are clear. You think that he will give you the city contracts.[17]

It is not without interest to oppose to this dialogue by Stevenson, and the conclusion which he draws from it, a passage by Pareto:

A certain proposition A can not be good unless it is formed by an honest

16 Calvin, *op. cit.*, Book I, chap. xviii, par. 1.
17 Charles L. Stevenson, *op. cit.*, p. 128.

man; I show that he who made this proposition is not honest, or that he was paid for doing it; thus I have shown that the proposition A is harmful to the country. This is absurd; and anyone who uses this reasoning has departed completely from the domain of reasonableness.[18]

To hold that the dishonesty of the author or the fact that he had a peculiar interest constitutes an argument invalidating his proposition or to reject this argument completely as irrelevant are two extreme positions which are equally oversimplified. In the first case, account is taken only of the person and the intentions attributed to him, to the neglect of the examination of the proposition advanced; in the second, only the proposition is looked at, apart from what is known concerning its author. Actually, in daily practice, we take account of both these factors, for what we know concerning the author permits us to understand the proposition better and to estimate its proper value. This shows that in this area practice is a great deal more varied than the analysis of theoretical thinkers, and the effect of the agent on the act is of an infinitely variable intensity. It is only at the extremes that it may be accorded an exclusive influence or entirely eliminated. We will see that one of these extremes is located in the region of theology and the other in that of science, inasmuch as science is considered as a system in itself.

We may cite on this subject a very interesting study by Mr. Asch,[19] who criticizes the procedures generally used in social psychology to determine the influence of prestige. These consist in asking subjects to what extent they agree with a judgment. Ultimately, the same judgment is presented to the same subject, but with a modification of the subject's knowledge of the author of the judgment. Mr. Asch shows quite well that the results attained do not at all demonstrate, as is generally supposed, that evaluations are modified exclusively in relation to the prestige accorded to the author. Indeed, the judgment estimated is not at all an invariable element which is evaluated by taking account of the prestige of the different authors to whom it is attributed. The judgment is not the same because, when it is attributed to one author rather than to another, it changes its significance; there is no simple change of value but a new interpretation, for the judgment is put in the new context of our knowledge of the person who is supposed to have enunciated it. There are, then, judgments, as there are acts, which we interpret by what we know concerning their author. The influence attributed in recent years to prestige and its power of suggestion is manifest less irrationally and simply than is generally supposed.

[18] Vilfredo Pareto, *Traité de Sociologie générale*, translated by Pierre Boven, II, par. 1756.

[19] Solomon E. Asch, "The Doctrine of Suggestion, Prestige, and Imitation in Social Psychology," *Psychological Review*, LV, 1948, pp. 250-276.

It is this interpretation of acts as dependent on what is known concerning their author which makes us understand the mechanism of prestige, and the transfer of value which it effects from the person having prestige to the most diverse of his acts. "What genius does not vindicate the works of his youth!" Malraux exclaimed.[20] And, indeed, anyone who considers the early works of a great artist cannot help seeing in them the foreshadowing of his future greatness. Thus recognition of outstanding value in a person even validates acts which precede the time when it becomes indisputably manifest. The author of works of genius created at different times *is* a genius; and this characterization attaches the acts to a stable quality of the person which shines as well into the years previous to the period of production of masterpieces as into the years which follow. It is not sufficient to say that the past guarantees the future—for the future may very well validate the past—but the stable makeup of the person does permit us to prejudge his acts and particularly his judgments. "There are persons," says Méré, "who recognize true merit and to please them is a good indication; but there are many more who do not have good judgment, and satisfying them should not cause too much rejoicing." [21]

We thus see how prestige may serve to validate acts, to give rise to inclinations to imitation, and to work out the idea of a model from which conduct may be copied. The use of this argumentative mechanism in knowledge has given rise to both the use and the abuse of arguments from authority.

When Cicero asked us to scorn works of art and wrote: "In your opinion what would be said by L. Mummius, who had such complete scorn of Corinth, if he saw one of these dandies lovingly fondling some chamber-pot made of Corinthian bronze?" [22] This argument has no interest unless L. Mummius has some prestige. In addition, we should notice that this scorn for Corinth, which can serve as a model, is at the same time an element of this prestige, for very often the authority to whom we refer is at the same time being justified. If there is no prestige, argument from the model becomes worthless. In the *Rhetorica ad Herennium* we find a humorous example which requires us to distinguish between an argumentative scheme and the conditions of its application. This work tries to give an example of an argument which is feeble because it argues from what is done to what ought to be done. It concerns a passage from the *Trinumnus* by Plautus: "It is very disagreeable to rebuke

[20] André Malraux, *Saturne: Essaie sur Goya*, p. 18.
[21] Méré, *op. cit.*, I, p. 77.
[22] Cicero, *De Paradoxe* 2.

114

a friend for a fault, but it is often useful and profitable: for today I shall rebuke my friend for what he has done." [23] The argument has scarcely any value because it is stated by a comic character, the old Megaronides. But this is not always the case. To be convinced of this, it is sufficient to remember the confessors of the faith.

Argument based on the idea that a model must be followed is stronger to the extent that the authority is not contested. When it is a question of divine authority, this authority even makes it possible to determine standards of goodness and of truth.

Very often the authority is based on competence as the only reason for the argumentative value of certain expressions. When the teacher says to his pupil, "I don't understand what you are saying," this usually means, "You have expressed yourself badly" or "Your ideas are not very clear on this point." Again, incompetence may be made use of as a criterion for the disqualification of everyone who is considered less competent than those who disclaim their own competence. This is the import of the argument used by Chevreul, president of the Parisian Academy of Sciences, when the attempt was made to disqualify the testimony of handwriting experts from the discussion of the authenticity of the manuscript presented by Michel Chasles.[24] This form of argument can have an outstanding philosophic importance, since it may destroy the competence not only of an individual or a group, with respect to a certain matter, but of humanity as a whole. When one denounces in himself the deficiencies of reason, this may be done in order to affirm the deficiencies of human reason in general. He does not present himself as an exception: quite the contrary, he creates the impression that others are in the same situation as he. In the extreme case, if all men are in the same situation, the problem is deemed insoluble.

Schopenhauer shows quite well the abuse of this argument which might occur, using the artifice of feigning incompetence in a ticklish situation.[25] Here we pass from rhetorical arguments to eristic and even sophistical argument. But it is because rhetorical argument has some value that it may be utilized in bad faith, just as counterfeiting would be inconceivable unless there were authentic bills having some value. And if sophistical argument differs from honest argument by the bad faith which is employed in it, in order to establish this bad faith in another we make

[23] Cicero, Rhetorica ad Herennium, chap. ii; cf. Plautus, Trinumnus, Act I, Scene I, verse 5.

[24] Andri Vayson de Pradenne, Les Fraudes en archéologie préhistorique, p. 297.

[25] Arthur Schopenhauer, "Eristische Dialektik," Kunstgriff 31, Sämtliche Werke, VI, p. 423.

use of the ensemble of rhetorical methods of argument which permit us to conclude from the acts to the intention. Sophistical argument thus provides double confirmation of the value and importance of rhetoric, for its value is confirmed both by those who imitate it in bad faith and by those who make use of it to discredit the pretenses of an adversary.

In analyzing successively the effect of the act on the agent and that of the agent on the act, we have been led to emphasize first one and then the other. But this is merely the artifice of analysis. The interaction is constant and is quite often explicitly seen.

We may gain the benevolence of the judges, we read in the *Rhetorica ad Herennium*, "by praising the courage, wisdom, kindness, and brilliance of their judgments, and by consideration of the esteem which they will merit, and the expectations which they must fulfill." [26] Thus we pass from the consideration of past judgments to an evaluation of the jury and from the good jury to the anticipated favorable verdict, which will itself elevate the prestige of the judges. Successive evocation of the act and the person, then of the person and the act, does not leave the mind at the point at which it started. The cumulative effect of these interrelationships is clear, as long as no use is made of a separating technique. We shall call this the "snowball" interaction. This may take place even in the case of a single act, since a work which does honor to its author will be itself all the more prized as the author is highly esteemed. But the snowball interaction is better revealed when there is a difference either in the time or in the nature of the acts to be performed. Its effect is then to allow the person or the agent to be a basis for expectations quite superior to those which his previous acts would have justified, had this interaction not taken place. We find an example of this in the reasoning which Whately cites, whereby, on the basis of the marks of divine benevolence in this world, we conclude concerning the splendor of the afterlife by way of the intermediate conclusion that God is benevolent.[27] No less than the intervention of a person is required to permit the passage from an observable realm to one entirely different, from the real world to the world of the future life. But there is more: the benefits which we expect in the afterlife infinitely surpass those we enjoy here below, which serve as the beginning point for a snowball argument.

Of course, the snowball interrelation implies that the act and the person mutually affect each other in the same direction. However, the interaction may operate in opposed directions. It is generally in such cases that use is made of certain techniques which prevent the interplay. It is these which we are going to analyze in the remainder of our study.

---

26 *Rhetorica ad Herennium*, i, chap. iv, p. 5.
27 Richard Whately, *Elements of Rhetoric*, p. 62.

The techniques which break or curb the interaction of the act and the person must be utilized when there is an incompatibility between the act and what is known concerning the person, that is to say, when the act requires a profound modification of our conception of the person which we refuse to make or when the person should confer on the act a value incompatible with the consequences which it involves, that is to say, with other connections which also influence its value.

The most effective technique for preventing the reaction of the act on the agent is to consider the latter as completely good or evil, that is, as a god or a demon. The most effective technique for preventing the reaction of the agent on the act is to consider the latter as a truth or the expression of a fact on which there is complete agreement, at least in the present circumstances. We will begin by examining these two techniques, which we will call "separation" techniques.

The introduction into our thought of a perfect and divine being gives the possibility of completely detaching the person from the act. Nevertheless, the notion of God is not always used in this manner, far from it. We are familiar with a series of arguments in which God is presented as operating in order to acquire prestige and is deemed to have done certain things to show his power, or as a sign of his power, which, being manifest in a natural order, permits belief in his actions in another order.[28]

Leibniz likewise refuses to neglect the works and consider only the creator. "And so," he writes, "I am very far from the sentiment of those who maintain that there are no rules of goodness and perfection in the nature of things, or in the ideas which God has of them, and that the works of God are good merely for the *formal reason* that God has made them. . . . *The creator is discovered by consideration of creation*." [29] Leibniz thus wishes to apply the same reasoning to God as to man. In the double transition from the person to the act and from the act to the person, the first transition is prior, since God is involved. But Leibniz does not wish to leave it at this; he wishes as well to understand why the world is good and to pass from the creation to the creator. But let us not forget that it is in virtue of the highly privileged first movement that he knows that the present world is the best of all possible worlds. However, if he makes use of the value of the creation to glorify the creator, he also knows how, in some cases, to prevent the action of the act on the agent, by making use of divine perfection. This he explains to us in the *Essay on Theodicy*, by imagining a man of extraordinary reputation in the following situation. He writes:

28 Blaise Pascal, *Pensées*, No. 560.
29 G. W. Leibniz, *Discours de métaphysique*, pp. 26-27.

A man might give such great and strong proof of his virtue and holiness that all of the most apparent reasons which could be held against him to charge him with a proposed crime, for example, larceny, or an assassination, would have to be rejected as the calumnies of false witnesses, an extraordinary accident which occasionally lays suspicion on the most innocent. Thus in a case in which all others would be in danger of condemnation, or questioning . . . this man would be unanimously acquitted by his judges.[30]

In this case, Leibniz continues, there would be no new law but the application of a "good logic of probability," since "this person has such admirable qualities, that in virtue of a good logic of probability we must have more faith in his words than in that of numerous others." Leibniz has used a human example as a basis for this justification, which he considers as rational, of a technique consisting in refusing all unfavorable effects of the act on the agent; but by that very fact, when the same technique is applied to God, it operates perfectly: "I have already remarked that anything which might be opposed to the goodness and justice of God, is merely an appearance, which would be damaging to a man, but which becomes as nothing when applied to God and when weighed with the demonstrations which assure us of the infinite perfection of his attributes."

We just as often encounter the independence of the person in relation to the act when it is a matter of negative values. Bossuet makes use of it in this curious passage:

We Christians must recognize that neither the sciences, nor a great mind, nor the other gifts of nature are very considerable advantages, since God permits them to be completely possessed by devils, his chief enemies, and thereby renders them not merely unfortunate, but even worthy of infinite scorn; that in spite of all these outstanding qualities, and miserable and impotent as we are, we are enviable to them, because our great God chooses to regard us with pity.[31]

It is qualities which are involved here, but the mechanism is the same as with acts. These qualities cannot modify the idea which we hold of the demon, but rather they are tainted thereby—they are devalued and do not constitute "very considerable advantages." The act or the quality is interpreted or minimized so that it cannot affect the agent, and it is completely subordinated to the nature attributed to the latter.

From the moment an act expresses a fact, the value which is attributed to it is completely independent of that of the person, so that we find ourselves in a situation the opposite of that in which the person is

[30] G. W. Leibniz, "Essais de théodicée," in Die philosophischen Schriften, edited by C. J. Gerhardt, VI, pp. 70-74.

[31] Jacques Bénigne Bossuet, "Sermons sur les démons," in Sermons, II, ii.

shielded from his acts. "A factual error subjects a wise man to ridicule," La Bruyère tells us. But this is evidently on condition that the fact is incontestable. No man has enough prestige to make us believe that $2 + 2 = 5$ or accept any testimony which seems to us contrary to experience. It is a matter of weighing the evidential value of the experience.

In this regard, Locke reminds us that

> to a man whose experience has been always quite contrary, and has never heard of anything like it, the most untainted credit of a witness will scarce be able to find belief: as it happened to a Dutch ambassador, who entertaining the king of Siam with the peculiarities of Holland . . . amongst other things told him "that the water in his country would sometimes in cold weather be so hard that men walked upon it, and that it would bear an elephant if it were there." To which the king replied "hitherto I have believed the strange things you have told me, because I look upon you as a sober, fair man: but now I am sure you lie!" [32]

In this account, experience and the generalizations which seem to be authorized by it are considered as a fact which surpasses any influence of the person. His act, since it is deemed incompatible with convictions drawn from experience, is treated as a falsehood, which is, in turn, considered a fact. The person can do nothing about it. And, conversely, the act is not without effect on the person, since the validity of all his previous assertions is damaged.

Anything which is considered as a fact is independent of the action of the person; this is why the status of the fact is shaken by using one means or another to attach its assertion to the character of the witness. Everyone knows the famous tale of the magician who was trusted by the king and had him put on clothes which, he said, were seen only by men above reproach. The king and his courtiers saw nothing but did not dare to say so until one day when a child, in his innocence, cried, "Why is the king naked?" The spell was broken. The magician had enough prestige to make perception serve as a criterion of everyone's morality until the indisputable innocence of a child destroyed this favorable prejudice. From the moment the perception was no longer tied to a judgment of value, everyone gave it its usual importance.

When does a judgment express a fact? As long, we have seen, as it is believed to be valid for a universal audience and (to avoid all discussion in this regard) has been included in a special discipline whose foundations are presumed to be accepted and whose criteria have been made the object of an explicit or implicit convention.

There is a number of scientific or practical techniques which at-

[32] John Locke, *An Essay concerning Human Understanding*, Book IV, chap. xv, par. 5.

tempt to obtain objectivity by separating the act from the agent either to describe it or to judge it. Behaviorism is one example; another is supplied by all competitions in which the contestants are judged on measurable performances or in which the work is judged without the name of its author being made known. In law a great many arrangements seek to characterize acts independently of the person committing them and even without concern for his intentions. In ethics such recourse to the fact without consideration of the intention is much less frequent. Still it is apparent that an ethics such as the Japanese, which is much more formalistic than Western ethics, may be considered as a morality of the act. Ruth Benedict cites a long list of Japanese school directors who committed suicide because the flames of a conflagration, with which they had nothing to do, threatened the portrait of the emperor which ornaments each educational institution.[33]

Detachment of the act and refusal to introduce into its evaluation any consideration concerning the person seem much more rationalistic than does the inverse technique. We have seen that Pareto ridicules the introduction of considerations concerning the author into estimation of the foundation of a proposition. In this he merely follows Bentham's view. We may note in this regard a remark by Whately, of which we cannot help admiring the insight on this point. "If the measure is a good one," says Bentham, "will it become bad because it is supported by a bad man?" And Whately replies, "It is only in matters of strict science, and that too, in arguing to scientific man, that the characters of the advisers (as well as all other probable arguments) should be wholly put out of the question." [34] Nevertheless, whatever the value of Whately's considerations, it cannot be denied that preoccupation with objectivity leads to the detachment of the act from the person because it is more difficult to obtain agreement concerning persons than concerning acts, or at least this seems to be the situation in virtue of the notion of a "fact." Someone is usually called "fair" because he judges the act without taking account of the person. It is true that this procedure often possesses indisputable advantages, the principal one being the facilitation of the agreement on criteria. But it must never be forgotten that it is no more than a procedure and may have serious disadvantages. The best proof of this is the recent attempts to individualize punishment.

The cases in which the interaction of the act and the person is entirely broken in one sense or another are relatively rare in social life, for they are merely limiting cases. Most techniques which are used for this are

[33] Ruth Benedict, *The Chrysanthemum and the Sword*, p. 151.
[34] Richard Whately, *op. cit.*, pp. 162-164.

not separation techniques but curbing techniques, which have the effect of restraining this interaction without completely annulling it.

One of these techniques is prejudice or, perhaps better, bias. An act committed by someone does not react on the conception which we have of this person, in so far as favorable or unfavorable prejudice permits maintenance of an adequation between the act and the person. The act is interpreted and judged in such a way that it need not modify our idea of the person, which, as we have already seen, supplies the context whereby the act is better understood whenever the act is not perfectly univocal. But if prejudice does permit the removal of a threatening inconsistency, it cannot be used when the inconsistency is too obvious.

The effect of bias or prejudice is quite often a blindness toward the value of an act and the transfer to it of other values stemming from the person. Avoidance of prejudice is thus a healthy separation between act and person. But if we put ourselves in the point of view of the normal interrelation of act and person, which seems to us primordial, prejudice appears as a curbing technique, a technique which is opposed to the continual renewal of the image of the person and contributes primarily to the stability of the person.

When we look at the role of bias and prestige, we see that it is prestige which may be considered as the force which assures the action of the agent on the act. It has an active and positive role and occurs at an earlier stage than that at which bias enters. Bias itself corrects an inconsistency between the act and the person and occurs when the latter must be shielded against the act. But though prestige may prepare for bias, they are not always linked, for bias may be based on other kinds of previous arguments.

In order to avoid giving the impression that we judge certain acts as a function of the person or that we suffer from prejudice, certain precautions must often be taken. One of them is to preface an unfavorable estimation of an act with certain eulogies of the person, and conversely. These eulogies are sometimes directed toward other acts, but with the intention of praising the person and making clear our own impartiality.

If the technique of prejudice is insufficiently established and the act stands out in spite of everything, it is possible to make a separation between distinct realms of activity in such a way that an act done in one of them will be considered irrelevant to the idea we form of the person, whose image is determined by the action of another realm. In different societies and different environments, these realms would not be determined in the same way. For example, to be hard-working or faithful in marriage may in certain cases be determinant for the image we form of the person, while in others they would be relegated to the reserve realm of acts of scant importance. The extent of these inactive realms is the object of an agreement, generally tacit, which comes under the same heading as the values and connections admitted by the group and even contributes to its characterization. It need hardly be said that the reserve realm of acts which are considered irrelevant may vary according to the person. Such acts as would be considered unimportant when attributed to a ruler would be essential to the idea we form of a person of lesser rank, and vice versa. It is the same with respect to the acts of a certain period of life—childhood, for example.

But we need not believe that the separation between the act and the person cannot be extended to the most important acts. Quite the contrary; in reality, the most important acts are also those which are watched, precisely because we know that they reflect on the image which we form of the person. But if we think that an act has been set up to create a certain impression, its indicative value is greatly reduced. This was emphasized by Schopenhauer, for whom the person colors and impregnates the least of his acts.[35] Indeed, it is in the little things which are least regarded that men indicate their true nature best.

In other cases, from the multiplicity of acts we retain only a single aspect, which alone is judged important. Sometimes we split the person into fragments having no mutual interrelation or frustrate the influence of the act on the person by crystallizing the latter at a particular stage of his existence. Jouhandeau traces the portrait of the woman who reduces her ego to what it once was and refuses to integrate her present actions into it, saying to her customers, "I am in the past; it is only my mummy that mends your shoes, Monsieur." [36] This technique is used much more often than would seem. Each time we make a rigid exception of past action, we crystallize the individual in some way. Thus shielded, he is endowed with some value but has lost his spontaneity.

Paulhan notices quite correctly the disagreeable impression we feel when we hear friends speaking of us.[37] According to him, this disagreeable impression is tied to the illusion of forecasts from the past. But it is not necessarily this which causes the impression, it being rather the fact that our acts and our person are linked by others in a mechanical and unchangeable fashion, as if our person had been arrested at a certain stage of its development. It is disagreeable to hear someone say of us, "He will certainly act nobly and sacrifice himself," because this act is presented simply as the consequence of the past and does not have the power to react on our future personality and re-create it for ourselves or others.

[35] Arthur Schopenhauer, "Zur Ethik," in *Parega und Paralipomena, Sämtliche Werke*, VI, p. 245.

[36] Marcel Jouhandeau, *Un Monde*, p. 34.

[37] Jean Paulhan, *Entretien sur des faits divers*, p. 67.

Along with these techniques of more general importance, whose richness we are very far from having exhausted, there are techniques of less importance, which merely seek to remove an incompatibility between the act and the person in a given circumstance.

One of them is recourse to the notion of an exception. The meritorious or blame-worthy act which seems incompatible with what we otherwise know of the person is considered as exceptional, to prevent the further transfer of its value to the person. Still it is often necessary to explain how this exceptional behavior could occur. If a friend wrongs us, we explain this behavior by ignorance or awkwardness, in order to avoid seeing in it causes which would shatter our friendly relations. It is on a conception of the same sort that we base the respectful recourse "from the pope poorly informed to the pope well informed." We thereby understand that the judgment which is opposed is not attributed to an imperfect faculty of judging but to badly informed counselors. It is thus possible to disapprove of the judgment, without modifying one's estimation of the person.

An extreme procedure consists in supposing that the act only apparently belongs to the person and that it was suggested or dictated by someone else or, still better, that someone else speaks through his voice. The person is reduced to the role of a witness. Bossuet asks, "May corrupt preachers bear the message of eternal life?" And he replies, carrying on Augustine's analogy to the vineyard and the bush, "The bush bears a fruit which does not belong to it, and is nonetheless the fruit of the vineyard for being supported by the bush" and "Do not scorn the grape on the pretext that it is found among the thorns: do not reject this doctrine because it is surrounded by evil: it still comes from God." [38]

Sometimes separation established between the person and his acts is an attempt not to protect the person but to see that the acts are given their proper value and are not lowered by the envy or ill repute with respect to their author. Chevalier de Méré tells us that "Caesar attributed his most admirable deeds to the favor of the Gods. However, Cato accuses him of believing in neither Gods nor Goddesses; Caesar merely understood the sentiments of the people." [39] Demosthenes does not hesitate to use the same technique: "Well, if I showed greater foresight than others in all circumstances, I do not mean to attribute it in any way to a special wisdom or some faculty on which I pride myself. No, these insights I owe to two causes which I shall explain: first, Athenians, to good luck . . . and second, to the fact that my judgments and my predictions

[38] Jacques Bénigne Bossuet, "Sermon des pécheurs," *op. cit.*, II, p. 489.
[39] Méré, *op. cit.*, II, p. 109.

are not paid for." [40] In this example the tie is only partially broken. Demosthenes attributes his good advice to luck but also to his own honesty. Indeed, the first reason might turn against him: if luck rules, why should it continue to favor him in the future? Now what is important, namely, confidence in his present forecast, he attributes equally to the honesty which his adversaries lack.

Recourse to luck or the goddess of fortune is a profession of modesty which, though it need not be taken too seriously, does permit the reduction of the effect of the act on the person. We may treat in the same manner other procedures, such as recounting a story as if it came from a third person or such as making judgments preceded by "they say that . . ." in place of "I suppose that . . ."—in brief, all those cases in which we attempt, as far as possible, to separate the act from the person in order to reduce the role of the latter to that of a witness or a mouthpiece.

It is in the realm of judicial debate that all these techniques are really applied to a happy hunting ground. It is there that we find all the procedures tying act and person or permitting the union of the two to be broken. The only conclusion which may be drawn from this is that the connection between act and person is merely a presumption and must never be considered a necessary tie. Among the techniques examined in the *Rhetorica ad Herennium*, the one known under the name of "deprecation" is very interesting from our point of view. "The accused admits the crime and its premeditation, but none the less implores mercy." And the author adds: "This could scarcely be done before a tribunal, unless we plead for a man who has been recommended by fine acts which are many and well-known." [41] At the extreme case, it is demanded that account be taken only of former acts which are put in opposition to the recent acts of the person. The argument at the same time implies the unity of the act and the person—without which previous acts would have no significance to the trial—and attempts to destroy this unity with respect to present actions. So conceived, this deprecation presumes that laudable acts express the true personality better than those which are harmful. It thus employs a double convention—that which ties the act to the person and that which permits them to be separated under certain circumstances. The duality of this convention alone permits this form of argument. The question is to note whether the destruction of the tie of act and person seems sufficiently justified under the given circumstances; but it must be emphasized that this destruction is invoked only in cases of difficulty.

The connection between act and person seems to us the prototype

[40] Démosthène, "Sur la paix," par. ii, in *Harangues*.
[41] Cicero, *Rhetorica ad Herennium*, i (*op. cit.*, chap. xiv).

of a series of ties which give rise to the same interactions and lend themselves to the same arguments: the connection between individual and group, the connection between an event and the epoch in which it occurs, and many other connections of coexistence of which the most general is that of act and essence. We have been able only to outline our observations concerning the relations between the act and the person. The study of other connections, the aspects in which they resemble the first, and those in which they are different, would carry us beyond the limits of this article. We will be satisfied if the preceding pages strengthen our readers in the idea that rhetoric, conceived as the study of methods of argument, may clarify the most diverse areas of human thought, from literature to epistemology and metaphysics, by way of law, morals, and religion.

HENRY W. JOHNSTONE, JR.

A NEW THEORY OF
PHILOSOPHICAL
ARGUMENTATION

In a heterodox age such as our own, for every philosophical outlook there is another which raises doubts about it, and the ingenuous thinker may well come to feel that only the reality of controversy itself is ultimately undeniable. This insight has often been tantamount to a cynical repudiation of all philosophies. A more hopeful and, indeed, more thoughtful alternative, however, would consist in developing the philosophical consequences of supposing that controversy is ultimately real. What is needed is a general theory of philosophical argumentation, a study of the conditions under which disputes among philosophers arise, are conducted, and may be assessed. For many reasons, the principles of philosophical argumentation seem *suorum generum*; they do not appear to be strictly identifiable with the canons of formal logic, scientific method, or any other hitherto established discipline. The most important of these reasons is that it is precisely the canons of logic and science which are among the controversial issues of contemporary philosophy. Other reasons will be discussed shortly.

In this situation, it is surprising that in recent years so little work has been done on the theory of philosophical argumentation. Indeed, the only sustained inquiry into it has been that undertaken by the logical positivists. But this inquiry is circumscribed by that very assumption whose doubtfulness has just been indicated; the assumption, namely, that the principles which govern philosophical disputes can be strictly identified with those of hitherto established methodologies.

The recent book *Rhétorique et philosophie* [1] offers an alternative to

---

[1] Ch. Perelman and L. Olbrechts-Tyteca, *Rhétorique et philosophie: pour une théorie de l'argumentation en philosophie*. Throughout the present discussion, parenthesized numbers will be used to refer to the pages of this work.

the positivistic approach. It accuses the positivist of adopting too narrow a conception of proof. "We are prepared to accept other arguments than those with which traditional logic, deductive or inductive, concerns itself. We shall consider as proof . . . any argument that diminishes our doubt, that quells our hesitations" (p. 123).

The basic task to which the authors of this book devote themselves is to explore the principles and important ramifications of the art of allaying philosophical doubts and hesitations—an art which they identify as rhetoric. This version of rhetoric is said to contrast with formal logic in several ways. In the first place, "while in logic, one always reasons at the interior of a postulated system, considered as taken for granted, in a rhetorical argument anything can at any time be called into question; one can always withdraw his adherence" (p. 26). Another difference is that in logic, one proof is sufficient to establish a given assertion, while in rhetoric many may be necessary. But the fundamental distinction is that although a logical proof is constraining, a rhetorical proof is not, but results only in a degree of assent to the thesis which the rhetorician proposes. And since degrees of assent are distinct from degrees of probability, rhetoric is independent of the theory of probability. Nor is it, furthermore, to be equated with the psychology of suggestion.

> The class of phenomena which we shall wish to study could undoubtedly serve as the object of a psychological research, seeing that the result at which [rhetorical] arguments aim is a particular state of consciousness, a certain intensity of adherence. But our concern is to grasp the logical aspect, in a very broad sense of the word, of the methods used, under the title of "proof," in order to obtain this state of consciousness (p. 3).

The use of the term "rhetoric" to connote the discipline which they do have in mind the authors attempt to justify in terms of its employment by ancient writers, especially Aristotle, whose third or panegyric kind of rhetoric [2] is said by them to correspond closely with the subject of their own investigation.

All eight chapters of *Rhétorique et philosophie* had appeared previously in various journals. Six of these articles were written by Professor Perelman alone; these are entitled, respectively, "Freedom and Ratiocination," "Absolute Philosophies and Relative Philosophy," "The Quest of the Rational," "On Proof in Philosophy," "Sociology of Knowledge and Philosophy of Knowledge," and "The Problem of Good Choice." These are largely preparatory or peripheral studies. In the two articles which seem most directly to develop the thesis of the book, "Logic and Rhetoric" and "Act and Person in Argument," [3] M. Perelman is joined by

[2] Aristotle, *Rhetorica*, 1358[b] 21-29.

[3] This article appears as Chapter 6 of the present volume.

Mme Olbrechts-Tyteca. In these chapters two important matters are discussed: the nature of the audience [4] in philosophical rhetoric and the techniques effective in dealing with this audience.

It is necessary to consider the audience of rhetorical argumentation because "rhetoric, in our sense of the word, differs from logic in that it is concerned not with abstract truth, categorical or hypothetical, but with adherence" (p. 18). And "since rhetorical argumentation aims at adherence, it essentially depends upon the audience to which it addresses itself, for what will be conceded by one audience will not be by another" (p. 19). And to produce or increase such adherence to his doctrine, the speaker can do no more than to exploit the assumptions or prejudices of his particular audience. The difference between philosophical and non-philosophical rhetoric is only that in the former, "one may make use only of premises admitted by everyone, or at least by that hypercritical assembly, independent of the contingencies of time and place, which one supposes oneself to be addressing" (p. 21). The universal audience to which the philosopher makes his appeal contrasts with the opposite extreme of the single respondent dramatized in the Socratic dialogue. In this case the rhetorician can readily ascertain what premises are actually conceded by his audience and, in making capital of these, can create the illusion that the argument concerns objective fact rather than opinion. But the universal audience affords no such assurance; it is in the last analysis only an image in the mind of the philosopher. "We invent a model of man—the incarnation of reason . . . which we seek to convince, and which varies with our knowledge of other men, or other civilizations, of other systems of thought, with what we take to be incontrovertible facts or objective truths" (p. 22). If certain individuals remain unmoved by his solicitations, the philosopher's only ultimate recourse is to regard them as irrational and thus excluded from the ideal audience which he supposes himself to be addressing. In so doing, "we shall pass, in reality, from the universal audience to the elite audience" (*ibid.*).

An obvious epistemological question arises here: how shall we distinguish the *bona fide* philosopher from one whose "elite audience" consists merely of figmentary interlocutors, who by definition will capitulate to his arguments? The reply is that "to address itself to this [elite] audience constitutes, in the case of an honest mind, the maximum effort of argumentation to which it can lay claim" (p. 39). To the extent that this statement appeals to the unexamined notion of the upright man, it seems unsatisfactory. But the suggestion that the genuine philosopher, as op-

---

[4] Throughout the present discussion, the words "audience" and "speaker" should be understood to cover situations involving the written as well as the spoken word.

posed to the charlatan, will use all the effective resources of rhetorical argumentation is helpful, since many of these devices are discussed at some length.

For Perelman and Olbrechts-Tyteca, most of the important techniques of rhetoric depend upon the fact that there is, in the mind of the audience, an interaction between the personality of the speaker and the propositions he asserts. If the speaker is trusted, his thesis will be received with less hesitation than otherwise, and if the thesis seems obviously true, the trustworthiness of its propounder will appear to be enhanced. La Bruyère is quoted as evidence that the complement of this latter relation likewise holds: "An error of fact throws a wise man into ridicule. A fact is more respectable than a lord-mayor." Objective fact is indeed one of the limiting points of the interaction; it is impersonal in the sense that its credibility is unaffected by the personality of the speaker. The other limit is the speaker regarded as perfect, since his sway over an audience cannot be diminished by any of his utterances, however absurd they may be. Thus science and theology represent extreme cases of the rhetorical situation. Most argumentation falls somewhere between these.

The rhetorical techniques which make use of this principle do so in striving either to inhibit or to reinforce the interaction. In the first case, the speaker will attempt to steer the argument toward either of the limits just mentioned; he will address his audience with an air of high authority, or he will efface himself in an attitude of objectivity. Both limits would seem to be involved when the acknowledged expert disqualifies himself; for "The incompetence of the competent man can be used as a criterion to disqualify all those whom one has no reason to believe more competent than him who has declared himself to be incompetent" (p. 69). This type of argument is often used by philosophers to establish the incompetence of man in general.

The relationship between a speaker and his utterances may, on the other hand, be reinforced by a constant reference from one to the other. This presupposes, of course, that both tend in the first place to be trusted by the audience. The authors discuss the ways of dealing with the interaction between a *proposition* and its *proponent* primarily in the wider context of the relation between the moral criticism of a *person* and that of his *acts* ("Act and Person in Argument"), but the former pair is a special case of the latter. "The connection between act and person seems to us the prototype of a series of relationships which give rise to the same interactions and the same arguments" (p. 84).

Various other modes of rhetoric are referred to, but not in any systematic fashion. The more closely an argument approaches the limit of pure mental suggestion, and the further it is from formal validity, the more important it will be to conceal rhetorically the use of rhetoric. "A fundamental procedure—well known and much used, but very effective—is to insinuate from the very beginning that one is not a persuasive speaker" (p. 37). Another procedure, which seems largely independent of the personality of the speaker, is to argue that a given proposal involves a difference of kind rather than one of degree, or vice versa. "When General Marshall was . . . fighting the 25% reduction of credits to Europe which the American Congress wished to impose, he asserted that from that time on it was no longer a question of 'reconstruction' but of 'assistance' " (p. 35). Again, one may attempt to disqualify a value by exhibiting it as merely a means to an end.

An interesting *obiter dictum* concerns the rhetorical tactic of accusing one's opponent of *petitio*: "Begging the question is not a logical fallacy . . . , for [logic] has never forbidden the use of the principle of identity. . . . The fact is that to commit a *petitio principii* is to regard as conceded a premise which one's interlocutor contests. The truth of the premise is not at issue, but only the adherence of the interlocutor" (pp. 127-128). And the matter of adherence is, of course, the essence of rhetoric.

Among the ramifications of this central theory of rhetoric are its bearings upon the contrast between absolute philosophies and relative philosophy, upon the sociology of knowledge, and upon the problem of freedom. Absolute ("premières") philosophies are those resting on unquestioned assumptions regarding reality, veridical cognition, or the nature of value, and would be exemplified by most traditional metaphysics. Such philosophies seem incapable of accounting for subjectivity, error, appearance, and other modes of disorder, and appear to be locked in endless contention with each other. Philosophical disagreements can be resolved only within relative ("régressive") philosophy; i.e., that whose postulates are open to revision when newly-encountered facts reveal incoherences in a previous formulation. But the revision "is neither automatic nor arbitrary; it is arrived at by a mind conscious of its own effort and of its responsibility, by a mind conscious of its engagement with the real and of its ultimate freedom of judgment." (P. 98. This is a quotation from an article by Gonseth.) Genuine choice is involved, and choice is influenced by argumentation. So relative philosophy is ultimately a product of rhetoric.

While absolute philosophies have been typical of times of social stability, ages of upheaval are characterized by a predominately relativistic temper of thought. This observation is intended to show the relevance of the sociology of knowledge to the study of philosophical argumentation. In general, the idea which the philosopher has of his universal audience "has varied in the course of history, [and this idea] has been influenced by the milieu in which one has lived, by the education he has received, and by all the other elements which determine the conceptions of the individual" (p. 140).

Intellectual freedom is neither submission to an externally imposed order nor absolute indeterminism; it is rather a feature of the rhetorical situation. In the case of two interlocutors, "we may consider as manifestations of freedom, in the first place, the attitude of the one who devises the arguments . . . and, in the second place, the behavior of the one who is content to grant or withhold his adherence to the theses which are presented to him" (p. 44). The first attitude corresponds to spontaneity of invention; the second to that freedom of commitment which is "the foundation of a community of minds" (*ibid.*).

The idea of rhetoric, then, sheds some light on traditional types and problems of philosophy—this much may be granted. And that *Rhétorique et philosophie* makes a solid contribution to the general theory of rhetoric is indisputable. In particular, the use the authors make of the concept of interaction is original and enlightening. But whether they have really succeeded in illuminating, to any considerable extent, the nature of philosophical argumentation itself is open to question. A general impression of the book is that most of the statements it makes about rhetoric, and most of the rhetorical techniques it discusses, do not apply peculiarly to the arguments of philosophers. The methods for inhibiting or reinforcing the interaction between a speaker's personality and his thesis are a case in point. These seem rather remote from any significant device of philosophical polemic. Whatever we may know of a philosopher's character has little to do with whether we accept or reject his position; the credibility of the Leibnizian theory of monads, for example, is not diminished by the statement that its author was somewhat of an opportunist in his personal conduct. Perhaps the rejoinder would be that such a theory approaches the impersonal limit of objective fact. But this is not satisfactory, for there is an obvious difference between a theory of monads, however "objectively" it may be presented, and objective fact as such—a difference which it would not be possible to conceal from any audience sufficiently enlightened to understand the theory of monads in the first place. This may be expressed by saying that the latter could not be confirmed or disconfirmed through any observation or series of observations; in Whitehead's phrase, it "could not fail of exemplification."

The ultimate reply might well be that the techniques based on interaction are not generally applicable to philosophical argumentation. This would bring into sharp relief the need for a clearcut distinction between philosophical and nonphilosophical rhetoric. The authors themselves regard this as a crucial problem and attempt to solve it by stipulating that the philosopher must address a "universal audience." The epistemological difficulties with this conception have already been pointed out. In addition it may be asked whether, even supposing these difficulties overcome, the stipulation makes any real sense; this question is especially justified in view of the fact that not a single concrete example of a genuine "universal audience" of philosophical rhetoric is given in the course of the entire book. (The audience which Pascal attempted to interest in the problem of the immortality of the soul is mentioned, but it seems clear that the intent here was didactic rather than purely philosophical.) If one tries to think of examples, he will be likely to think of moral appeals to the human race, like the Sermon on the Mount and the Communist Manifesto. But the "universality" of the audience in such cases is not at all what the authors seem to intend it to be. It is primarily a rhetorical impression of universality insinuated by the speaker into the minds of his audience for the sake of united action, rather than an idea of "reason incarnate" grasped by the speaker himself. Nor is it clear that this type of appeal is really philosophical, since neither analysis nor speculation is likely to be involved. In any event, no theory of philosophical argumentation which omits these traditional activities of philosophers can be regarded as adequate.

The point may be pressed further by asking what audience *is* addressed by the arguments of analytic or speculative philosophers. For the present writer, an irresistible reply is that it consists of those whom the philosopher wishes to disabuse of error. For Plato, it included the Sophists; for Hume, the Rationalists; for Hegel, the Intuitionists. But in no case would it include the whole world. It would exclude at least those whom the philosopher regarded as his allies. But oddly enough, the authors insist that "The author ought . . . . himself to be included in this [universal] audience"! (p. 21)

M. Perelman and Mme Olbrechts-Tyteca might well reply here that philosophical argumentation may be not only polemical or negative but also constructive, and that only the latter variety of it is addressed to a universal audience. If this is what they meant, it is a serious defect in their exposition not to have said so, for the distinction between "argument" in the sense of "attack" and the same word in the sense of "proof" is fundamental. And, aside from the interesting question whether there has ever been an effective philosophical "proof" which was not actually an attack, the objection may be raised that it is not very helpful to suppose that seemingly constructive philosophical arguments are addressed to a universal audience. For of all proofs, those which have the clearest claim to a universal audience are scientific demonstrations; here all of the authors' observations, including those on the passage to an elite audience as the result of the speaker's identification of recalcitrance with irrationality, are borne out with complete success. Mere universality gives no clue as to how one might distinguish constructive philosophy from scientific exposition.

In discussing the relations between philosophy and science, M. Perelman does distinguish the "responsibility" of the former from the "technicity" ("technicité") of the latter (pp. 98, 115, 117). He does this in such a way as to suggest the traditional view that philosophy is concerned with Reason and science with the Understanding. If Reason and Understanding could be regarded as distinctive modes of the universal audience —and the authors do refer to this audience in its philosophical version as "the incarnation of reason"—then perhaps the difference between philosophy and science could be maintained. But is it not a distortion of the philosopher's purpose to say that he addresses his arguments to Reason? A much more natural description of philosophical argumentation is that it is addressed to an unspecified or, if specified, particular audience, and that Reason is the means, mode, vehicle, or language of the argument.

If all the foregoing objections are valid, one wonders whether there is really any promise after all in the attempt to define philosophical argumentation in terms of rhetoric. This doubt is fortified by the reflection that the philosopher's aim in arguing has usually been more than merely to secure adherence to his thesis. More specifically, no conscientious philosopher would be satisfied by assent brought about by methods concealed from his audience. Philosophical controversy is essentially a bilateral affair; it is genuine only when each party to it makes available to the other all the argumentative devices that he uses. The authors, in fact, are careful to point this out (p. 18). But they also realize, indeed emphasize, the fact that "rhetoric" has commonly been used in a sense at least neutral to the distinction between unilateral and bilateral persuasion. And at no point in the book is it made clear that the rhetorical techniques employed in philosophical argumentation would be essentially bilateral.

It should be stressed, however, that the problem here does not arise from any mere oversight on the part of the authors. It is rather a consequence of a systematic refusal to suppose that there is any difference, except one of degree, between Rhetoric and the discipline which has traditionally been called "Dialectic." Aristotle, whom it is germane to quote here, in view of the importance which the authors attach to his *Rhetorica*, defined "Dialectic" as "a line of inquiry whereby we shall be able to reason from opinions that are generally accepted about every problem propounded to us," [5] and went on to define "Rhetoric," "the counterpart of Dialectic," [6] as "the faculty of observing in any given case the available means of persuasion." [7] But an age of "Relative Philosophy" distrusts the notion that there is any *bona fide* "reasoning" from "generally

---

[5] *Topica*, 100ᵃ 18-20, Pickard-Cambridge translation.

[6] *Rhetorica*, 1354ᵃ 1, Roberts translation.

[7] *Ibid.*, 1355ᵇ 25-26.

accepted" (i.e., philosophical) opinion. To it, such reasoning smacks of the inflexibility and intellectual despotism of "Absolute Philosophies." Because they regard all philosophical positions as the product of a free and tentative choice, the authors are satisfied to suppose that no objective dialectic of ideas is operative in this area. Yet the fact that there must be such a dialectic is shown not only by the results but also by the method of the present criticism; for the statement that certain difficulties arise from a systematic repudiation of the distinction between rhetoric and dialectic is not intended necessarily to persuade anyone; it is only a kind of reasoning from generally accepted opinion. The final account of philosophical argumentation will have to be given by a philosophy which endorses dialectic while avoiding the absolutism which this book justly opposes.

The preface to *Rhétorique et philosophie* had been undertaken by the late Professor Émile Bréhier, who unfortunately died before he had finished writing it. The paragraphs which are printed, however, suggest a line of criticism similar to that adopted here. The very last passage seems especially relevant; it reads: "Rhetoric seeks to justify a thesis by relying upon a general knowledge of men, of their characters, of their passions; it is an art of obtaining assent. The dialectician seeks to try ("éprouver") the intellectual force of. . . ."

Never, to the present writer's knowledge, has death interrupted a more interesting sentence.

CH. PERELMAN

REPLY TO
HENRY W. JOHNSTONE, JR.[1]

First of all, I want to thank Mr. Johnstone very sincerely for having, through his discussion, made known some of our ideas on argumentation. Contacts between philosophical circles speaking different languages are not frequent enough and every opportunity to multiply them should be welcomed. It would be unfortunate if such opportunities should raise misunderstandings, for which we ourselves might involuntarily be at least partially responsible.

For instance, I know that Mr. Johnstone himself is fundamentally interested in philosophical argumentation—as may be seen from the articles he has published recently.[2] As far as we are concerned, our main interest is in the construction of a philosophical theory of argumentation and in the elaboration of a treatise dealing with argumentation in general. The subtitle, of our book *Rhétorique et philosophie* seems, however, to have lent itself to a misunderstanding: "Pour une théorie de l'argumentation en philosophie," was intended to show that our contention was that a place should be given, in philosophy, to a theory of argumentation. It is true that in my article "De la preuve en philosophie," I pointed out that philosophy itself cannot be adequately understood without reference to a theory of argumentation, but this contention is only a particular application of our general thesis.

Fundamentally our thesis stresses the opposition between (formal) demonstration and argumentation. It expresses our disappointment arising from the observation that logic is nowadays reduced to the study of

[1] See "A New Theory of Philosophical Argumentation," reprinted as Chapter 7 of the present volume.

[2] "Philosophy and *Argumentum ad Hominem*," *Journal of Philosophy*, XLIX, 1952, pp. 489-498. "The Methods of Philosophical Polemic," *Methodos*, V, 1953, pp. 131-140. "The Nature of Philosophical Controversy," *Journal of Philosophy*, LI, 1954, pp. 294-300.

formal reasoning, and that so far as the Aristotelian distinction between analytical and dialectical proofs is concerned, the whole field of dialectical reasoning has been neglected. We feel that this narrowing of the field of logic is disastrous for the methodology of the human sciences, for law and for all branches of philosophy. Our purpose is thus a general one and we think that to say, as Mr. Johnstone does, that our main task is "to explore the principles and important ramifications of the art of allaying philosophical doubts and hesitations" (p. 127) is to restrict it unduly: we certainly are interested in this problem, but only as a special case of a general theory of argumentation.

Besides, we have nowhere identified the subject of our investigation with the study of the epideictic or panegyric kind of discourse (p. 127), since our theory has a very general scope. What we claim is that light can be shed on the nature and function of epideictic discourse by showing that argumentation like all persuasive discourse, is directed towards increasing the intensity of adherence to certain theses, that this intensity can always be increased, and that, because of this feature, arguments aiming at adherence are different from proofs directed toward truth: this should make it possible to understand in what fashion a logic of value judgments, conceivable only within the framework of a theory of argumentation, will differ from a logic concerned with the truth of propositions.

This much being said, we come back to the main point in the discussion of Mr. Johnstone, which bears on our divergent conceptions of philosophical argumentation. For Mr. Johnstone, the latter is fundamentally *ad hominem*; it is critical and dialectical, and for this reason local, neither having value for everybody nor even claiming universal assent: so science and philosophy would essentially differ from each other.

We, for our part, are easily induced to acknowledge that criticism in philosophical matters is often *ad hominem* but not necessarily so. We believe in the possibility of external criticism, with reference to generally admitted theses, which are explicitly or implicitly in opposition to those of the philosopher. Curiously enough it happens to be this conception that Mr. Johnstone himself adopts for his own account, when he opposes to rhetoric, defined in our terms, the dialectic of Aristotle as "a line of inquiry whereby we shall be able to reason from opinions that are generally accepted about every problem propounded to us." (p. 133) This means that our own conception is really akin to dialectical argumentation, as understood by Aristotle, and which the latter opposes to Mr. Johnstone's type of *ad hominem* argumentation. Aristotle would rather have characterized this as examinational or critical.[3]

In our view, philosophical argumentation, especially when it is con-

[3] *De Sophisticis Elenchis*, 165[b] 1-5.

structive—we must stress the fact that Mr. Johnstone's conception disregards the techniques used by a philosopher in developing his own system—is dialectical in the sense of Aristotle. It starts from generally accepted propositions. But what are these, if not propositions accepted by the universality of reasonable minds, as the philosopher conceives this universality? In this sense we say that for a philosopher it is not enough to persuade some particular audience—that would be merely *ad hominem* —but he claims to convince a universal audience: his argumentation is not *ad rem*—this characterization makes no sense—but *ad humanitatem*. It is true that every philosopher may have a different vision of such an audience—and on this point psychology and sociology of knowledge may properly intervene—but we are faced with a philosophical argument only when the reasonings advanced at least *claim* to be valid for everybody. This should enable us to understand, without the incredulity expressed by Mr. Johnstone (p. 132), why the author himself must be included among the members of such an audience.

How then, asks Mr. Johnstone, can we distinguish philosophy from science? Properly, through the part played in philosophy by argumentation. The use of conventionally admitted experimental and deductive techniques, reduces, in science, the room for argumentation. It is only when it is a question of hypotheses, or of the appreciation of facts outside the technical field, that scientific and philosophical argumentation tend to blend. In philosophy, one does not try to establish facts but one argues them, in such a way, however, as to claim that this kind of reasoning should be admitted by everyone. Were it not for this claim, it would be difficult to distinguish the philosophical discourse, from the political, legal or theological one.

HENRY W. JOHNSTONE, JR.

PERSUASION AND VALIDITY

IN PHILOSOPHY

It has often been asserted that philosophical statements are noncognitive —that they do not convey genuine knowledge. With this assertion I am inclined, for various reasons, to agree. But I do not agree with a conclusion that is sometimes drawn from the assertion that philosophical statements are noncognitive. This is the conclusion that there can be no valid arguments supporting philosophical statements. It is certainly not obvious, I admit, that valid argumentation could yield a noncognitive conclusion. Of course, a formally valid argument with at least one noncognitive premise could have a noncognitive conclusion; this is shown, for example, by recent work on the Logic of Imperatives.[1] But this observation is not to the point. Those who deny that noncognitive philosophical statements can be the conclusions of valid arguments are not thinking of validity in a purely formal sense. What they have in mind is rather the notion of a valid argument as one leading to a necessary conclusion—a conclusion, in other words, which, in view of the argument, it is obligatory to accept. Now the existence of an obligation to accept a statement seems to create a presumption that what the statement expresses is an item of knowledge. There has been a strong tendency to suppose that the conclusion of any argument valid in this sense must be cognitive, from which it would follow that no noncognitive statement could be the conclusion of a valid argument.

But the contention that all the arguments employed by philosophers to reach noncognitive conclusions are invalid seems to require some further explanation. Is it through sheer naïveté that the philosopher uses invalid arguments? While this interpretation may hold in certain cases, it fails to do justice to the fact that some philosophers obviously capable of distinguishing valid from invalid arguments have argued for conclusions that would surely be noncognitive if any philosophical statements

[1] See R. M. Hare, *The Language of Morals*.

are. Leibniz, for example, who stated that "All is for the best in this best of possible worlds," was one of the keenest logicians of all times. Perhaps, then, the philosopher uses invalid arguments for the same reason that the scientist does; namely, because philosophical arguments to noncognitive conclusions are inductive, and no inductive argument could be, strictly speaking, valid. A moment's reflection, however, serves to show that the arguments in question are not inductive. For inductive arguments must surely have cognitive conclusions. There is finally the possibility that the philosopher deliberately uses invalid arguments in the effort to persuade —that his ulterior motives for seeing to it that certain noncognitive philosophical statements are accepted are sufficiently strong, in other words, to drive him to provide rationalizations for these statements, genuine reasons being unavailable. This explanation is itself persuasive, and needs to be reviewed with considerable care.

The view that the philosopher who argues to a noncognitive conclusion is aiming to persuade his audience to accept it, even though he may know perfectly well that the argument is invalid, might seem to raise questions about the candor of such a philosopher. Yet if there are no valid arguments to noncognitive conclusions, he is surely not attempting to do dishonestly what other people are capable of doing honestly. In resorting to persuasion, futhermore, he may be performing a function vital to the maintenance of society, since it is not valid but persuasive arguments, whether valid or not, that evoke action. The choice that faces the philosopher is not between valid and invalid argumentation, but between argumentation that serves a social purpose and argumentation that does not. Under these circumstances, it is altogether unrealistic to accuse the philosopher of failing to be candid.

One may be tempted to dismiss this view by simply saying that not all philosophical arguments leading to noncognitive conclusions are intended to evoke action. But this reply might well invite the retort that the philosopher who is not concerned with action is not attending to his proper business. It is perhaps better to answer in terms of a closer examination of the actual properties of philosophical arguments in general, in the hope that this will serve not only to distinguish the use of such arguments from the use of arguments intended to persuade but also to contribute to a positive account of validity in the case of the former.

I shall begin by remarking that it is commonly supposed that anyone who makes a philosophical statement is under some obligation to respond to the criticisms of those to whom the statement is addressed. The philosopher unwilling to discuss his own explicit philosophical statements with others inevitably invites questions regarding his right to be considered a philosopher. He need not, of course, reply to all criticisms or questions. But associated with any philosophical statement is a class of criticisms and questions more or less relevant to the statement, and with these he must deal. His critic is naturally under a similar obligation.

The obligation that I am pointing to here is no more than an aspect of the disorientation produced by a philosophical statement or question uttered out of any argumentative context. What appears to an observer as the phenomenological incompleteness of such a statement appears both to its propounder and to its critics as an ethical incompleteness—as a promise that he must now attempt to fulfill. The discussion to which this promise commits him has, within his point of view, the same function as the genetic story that the observer wants to be told: both are required in order to mitigate what is essentially the same incompleteness. The argument for a philosophical statement—that is, the attempt to support it— is to the résumé of events leading to the statement—the argument for it in another sense—as inner is to outer.

The situation described so far, however, might not appear to differ essentially from the conditions that give rise to argumentation primarily intended to persuade. The man who wishes to persuade usually cannot hope to do so merely by making a statement. He, too, must fulfill whatever promise is implicit in his having made the statement. Unless he is regarded as a prophet, he must be willing to discuss it with others and defend it against their objections. Not every objection will be relevant, but there will be a class of possible relevant objections.

It is important to notice, however, that in discussing his position, the philosopher is not satisfying a requirement of exactly the same sort as the requirement that is satisfied when the man who intends to persuade is willing to discuss what he has to say. The latter must support his views because if he does not, he is not likely to be very effective in persuading, owing to the fact that statements ordinarily have less persuasive impact in isolation than they do in an argumentative context. In addition, his audience may be disappointed by his failure to keep the promise that his utterance seemed to imply. The philosopher, on the other hand, must discuss *his* position, not in order to achieve effectiveness, but simply because he has accepted the obligation to undertake the discussion promised by his initial statement, regardless of the consequences of this discussion.

But even if the persuasive speaker—I use the word "speaker" as an obvious abbreviation for "speaker or writer"— were obligated to discuss his assertions for the same reasons that account for the philosopher's obligation, there would remain essential differences between the persuasive speaker's *method* of discussion and the philosopher's method. The aim of the merely persuasive speaker is to secure adherence to his point of view. This aim is difficult to achieve in the measure that his audience is aware that he is trying to achieve it. To the extent that the rhetorical techniques used by a speaker are recognized by his audience, that audience is alienated or left unmoved rather than persuaded. There are no doubt many individuals who enjoy surrendering themselves to a powerful speaker. But once the technical sources of the speaker's power become evident, this surrender loses its enchantment. Such sources of power are, of course, capable of being appreciated as techniques. But to appreciate the artistry of a rhetorical technique and to be persuaded by that technique are two different things. The point is not merely that people want, or think that they want, to be told the truth rather than to be managed. As a psychological generalization, this observation is in fact open to serious doubts. The point is rather that it is impossible to be persuaded by a technical device at the same time that one sees it as merely a device. This is true even if on occasion a persuasive speaker may explicitly avow his intention to persuade his audience, and even call the attention of the latter to the rhetorical devices that he uses. For such a performance could itself be an effective technique of persuasion, provided that it were not recognized as a technique. Rhetoric is perfect only when it perfectly conceals its own use. To be assured of effectiveness, a speaker must operate unilaterally upon his audience, and at the same time prevent it from seeing that he is operating unilaterally.

None of these considerations, however, would seem to affect the way in which the philosopher must conduct the defense or clarification of his position. No philosopher worthy of the name would wish to secure assent to his position through techniques concealed from his audience. One reason for this is that it would be impossible for him to evaluate such assent philosophically. Did his interlocutor really understand his position or not? In the situation in which the use of rhetoric is in order, this question is, of course, pointless; so long as the interlocutor *acts* in the required fashion, the rhetorical argument has been effective. But it is philosophically important to know whether one's interlocutor did understand one's position or not, if only because the problem of comparing the implicit content of two explicitly similar avowals is always relevant to a philosophical discussion.

It is not only for this reason that the philosopher attempts to avoid the use of unilateral techniques of argumentation. Another reason is that he wishes to test his assertions against the criticism of his colleagues. He naturally wants his point of view to prevail. But no philosophical purpose is served when a point of view prevails only because its author has silenced criticism of it through the use of techniques that are effective because they are concealed from the critics.

It is perhaps tempting to suppose that the whole point might be put much more briefly by simply saying that the philosopher is obligated to tell the truth. Yet while this is perhaps suggestive of the distinction

I am trying to draw between the philosopher and the persuasive speaker, it is not sufficient. For the latter may intend to do no more than to carry out the obligation to tell the truth. But the kind of truth that he wishes to tell requires him to consider various ways of telling it, some more persuasive than others. The kind of truth the philosopher wishes to tell, on the other hand, is rendered less rather than more acceptable when persuasive ways of telling it are deliberately chosen. It is acceptable only to the extent that telling it is tantamount to putting it to the test critically.

The philosopher's method of discussion is thus one that avoids the use of unilateral techniques. It is, in fact, essentially a bilateral method, in the sense that the philosopher is obligated not only not to conceal from his audience any of the techniques he uses in arguing, but also to make available to it all the techniques that he does use. For if he is unwilling to submit to the very arguments he uses against others, he thereby shows that it is not criticism but persuasion that interests him. In itself, of course, this consideration is not sufficient to distinguish philosophical from rhetorical argumentation. For a unilateral appeal to emotions, to authority, to laughter, or to force does not become a philosophical discussion merely as the result of becoming bilateral, as, for example, when A, who has been ridiculed by B, ridicules B in return. Such a discussion is at best an alternation of assaults which each participant would like the exclusive right to indulge in, because he sees that his own advantage is diminished by his opponent's use of the same technique. The philosopher, on the other hand, sees that there is an advantage in the adoption of his techniques by others, because that adoption constitutes an authorization of his use of them. Conversely, each new mode of criticism to which he is willing to submit increases the arsenal of criticisms that he can in turn make use of.

Having drawn a number of distinctions between philosophical arguments and arguments intended to persuade, I want to return to the topic of validity. Let us recall that those who deny that a philosophical argument can be valid if its conclusion is noncognitive are not denying that such an argument could be *formally* valid. What they are denying is rather that it could ever be obligatory to accept the conclusion of such an argument, in view of the argument. Now I have already tried to show that the philosopher is obligated to discuss his views. But the obligation to discuss could scarcely exist unless the philosopher were also obligated to accept the *results* of the discussion. One cannot at one and the same time suppose both that the parties to a discussion are obligated to be parties thereto, and that they are also free at any time to ignore what has been said during the course of the discussion. From this I conclude that it can be obligatory for someone to accept the conclusion of a philosophical argument, in view of the argument; and thus not only that a valid philosophical argument is possible, but also that this possibility exists whether the conclusion of such an argument is regarded as cognitive or noncognitive.

Although it is my view that the philosopher is under a general obligation to embark upon discussion, I do not wish to suggest that there are any specific conclusions that he is obligated to accept. Any discussion that he pursues will surely depend, at least partly, upon the point of view that he is defending and upon his interlocutors' criticisms of it. The obligation to accept one conclusion rather than another will arise from the discussion itself.

There may still be something puzzling about the idea of a valid argument to a noncognitive conclusion. When an argument establishes the obligation to accept its conclusion, how can that conclusion fail to be cognitive? But the notion of a valid argument as one leading to a conclusion which, in view of the argument, it is obligatory to accept does not specify whether the obligation to accept the latter is imposed on everyone or just on certain individuals. If the obligation is imposed on everyone, the conclusion is clearly cognitive, which is equivalent to saying that if the conclusion is noncognitive, the obligation is not imposed on everyone.[2] In particular, if, as I have attempted to show on independent grounds, all philosophical conclusions are noncognitive, then not everyone can be obligated to accept any such conclusion. Whenever a philosophical argument is valid, some individuals, but not all, are obligated to accept its conclusion.

If there is any residual difficulty, it lies in the idea of a conclusion that some, but not all, are obligated to accept. But there should be no mystery about this. Few indeed are the obligations that are imposed on everyone. Most obligations arise from commitments made by specific individuals, or by groups of them, and are not imposed upon those who have not made the relevant commitments. A promise is a common example of such a commitment. If in uttering a philosophical statement an individual has implicitly made a promise, then he, but not necessarily everyone, is obligated to keep that promise. He will find that as a result of his initial commitment, he must accept conclusions that not everyone need accept.

An example of what I am trying to say—one of a great many that

[2] The converse of this statement is sometimes assumed; to wit, "If not everyone is obligated to accept a certain conclusion, the latter must be noncognitive." Thus examples putatively showing that the obligation to accept certain statements (e.g., "Killing is wrong.") is effective only for certain cultures or at certain periods of history may be adduced in the effort to show that such statements are noncognitive. This reasoning, however, seems inconclusive, because there are many cognitive statements that no one is obligated to accept; namely, those whose truth has not yet been established.

might equally well have been chosen—is the discussion between Socrates and Thrasymachus in Plato's *Republic*. Having asserted that justice is the interest of the stronger, Thrasymachus asks why his audience does not praise him. Now such applause might indeed have been appropriate if this assertion had been regarded as the utterance of a somewhat prophetic orator. But it is not so regarded, at least by Socrates. Before praising Thrasymachus, he must first understand him. The questions he begins forthwith to raise serve to remind Thrasymachus that he must now fulfill the obligation of clarifying and defending his assertion. Nor is Thrasymachus unwilling to be reminded. Once Socrates' queries begin, Thrasymachus is no longer an orator seeking praise but a philosopher trying to keep a promise. There are times when he attempts to revert to a rhetorical role —accusing Socrates, for instance, of being a slanderer. But further references to his obligation to maintain his end of the discussion are sufficient to force him back to a philosophical level. Having undertaken the discussion, he has no right to abandon it. He must, furthermore, accept the results of the discussion, including, for example, the distinction between the strict and the popular sense of the word "ruler." Also, the obligation to accept this conclusion and certain others is imposed not on everyone, but on Thrasymachus and perhaps on some others who take a position similar to his. It is not, for example, imposed on those who participate in discussions in which it would be entirely pointless to introduce this distinction. Nor is it imposed on anyone who departs from the premise or assumption that it makes no sense to talk about the ideal practitioner of an art, as opposed to the actual practitioner. Socrates and Thrasymachus, on the other hand, hold in common the view that this kind of talk does make sense, and since it is a kind of talk directly related to the thesis that justice is the interest of the stronger, the distinction in question is far from pointless for them. This may be put positively by saying that they are under an obligation to consider the distinction, thus that the argument through which they are led to it is valid. But the question whether this argument is *formally* valid simply does not arise. The fact that Thrasymachus, having asserted that justice is the interest of the stronger, must, in view of his assumption that it makes sense to talk about the ideal practitioner of an art, go on to distinguish between the strict and the popular sense of the word "ruler" (an obligation surely not imposed on everyone) has nothing to do with the *form* of the argument here employed. To analyze this form would be beside the point.

One other idea that receives especially solid exemplification in the same passage is that philosophical discussions are bilateral. It is only because Socrates has compared the ruler to a shepherd that Thrasymachus is entitled to do so. Thrasymachus leaves no doubt that he is gratified by this unexpected authorization to use what he considers to be a devastating analogy.

The view that a valid philosophical argument obligates some individuals, but not all, to accept its conclusion serves as a reminder of the existence of genuine philosophical disagreement. It implies that any philosophical statement must be a source of disagreement between those obligated to accept it and those not so obligated. Such disagreement is radical, in the sense that it cannot be overcome through compromise. When two or more arguments lead to incompatible conclusions, compromise can be achieved only by correcting at least some of the arguments in such a way as to remove the incompatibility. But when all the arguments in question are valid, they are not subject to correction at all, so that no compromise is forthcoming.

The character of philosophical disagreement is further suggested by some remarks regarding the role of disagreement in rhetoric. Persuasive argumentation is pointless unless there is an initial disagreement that it aims to overcome. But it is impossible unless it can make use of beliefs, attitudes, prejudices, or explicit premises adopted by its audience. These constitute an initial area of agreement, in the sense that if the speaker appeals to them, the audience will not protest. There is no reason, however, why the speaker himself need espouse such beliefs, attitudes, prejudices, or premises; it is sufficient for him to be able to rely on his audience's espousal of them. Regardless of whether the speaker shares the preconceptions of his audience, and regardless of whether he actually believes in the conclusion he is attempting to promote, it is always possible, in principle, to regard him as uncommitted; for the actual commitments of the speaker do not enter into the analysis of his rhetorical success. (Of course, if his audience thinks that his actual commitments are incompatible with the conclusion he is advocating, his success will be diminished; but we can still analyze this situation without referring to the speaker's actual commitments as such.) From the point of view of the analysis of persuasion, the role of the speaker is to treat his audience as an object. He must begin by assessing as accurately as possible the initial area of agreement. He must then consider how best to exploit this preliminary situation in order to persuade his audience to accept the statements he wants it to accept—statements with which it is not yet in agreement. His task is to manipulate his audience so as to secure agreement. All relevant disagreements must be overcome. Furthermore, the attempt to overcome disagreement must itself be concealed. For the audience will wish to reserve the right to disagree with the speaker and is likely to react in an adverse fashion if it feels that he is ignoring this right. This phenomenon is probably closely related to the impossibility of persuading through a technique that is seen as a mere technique.

The wish of an audience to reserve the right to disagree with the speaker addressing it may be viewed as a desire on its part to come to its own conclusions. It is just such spontaneity, however, that the speaker must suppress, or at least restrict, if he is to perform his role of manipulating his audience. Yet he must always create the illusion that he is inviting the latter to come to its own conclusions; for if he does not, it will exercise a residual spontaneity of judgment, lying inevitably beyond his control, to reach the conclusion that its right to reach its own conclusions is being threatened. One may think of this reaction as a process through which an audience in turn comes to regard the speaker addressing it as an object whose harmful properties are well known but can be rendered ineffective by means of equally well-known precautions. This seems an appropriate fate for the speaker who has too bluntly attempted to deal with his audience as an object.)

In the rhetorical situation, then, disagreement exists only to be overcome through the exploitation of an initial agreement, and the desire of an audience to reach its own conclusions must be circumvented. In philosophical discussions, on the other hand, whether there is an initial agreement or not, it cannot be exploited to overcome disagreement, since the latter is radical, permitting no compromise. What must be exploited is just the desire of each participant to reach his own conclusions. A conclusion has no philosophical use if it is not reached freely. To be philosophically useful, it must represent the unconstrained attempt on the part of its advocate to fulfill his obligation to defend and clarify his position. Thus philosophical discussion is, in effect, a collaborative effort to maintain the conditions under which disagreement is possible. If it has arisen from an initial disagreement engendered by valid arguments to incompatible conclusions, it can proceed only by inviting further valid arguments from its participants, because it is precisely by employing valid arguments that each participant achieves the perfect exercise of his right to reach his own conclusions. This account may suggest a kind of monadism of philosophical positions—a plurality of positions, each obeying its own inner law of development but wholly incapable of interacting with the others. In fact, however, it contains the germ of what I want to say about the ways in which philosophical positions do interact. Interaction of this type, which is appropriately referred to as "philosophical controversy," is possible only because philosophical discussion, in order to maintain itself, must *exploit* the desire of each participant to reach his own conclusions, and must *invite* him to argue validly. When the motive to maintain the discussion is lacking, philosophical positions do, in fact, tend to become monadistically isolated from each other; and this isolation owes itself to the radical nature of their disagreements with each other. When this motive is present, on the other hand, the disagreements are no less radical, but it is possible for the partisan of one position to invite a partisan of another to develop through unconstrained argument the consequences of a statement the latter has made. Since such consequences may prove to be an unexpected source of embarrassment to the individual who develops them, it is an effective technique of philosophical controversy to invite one's opponent to come to his own conclusions. Indeed, in the absence of the possibility of compromise, it is the only effective technique.

The success of the rhetorical speaker will depend upon the extent to which there are beliefs, attitudes, prejudices, or premises constituting an initial area of agreement on the part of his audience. Thus the speaker whose audience is most uniform in membership is likely to have the greatest chance of success. The audience of rhetoric is therefore essentially limited. It is unlikely that there are any statements that mankind as a whole could be persuaded to accept, because it is unlikely that there is any area of agreement to which all men would subscribe. The view has been taken, however, that there are arguments addressed to mankind as a whole; to wit, the ones employed by the philosopher.[3] Such a view has the same source as the view of philosophical argumentation that I have been taking in this chapter: both arise from the feeling that the arguments employed by the philosopher are somehow different from those the persuasive speaker employs. But here, I think, the similarity ends. There are, in my opinion, two basic difficulties with the view that philosophical arguments are addressed to mankind as a whole. First, it has not been made clear how mankind as a whole could constitute an audience or what the philosopher could be intending to accomplish by addressing such an audience. According to the authors who take the view in question, the audience that the philosopher addresses has, in the last analysis, only an ideal existence: "We invent a model of man—the incarnation of reason . . . which we seek to convince, and which varies with our knowledge of other men, or other civilizations, or other systems of thought, with what we take to be incontrovertible facts or objective truths." [4] If certain individuals remain unmoved by his solicitations, the philosopher's only recourse is to regard them as irrational and thus as excluded from the ideal audience that he supposes himself to be addressing. In so doing, he substitutes the idea of an elite audience for that of a universal one. We seem to be left with the tautology that the philosopher addresses the audience that he addresses. But this has no tendency to show that the audience which the philosopher does address is mankind as a whole. Nor does it clearly indicate what transaction the philosopher is undertaking with his audience. What does it mean to "convince" a model that one has invented?

The second difficulty is that the radical nature of philosophical disagreement seems to diminish the force of the contention that the

[3] See Ch. Perelman and L. Olbrechts-Tyteca, *Rhétorique et philosophie* and *Traité de l'Argumentation.*

[4] *Rhétorique et philosophie*, p. 22.

arguments of philosophers are addressed to a universal audience. If disagreement plays a fundamental role in philosophical argument, as I think it does, then the audience of such argument, like the audience of rhetorical argument, must be limited. What distinguishes one limited audience of philosophical argumentation from another is the impossibility of resolving the issues between the two audiences by compromise. In this situation, the arguments effective against one audience would seem pointless to the other. It would appear that no philosophical arguments addressed to mankind as a whole could be effective. This again raises a question about the point of saying that they are so addressed.

It has been objected that my characterization of philosophical argumentation emphasizes criticism or polemic, and that if I had paid proper attention to arguments of a constructive type, my results would have been compatible with the contention that the latter are addressed to a universal audience.[5] Now I admit the importance of the distinction between critical and constructive philosophical argumentation. Nevertheless, throughout this chapter what I have been attempting to characterize is philosophical discussion in general, whether critical or constructive in intent. I have tried to exhibit such discussion as the response to an obligation to amplify and defend. I see no reason why such a response would necessarily be confined either to criticism or to constructive elaboration. Both activities are appropriate to an obligation of the sort that I have in mind. Nor is there any reason why constructive arguments should, any less than critical arguments, constitute an effort to maintain the conditions of disagreement—an effort, that is, to invite the audience to reach its own conclusions. A constructive conclusion to which an audience acquiesces merely because it has been persuaded to do so is as philosophically useless as a critical conclusion reached under the same circumstances.

There is, nonetheless, an appealing quality in the idea that philosophical arguments are addressed to a universal audience. For this is a way of recapitulating the agelong theme that philosophy is fundamentally an exercise of reason. I do not take exception to this theme. I want only to raise the question whether reason must involve universality in the way it has usually been supposed to. There may be truths reached by reasoning that are equally acceptable to all rational beings. But if such truths exist, they are entirely without content. My view, however, is that the results of philosophical reasoning have content. Hence reason in its philosophical use cannot be universal.

[5] See Ch. Perelman, "Reply to Henry W. Johnstone, Jr.," reprinted as Chapter 8 of the present volume.

MAURICE NATANSON

RHETORIC AND PHILOSOPHICAL ARGUMENTATION

The species "philosophical argumentation" stands to the genus "argumentation" in a rather special relationship, for included within the former is the rationale of the latter. The logic of argumentation is the theme of philosophical argumentation. Clearly, then, by philosophical argumentation is meant a subsidiary discipline of tremendous depth and with great implications. It is not the arguments philosophers employ which constitute the subject matter of philosophical argumentation but rather the nature of argumentation as such within philosophical discourse. However, it is through the study of philosophical arguments that we come to appreciate the problems of philosophical argumentation. A first approach to the nature of what is distinctive about philosophical argumentation may then be made by considering briefly the features of philosophical arguments. Some preliminary distinctions may prove to be valuable.

First, philosophical arguments are essentially *a priori* in character; i.e., they are not about matters of fact. They differ from mathematical and purely formal arguments to the extent that they have experiential or phenomenological bearing. Isaiah Berlin once put the matter this way: If you have a factual question you go to a scientist for the answer; if you have a formal question you go to a mathematician for the answer; but if your question is neither factual nor formal, you go to a philosopher for help. An equivalent expression of the same position is made by George Santayana in his Preface to *Scepticism and Animal Faith.* "Here is one more system of philosophy," Santayana writes. "If the reader is tempted to smile, I can assure him that I smile with him, and that my system . . . differs widely in spirit and pretensions from what usually goes by that name. . . . I am merely attempting to express for the reader the principles to which he appeals when he smiles." [1]

[1] George Santayana, *Scepticism and Animal Faith,* p. v.

Second, philosophical arguments are never synonymous with their techniques of articulation; modes of argument are not the same as philosophical arguments. Thus, one may show that a certain form of argument is invalid—traditional syllogistic fallacies, for example—without concluding that what is being argued is philosophically unacceptable. Philosophic content appears to transcend its formal vestment.

Third, the relationship between speaker (or writer) and audience is different in philosophy from other fields; accordingly, a rather special problem arises in trying to understand philosophical arguments in relation to their authors and the audiences they are intended to address. Here we enter a still wider region in which rhetorical considerations become relevant, indeed central. I prefer to approach this set of problems in the context of a recent and admirable book, *Philosophy and Argument* by Henry W. Johnstone, Jr. In a section on "Persuasion and Validity in Philosophy" [2] Johnstone discusses the relationship between author and audience. He contrasts in particular the differences between the speaker as rhetorician and the speaker as philosopher. A summary statement of some of the differences he finds may prove helpful at this point:

1. The aim of the rhetorician is to persuade his audience; the aim of the philosopher is to explain his position.

2. The persuasive speaker must necessarily hide his rhetorical technique if he is to succeed as a persuader of men; the philosopher fails if he knowingly or designedly conceals his techniques.

3. The rhetorician argues unilaterally toward his audience; the philosopher proceeds bilaterally toward his colleagues. [3]

The method of the philosopher, then, according to Johnstone, is necessarily and essentially bilateral: "The philosopher is obligated not only not to conceal from his audience any of the techniques he uses in arguing, but also to make available to it all the techniques that he does use." [4] It would appear on this account that rhetoric and philosophy are disparate activities. To the extent that the philosopher deliberately chooses rhetorical devices to make his position more attractive, he fails in his professional role. [5]

Through Johnstone's argument we have now come to one view of what characterizes, in decisive fashion, a philosophical argument and differentiates it from other modes of argumentation, especially those employed by the rhetorician. The philosopher is professionally committed to

[2] Reprinted as Chapter 9 of the present volume.
[3] Johnstone, p. 142.
[4] Johnstone, p. 142.
[5] Cf. Johnstone, pp. 139-141.

a "nothing may be concealed" mode of expression. If he fails it must be because of his inability or inexactitude, not because of a choice to hide something. The philosopher, on this account, turns out to be an open man. His methodology must remain as much available for inspection as his conclusions and supporting reasons. The total philosophical machinery is involved, then, in philosophical argumentation. Rhetoric, on the contrary, is grounded in the principle of disguise. Even if the rhetorician's motives are noble and his conclusions sound, his devices are chosen from a different base, one that bears a secretive nature. The machinery of his method is never open for inspection while the engine of his argument is in operation. But a further question arises to complicate the present discussion. If the speaker as rhetorician and the speaker as philosopher are qualitatively different, what about their respective audiences? Are there distinctive differences in audiences as well? The differences to be noted here are not between audiences as such but rather between different relationships to audiences speakers stand in. The relationship of the rhetorician to his audience is not that of the philosopher to his audience. As Johnstone points out, persuasive argumentation hinges upon the fact that the rhetorical speaker must have an initial disagreement with his audience which he struggles to overcome by making use of attitudes, beliefs, and prejudices held by that audience. In philosophical argumentation, however, the philosopher does not have the right to take advantage of either his audience's disagreements or its fundamental assumption, as Johnstone notes:

In the rhetorical situation, disagreement exists only to be overcome through the exploitation of an initial agreement, and the desire of an audience to reach its own conclusions must be circumvented. In philosophical discussions, on the other hand, whether there is an initial agreement or not, it cannot be exploited to overcome disagreement, since the latter is radical, permitting no compromise. What must be exploited is just the desire of each participant to reach his own conclusions. A conclusion has no philosophical use if it is not reached freely. To be philosophically useful, it must represent the unconstrained attempt on the part of its advocate to fulfill his obligation to defend and clarify his position. Thus philosophical discussion is, in effect, a collaborative effort to maintain the conditions under which disagreement is possible.[6]

But before proceeding further with the analysis of our problem, it is necessary to admit a rather central point into the discussion of audiences: the rhetorician's audience may be specified; the philosopher's audience is specifiable with great difficulty. To whom is the philosopher really addressing his arguments? Obviously, all sorts of answers are possible: to other professional philosophers, to graduate students in his field, to philosophically trained laymen or specialists in other related fields. But to an-

[6] *Ibid.*, p. 146.

swer in this way is to admit of essential ambiguities. Clearly, the question here is not, Who is professionally qualified to understand what the philosopher has written? Is the philosopher interested in addressing any individual capable of comprehending his arguments? What about the more nearly human factors of time and place? Surely, a philosopher answering another philosopher in a journal article is primarily interested in an immediate response, discussion of his views, etc., and not in what future philosophers will think of his arguments two or three thousand years hence. But psychological considerations must be kept to one side, and practical considerations as well. We are interested, in the immediate context, in what is professionally germane to the philosopher's activity *qua* philosopher. And here it is possible to say, candidly, that the philosopher's audience is at best a problematic concept. At one extreme the philosopher is addressing his fellow philosophers active on the professional scene. At another extreme it can be argued, as Perelman and Olbrechts-Tyteca do in *Rhétorique et philosophie*,[7] that philosophical arguments are addressed to mankind, a universal audience. Accordingly, the proper audience of the philosopher is an ideal-type, a model, or universal construct, having only an ideal existence. At this point I propose to part company with Johnstone's analysis and to turn to certain problems it raises for rhetoric and philosophy. What follows now is a forward-looking summary of my argument.

Whatever the philosopher *believes* himself to be doing, there is immanent within his professional activity something antecedent to either a unilateral or a bilateral mode of procedure: there is a mono-lateral or proto-lateral activity. To translate simply: the philosopher is trying to uncover something about himself. Philosophical activity is self-discovery. Philosophical reports, spoken or written, are self-reports first, arguments later. "First" here is intended in a logical, not a chronological sense. Even if the argument is chronologically first, its probing is a matter of uncovering its original intent in relationship to the self that intended it. The self that seeks an alter ego, the philosopher who looks for an interlocutor, the teacher in quest of his student—all are involved in a primary situation in which rhetoric and philosophy are integral, although the problem of rhetorical technique gives way to the underlying question of philosophical communication. The philosophical form closest, in this sense, to the original fusion of rhetoric and philosophy is dialogic philosophy in the Socratic tradition. The mode of argument that is generated out of this tradition is at once distinctively and truly philosophical as well as

---

[7] Ch. Perelman and L. Olbrechts-Tyteca, *Rhétorique et philosophie: pour une théorie de l'argumentation en philosophie.* See p. 20 ff., esp. p. 22. Cf. Johnstone, p. 147 and see Ch. Perelman, "Reply to Henry W. Johnstone, Jr.," reprinted as Chapter 8 of the present volume.

rhetorical. Persuasion, however, will be treated as dialectical transformation of the self through indirect argumentation. The category of "indirection" is the operative one here; Socrates, Montaigne, and Kierkegaard may serve as triple moments in the exploration of indirect argumentation. It may be well to note that I have chosen a very special aspect of philosophical argumentation as a basis for going beyond Johnstone's position. This is at once the weakness and the strength of what follows. I am not concerned with classical rhetoric. I am not concerned with the full range of all philosophical argumentation. But neither am I concerned to present a compromise of any order, for I believe that my special case generates decisively important features of both philosophy and rhetoric. Here, then, is a philosophical approach to rhetoric through the mode of indirect argumentation.

The image of Socrates is prominent in the writings of both Montaigne and Kierkegaard; the humanity of Socrates invites the pleasure of the later thinkers. "Socrates' purpose was not vague and fanciful," Montaigne writes; "his aim was to furnish us with things and precepts that are really and more directly serviceable to life." [8] And Kierkegaard celebrates the same common touch. But far from simple utility being at issue, it is a fundamental method of procedure that is in question here. Montaigne is not suggesting that Socrates is a good philosopher because his activity was pragmatically helpful. Far from being helpful, it was severely hurtful. The point of Montaigne's consideration of Socrates lies in a different direction, then. To understand Montaigne on Socrates it is necessary to turn to Montaigne on Montaigne, his central subject. Self-knowledge is the clue to as much of our comprehension of the world as man can gain. For Montaigne, we can be certain of very little indeed: but we can achieve apodictic knowledge of ourselves. The proper course of knowing can consist only in determining the limits of the self, and for Montaigne those limits are not to be found in exalted places but rather in commonplace circumstances. The world of daily life carries within it the secret of our being. Socrates more than any other philosopher was first of all simply himself; that was his art and his genius. "He was besides," Montaigne writes, "always one and the same, and raised himself not by fits and starts, but by his natural temperament, to the highest pitch of vigour. Or to speak more correctly, he raised nothing, but rather brought down, reduced and subjected vigour to its natural and original pitch, as well as all asperities and difficulties." [9] Self-knowledge, then, presupposes an epistemic condition: knowledge is within the person, and teaching must be

[8] "Of Physiognomy," *The Essays of Montaigne,* translated by E. J. Trechmann, II, p. 509.
[9] *Ibid.,* pp. 509-510.

restricted to a process of dialectical occasioning. To learn is to confront another and thereby come to confront oneself. Here is the first lesson in philosophical indirection.

Kierkegaard carries on Montaigne's theme:

> From the standpoint of the Socratic thought every point of departure in time is *eo ipso* accidental, an occasion, a vanishing moment. The teacher himself is no more than this; and if he offers himself and his instruction on any other basis, he does not give but takes away, and is not even the other's friend, much less his teacher. Herein lies the profundity of the Socratic thought, and the noble humanity he so thoroughly expressed, which refused to enter into a false and vain fellowship with clever heads, but felt an equal kinship with a tanner; whence he soon "came to the conclusion that the study of Physics was not man's proper business, and therefore began to philosophize about moral matters in the workshops and in the market-place" . . . but philosophized with equal absoluteness everywhere.[10]

Here is the second lesson in philosophical indirection.

And now by indirection we arrive at a new way of differentiating philosophical argumentation from all other modes of argumentation. What is at issue in the philosopher's argumentation is himself. There is no ideal observer in philosophy any more than there is an agreed upon and necessary starting point. Each philosopher must be a beginner because philosophy is a science of beginnings. One contemporary philosopher, Edmund Husserl, would have preferred to call philosophy "archeology" had that term not already been taken for a separate discipline. Philosophy is a science of origins, of roots, of foundations or beginnings.[11] As a foundation digger, then, the philosopher is confronted first of all with himself; he is his own primary datum. How is he to describe himself, talk about himself, converse with himself? Is the philosopher an ideal observer of his own being? And can the philosopher's reports stand as evidence for other philosophers? The notion of philosophical indirection is an effort to explore some of these interrelated questions. In the Socratic-Kierkegaardian tradition we have discussed, the following style of answer arises.

There can be no substitution in philosophy proper, i.e., I cannot stand in relationship to your findings as you do or should. My task is to uncover my own truth, or more properly, my own relationship to truth. To say with Kierkegaard that "truth is subjectivity" is to locate the domain of the true in vital nexus with the inquiring agent—not the ideal or artificial observer but the unique and but once given ego. It is not truth that interests Kierkegaard, but himself in relationship to truth. Philosophical argument is not rendered impossible; instead it can operate ex-

[10] Sören Kierkegaard, *Philosophical Fragments*, pp. 6-7.
[11] See Herbert Spiegelberg, *The Phenomenological Movement*, I, p. 82.

istentially only by means of indirect communication, by what we have called indirection. I am now suggesting that this procedure has a logic of its own which can tell us much about philosophical argumentation and rhetoric as well. But some cautions must be taken. Once again, I repeat that my analysis by no means is intended to handle the total range of philosophical thought. There are major arguments in the history of philosophy in the fields of logic, epistemology, and metaphysics which are untouched by what I have to say here. Nor will the implications of my argument for rhetoric pertain to the full range of that discipline. I content myself with small conclusions in the hope that meaningful questions of a larger scope may be articulated. This itself is an instance of indirect procedure, and what follows now is a third lesson in philosophical indirection.

What one thinker finds in another transcends the former's arguments and relates instead to his mode of argumentation. The latter has an overt and a covert form. The overt mode of philosophical argumentation in Hume's analysis of causation or in Kant's transcendental deduction presents itself directly for examination. What is hidden is not intended to be hidden; rather Hume and Kant failed to make themselves clear to the extent that their methodological procedures remain obscure. Here we agree with Johnstone's analysis of bilateral argumentation. The philosopher's prime responsibility is to make his argumentation as clear as his arguments. But this pertains to overt argumentation alone. There is also what I have termed the covert mode of philosophical argumentation. It is here that indirection enters, and it is here that rhetoric enters, for it is here that the essential being of the philosopher, his subjectivity, is at issue. Prior to arguments there is argumentation, and argumentation involves the style of the philosopher's existence. What kinds of questions does he take as significant? What order of problem presents itself to him as having primary force? What is it he is essentially striving to do in his philosophizing? We look to men for answers to these questions as much as we look to their works. Or to express it differently, we look to works as indirect clues to their authors. The result of our inquiry is not an esoteric domain of personality that presents itself; rather, it is a protoargumentative level of suasion that is encountered here. I prefer to think of it as an aspect of rhetoric.

At the level of covert argumentation, the philosopher *does* make a choice about his mode of procedure, the style of his presentation, the ultimate technique he is going to employ. One such radical choice is to proceed by means of philosophical indirection, and that choice precludes the philosopher's making his dialectical technique, his mode or argumentation, available in his argument. At least in one important instance, then, Johnstone's criterion for what sets apart philosophy and rhetoric breaks down. Indeed, his differentiating point is precisely what unites philosophy and rhetoric at this juncture. To be sure, the instance is a limited one—all philosophers do not fall in the camp of Socrates, Montaigne, and Kierkegaard. Yet there is an importance to a connection once seen that ought not to be dropped or abandoned. Expanded beyond its formulation here, the notion of a proto-argumentative procedure involving the subjectivity of the philosopher would lead to what might be termed the rhetoric of commitment not merely to his work but to the overriding importance of his problems. One can sense such commitment in philosophers as different as Husserl and Wittgenstein. The problem is not a psychological one. I am not talking about the "personalities" of philosophers.

The specific arguments philosophers use are not synonymous with the underlying structure of philosophical argumentation. Concrete arguments are rooted in a more primordial ground, the fundamental intent of the philosopher. When that intent is shared and sympathetically taken up, philosophers seem to attract and even educate each other; dialogue is possible. When that intent is clearly unshared, only arguments are possible. The analysis of arguments is the proper business of theory of argumentation, but the consideration of fundamental intent is generated out of philosophical indirection alone. The resonance a philosopher feels with a point of view or a thesis involves a rhetorical presupposition. Rhetoric in this sense is concerned with proto-argumentation and a primordial choice of styles of philosophizing. Its ultimate subject matter is the unique person committed in his uniqueness to a way of seeing and having a world. Perhaps another name for what I have in mind here is *ethos*. If this suggestion is warranted, then it might be fairly said that I have interpreted the philosophical self in rhetorical terms. Philosophical indirection, however, is less concerned with rhetoric as persuasion than it is with rhetoric as involvement. The alter ego is to be freed, not overcome. The philosopher achieves his own freedom in helping the other to free himself. This is the final lesson in philosophical indirection.

BIOGRAPHICAL NOTES

Donald C. Bryant was born in New York City in 1905. He received his B.A., M.A., and Ph.D. from Cornell University. Before going to the State University of Iowa, where he is now Professor of Speech, he was Chairman of the English Department at Washington University, St. Louis, Missouri. Mr. Bryant has been editor of the *Quarterly Journal of Speech*. Books he has written or edited include *Edmund Burke and His Literary Friends*, *Papers in Rhetoric*, and *The Rhetorical Idiom*.

P. Albert Duhamel was born in 1920. In 1945 he was awarded the Ph.D. degree by the University of Wisconsin. He has taught at the University of Chicago, and is at present associated with Boston College. Mr. Duhamel is co-author of *Rhetoric: Principles and Usage*, *Persuasive Prose*, and *Literature: Form and Function*.

Hoyt H. Hudson was a Nebraskan, born in 1893. He studied at Huron College, the University of Denver, and the University of Chicago, before taking his Ph.D. at Cornell in 1923. He taught at Cornell, Swarthmore, the University of Pittsburgh, Princeton (where he became Chairman of the English Department), and Stanford. He was editor of the *Quarterly Journal of Speech* from 1933 until 1935. Among his books are *Principles of Argument and Debate* (with J. W. Reeves) and translations of Kant, *Religion within the Limits of Reason Alone* (with T. M. Greene) and of Erasmus, *The Praise of Folly*. Mr. Hudson died in 1944.

Henry W. Johnstone, Jr. was born in 1920. He did his undergraduate work at Haverford College, and received his Ph.D. from Harvard. Before going to The Pennsylvania State University, where he is Professor of Philosophy, he taught at Williams College. He was a Belgian-American Educational Foundation Fellow in 1957 and a Fulbright Lecturer at Trinity College, Dublin, Ireland, 1960-61. Among his books are *Elementary Deductive Logic*, *Philosophy and Argument*, and *Natural Deduction* (with John M. Anderson).

Maurice Natanson is a native of New York City, where he was born in 1924. He holds the Ph.D. degree from the University of Nebraska, and is also a Doctor of Social Science from the New School for Social Research, where he studied for two years as an American Council of Learned Societies Scholar. He is at present Professor of Philosophy at the University of North Carolina. Mr. Natanson's books include *A Critique of Jean-Paul Sartre's Ontology*, *The Social Dynamics of George H. Mead*, *Literature, Philosophy, and the Social Sciences*, and *Philoso-*

phy of the Social Sciences: A Reader. He was Distinguished Visiting Professor at The Pennsylvania State University in 1963 and Visiting Professor at the University of California at Berkeley, 1964-65.

Lucie Olbrechts-Tyteca was born in Brussels in 1899. She was trained in literature, social sciences, and economics at the University of Brussels. For a time her main interest was in social psychology. But with the feeling that "social psychology had too much of a tendency to take it for granted that the irrational and suggestion prevailed in human relations as soon as one left the serene city of the scientists," she began working on problems of rhetoric and argumentation with Perelman in 1947. Their collaboration produced two books and a number of articles, as well as several papers that Mme Olbrechts-Tyteca wrote alone.

Robert T. Oliver was born in 1909. He was educated at Pacific College, the University of Oregon, and the University of Wisconsin, from which he received his Ph.D. in 1937. He taught at Bucknell and Syracuse, and is now Chairman of the Department of Speech at The Pennsylvania State University. Among his books are *Syngman Rhee, Four Who Spoke Out,* and *The Psychology of Persuasive Speech.*

Chaïm Perelman was born in Warsaw in 1912 and emigrated to Belgium in 1925. He received doctoral degrees in Philosophy and Law from the University of Brussels, where he is now Professor of Philosophy. He has organized and held offices in many international philosophical societies and congresses and has lectured all over the world. Together with L. Olbrechts-Tyteca he wrote *Rhétorique et Philosophie* and *Traité de l'Argumentation,* and he is the author of *The Idea of Justice and the Problem of Argument.* In 1962, M. Perelman was Distinguished Visiting Professor of Philosophy and Speech at The Pensylvania State University. In the same year he also won the Prix Franqui, the highest award given by the Belgian Government for scholarly or scientific work.

Richard M. Weaver was a native of Asheville, North Carolina. Born in 1910, he was educated at the University of Kentucky, Vanderbilt University, and Louisiana State University, where he received his Ph.D. in 1943. Among the institutions at which he taught were Texas A.&M., Louisiana State, and the University of Chicago, where, as Professor of English, he taught courses on writing. Just before his death in 1963 he had accepted a call to Vanderbilt. His books include *Ideas Have Consequences, The Ethics of Rhetoric,* and *Visions of Order,* published in 1964.

BIBLIOGRAPHY

The following list is intended to be selective, not comprehensive. It includes authors and titles referred to in the book and some additional sources. Occasionally, a different edition of a work than that referred to in the text has been included. Further references can be found in James W. Cleary and Frederick W. Haberman, A *Bibliography of Rhetoric and Public Address*, 1947-1962, Madison, Wisconsin: University of Wisconsin Press, 1964; Albert R. Kitzhaber, A *Bibliography on Rhetoric in American Colleges, 1850-1900*, Denver, Colorado: Bibliographical Center for Research, Denver Public Library, 1954; Raymond Klibansky (editor), *Philosophy at the Mid-Century: A Survey*, 4 volumes, Firenze: La Nuova Italia Editrice, 1961; Gilbert Varet, *Manuel de Bibliographie Philosophique*, 2 volumes, Paris: Presses Universitaires de France, 1956. Also see the bibliographies in Fogarty, *Roots for A New Rhetoric*; Perelman and Olbrechts-Tyteca, *Traité de L'Argumentation*; and *Logique et Analyse* (cited below).

Adams, John Quincy, *Lectures on Rhetoric and Oratory*, with an Introduction by J. Jeffrey Auer and Jerald L. Banninga, 2 vols., New York: Russell and Russell, 1962.

Adler, Mortimer, *Dialectic*, New York: Harcourt, Brace, 1927.

Agee, James, and Walker Evans, *Let Us Now Praise Famous Men*, Boston: Houghton Mifflin, 1941.

Aiken, Henry David, "The Revolt Against Ideology," *Commentary*, Vol. XXXVII, 1964, pp. 29-39.

Aly, Bower, "The Rhetoric of Semantics," *Quarterly Journal of Speech*, Vol. XXX, 1944, pp. 23-30.

Anderson, Raymond E., "Kierkegaard's Theory of Communication," *Speech Monographs*, Vol. XXX, 1963, pp. 1-14.

Aristotle, *The Art of Rhetoric*, edited and translated by John Henry Freese, New York: G. P. Putnam, 1926.

———, *The Basic Works of Aristotle*, edited by Richard McKeon, New York: Random House, 1941.

———, *The Rhetoric of Aristotle*, translated by Lane Cooper, New York: D. Appleton, 1932.

———, *The Rhetoric of Aristotle*, translated with an analysis and critical notes by J. E. C. Welldon, London: Macmillan, 1886.

———, *Rhetoric and Poetics*, translated by W. Rhys Roberts, New York: Modern Library, 1954.

———, *Rhétorique*, translated by Médéric Dufour, 2 vols., Paris: Collection des Universités de France sous le patronage de l'Association Guillaume Budé, 1932.

———, *The Works of Aristotle*, edited by W. D. Ross, Vol. XI includes *Rhetorica*, translated by W. Rhys Roberts, Oxford: Clarendon Press, 1959.

———, ———, Vol. I includes *Topica* and *De Sophisticis Elenchis*, translated by W. A. Pickard-Cambridge, London: Oxford University Press, 1928.

Aron, Raymond, *Introduction à la philosophie de l'histoire: essai sur les limites de l'objectivité historique*, Paris: Gallimard, 1948. (English translation: *Introduction to the Philosophy of History: An Essay on the Limits of Historical Objectivity*, translated by George J. Irwin, Boston: Beacon Press, 1961.)

Asch, Solomon E., "The Doctrine of Suggestion, Prestige, and Imitation in Social Psychology," *Psychological Review*, Vol. LV, 1948, pp. 250-276.

Atkins, J. W. H., *Literary Criticism in Antiquity: A Sketch of its Development*, 2 vols., Cambridge: The University Press, 1934.

Augustine, St., *Concerning the Teacher and On the Immortality of the Soul*, translated with a Preface by George G. Leckie, New York: Appleton-Century-Crofts, 1938.

Ayer, A. J., *Philosophy and Language: An Inaugural Lecture delivered before the University of Oxford on 3 November 1960*, Oxford: at the Clarendon Press, 1960.

————, review of Perelman and Olbrechts-Tyteca, *Rhétorique et Philosophie*, *Revue Internationale de Philosophie*, Vol. VII, 1953, pp. 157-159.

Bacon, Francis, *The Advancement of Learning*, New York: E. P. Dutton, 1934.

————, *Essays*, Introduction by William H. Hudson, New York: Thomas Y. Crowell, 1901.

————, *Selected Writings*, Introduction by Hugh G. Dick, New York: Modern Library, 1955.

Bain, Alexander, *English Composition and Rhetoric: A Manual*, New York: D. Appleton, 1867.

Baldwin, Charles S., *Ancient Rhetoric and Poetic*, New York: Macmillan, 1924.

————, *Medieval Rhetoric and Poetic*, New York: Macmillan, 1928.

Barzun, Jacques, *Science: The Glorious Entertainment*, New York: Harper and Row, 1964.

Belaval, Yvon, *Les Philosophes et leur langage*, Paris: Gallimard, 1952.

Bell, Daniel, *The End of Ideology: On the Exhaustion of Political Ideas in the Fifties*, Glencoe, Illinois: Free Press, 1960.

Benedict, Ruth, *The Chrysanthemum and the Sword: Patterns of Japanese Culture*, Boston: Houghton Mifflin, 1946.

Bird, George L. and Frederick E. Merwin, (editors) *The Press and Society: A Book of Readings*, New York: Prentice-Hall, 1951.

Bitzer, Lloyd F., "Aristotle's Enthymeme Revisited," *Quarterly Journal of Speech*, Vol. XLV, 1959, pp. 399-408.

Black, Edwin, "Plato's View of Rhetoric," *Quarterly Journal of Speech*, Vol. XLIV, 1958, pp. 361-374.

Black, Max, *Language and Philosophy: Studies in Method*, Ithaca, New York: Cornell University Press, 1949.

————, *Models and Metaphors: Studies in Language and Philosophy*, Ithaca, New York: Cornell University Press, 1962.

Blair, Hugh, *An Abridgment of Lectures on Rhetoric*, Philadelphia: Key, Meilke, and Biddle, 1832.

————, *Lectures on Rhetoric and Belles Lettres*, London: T. Tegg and Son, 1838.

Blish, James, "Rituals on Ezra Pound," *Sewanee Review*, Vol. LVIII, 1950, pp. 185-226.

Boissier, Gaston, "Les Écoles de Déclamation à Rome," *Revue des Deux Mondes*, Vol. XI, 1902, pp. 481-508.

————, *La Fin du Paganisme: Étude sur les dernières luttes religieuses en Occident au quatrième siècle*, Paris: Hachette, 1891.

Booth, Wayne C., *The Rhetoric of Fiction*, Chicago: University of Chicago Press, 1961.

Bosco, Nynfa, "Perelman e un rinnovamento della retorica," *Filosofia*, Vol. VI, 1955, pp. 601-613.

Bossuet, Jacques Bénigne, *Sermons*, 4 vols., Paris: Garnier, 1889-1891.

Brembeck, Winston Lamont, and William Smiley Howell, *Persuasion: A Means of Social Control*, New York: Prentice-Hall, 1952.

Brigance, William Norwood, "General Education in an Industrial Free Society," *Quarterly Journal of Speech*, Vol. XXXVIII, 1952, pp. 177-183.

Britton, Karl, *Communication: A Philosophical Study of Language*, London: Kegan Paul, Trench, Trubner, 1939.

Bryant, Donald C., "Aspects of Rhetorical Tradition: The Intellectual Foundation," *Quarterly Journal of Speech*, Vol. XXXVI, 1950, pp. 169-176 and 326-332.

————, "Some Problems of Scope and Method in Rhetorical Scholarship," *Quarterly Journal of Speech*, Vol. XXIII, 1937, pp. 182-189.

————, (editor) *Papers in Rhetoric*, Saint Louis, 1940.

————, (editor) *The Rhetorical Idiom: Essays in Rhetoric, Oratory, Language, and Drama presented to Herbert August Wichelns*, Ithaca, New York: Cornell University Press, 1958.

Burgess, Theodore C., *Epideictic Literature*, Chicago: University of Chicago Press, 1902.

Burke, Edmund, *Correspondence*, edited by Charles William and Sir Richard Bourke, London: F. and J. Rivington, 1844.

Burke, Kenneth, *Counter-Statement*, 2nd ed. rev., Los Altos, California: Hermes Publications, 1953.

————, *A Grammar of Motives*, New York: Prentice-Hall, 1945.

————, *The Philosophy of Literary Form*, Baton Rouge, Louisiana: Louisiana State University Press, 1941.

————, *A Rhetoric of Motives*, New York: Prentice-Hall, 1950.

————, "Rhetoric—Old and New," *Journal of General Education*, Vol. V, 1951, pp. 202-209.

Calvin, John, *Institution de la religion chrétienne*, edited by Frank Baumgartner, Geneva: E. Béroud, 1888 (English translation: *Institutes of the Christian Religion*, edited by John T. McNeill, translated by Ford Lewis Battles, 2 vols., Philadelphia: Westminster Press, 1960).

Campbell, George, *The Philosophy of Rhetoric*, 7th ed., London: Printed for William Baynes and Son, 1823.

――――, *The Philosophy of Rhetoric*, edited by Lloyd F. Bitzer, with a Foreword by David Potter, Carbondale, Illinois: Southern Illinois University Press, 1963.

Caplan, Harry, "Classical Rhetoric and the Medieval Theory of Preaching," in *Historical Studies of Rhetoric and Rhetoricians*, edited by Raymond F. Howes, Ithaca, New York: Cornell University Press, 1961, pp. 71-89.

Cassirer, Ernst, *An Essay on Man*, New Haven, Connecticut: Yale University Press, 1944.

――――, *Language and Myth*, translated by Susanne K. Langer, New York: Harper, 1946.

Caxton, William, *The Mirrour of the World*, edited by Olliver H. Prior, New York: Oxford University Press, 1913.

Chase, Stuart, *The Tyranny of Words*, New York: Harcourt, Brace, 1938.

Christopherson, Myrvin F., "Speech and the 'New' Philosophies Revisited," *Central States Speech Journal*, Vol. XIV, 1963, pp. 5-11.

Cicero, *The Basic Works*, edited by Moses Hadas, New York: Modern Library, 1951.

――――, *Brutus. On the Nature of the Gods. On Divination. On Duties*, translated by Hubert M. Poteat, with an Introduction by Richard McKeon, Chicago: University of Chicago Press, 1950.

――――, *De Oratore*, translated by E. W. Sutton and completed by H. Rackham, 2 vols., in the Loeb Classical Library, Cambridge, Massachusetts: Harvard University Press, 1959.

――――, *Rhetorica ad Herennium*, translated by Harry Caplan, in the Loeb Classical Library, Cambridge, Massachusetts: Harvard University Press, 1954.

――――, *Rhetorica ad Herennium*, in Oeuvres Complètes, translated by M. Nisard, Paris: Didot, 1859.

Clark, Donald Lemen, *Rhetoric and Poetry in the Renaissance: A Study of Rhetorical Terms in English Renaissance Literary Criticism*, New York: Columbia University Press, 1922.

Clevenger, Theodore, Jr., "Toward an Understanding of Experimental Rhetoric," *The Pennsylvania Speech Annual*, Vol. XXI, 1964, pp. 23-27.

――――, "The Place of Rhetoric in a Liberal Education," *Quarterly Journal of Speech*, Vol. XXXVI, 1950, pp. 291-295.

――――, *Rhetoric in Greco-Roman Education*, New York: Columbia University Press, 1957.

Clippinger, Erle Elsworth, *Written and Spoken English: A Course in Composition and Rhetoric*, rev. ed., New York: Silver, 1924.

Collingwood, R. G., *An Autobiography*, Oxford: Oxford University Press, 1939.

――――, *An Essay on Philosophical Method*, Oxford: Clarendon Press, 1933.

Cope, E. M., *An Introduction to Aristotle's Rhetoric*, London: Macmillan, 1867.

――――, "On the Sophistical Rhetoric," *Journal of Classical and Sacred Philosophy*, Vol. III, 1856, pp. 34-80 and 253-288.

Cox, Leonard, *The Arte or Crafte of Rhethoryke*, edited with an Introduction and notes by Frederic Ives Carpenter, Chicago: University of Chicago Press, 1899.

Crawshay-Williams, Rupert, *Methods and Criteria of Reasoning: An Inquiry into the Structure of Controversy*, New York: Humanities Press, 1957.

Croissant-Goedert, Jeanne, "La Classification des sciences et la place de la rhétorique dans l'oeuvre d'Aristote," *Actes du XI Congrès International de Philosophie*, Vol. XIV, 1953, pp. 269-275.

de Laguna, Grace A., *Speech: Its Function and Development*, Bloomington, Indiana: Indiana University Press, 1963.

de Méré, Chevalier, *Oeuvres complètes*, Vol. III, Paris: Collection des Universités de France, 1930.

Demos, Raphael, "On Persuasion," *Journal of Philosophy*, Vol. XXIX, 1932, pp. 225-232.

Démosthène, *Harangues*, translated by Maurice Croiset and G. Mathieu, 4 vols., Paris: Collection des Universités de France, 1924-1947.

De Quincey, Thomas, *Collected Writings*, edited by David Masson, Vol. X, London: A. and C. Black, 1897.

Diels, Hermann, *Die Fragmente der Vorsokratiker*, 9th Auflage, edited by Walther Kranz, Berlin: Weidmann, 1959.

Donne, John, *Sermons: Selected Passages*, with an Essay by Logan Pearsall Smith, Oxford: The Clarendon Press, 1919.

Edie, James M., "Expression and Metaphor," *Philosophy and Phenomenological Research*, Vol. XXIII, 1963, pp. 538-561.

Erasmus, Desiderius, *The Essential Erasmus*, selected and newly translated with Introduction and Commentary by John P. Dolan, New York: New American Library, 1964.

Eubanks, Ralph T., and Virgil L. Baker, "Toward an Axiology of Rhetoric," *Quarterly Journal of Speech*, Vol. XLVIII, 1962, pp. 157-168.

Farnham, Willard, *Medieval Heritage of Elizabethan Tragedy*, Berkeley, California: University of California Press, 1936.

Fénelon, François, *Dialogues on Eloquence*, translated with an Introduction by Wilbur Samuel Howell, Princeton, New Jersey: Princeton University Press, 1951.

Ferrater Mora, José, *Diccionario de Filosofía* (article on "Retórica"), Buenos Aires: Editorial Sudamericana, 1958.

Feys, Robert, "Logique," in *Philosophy in the Mid-Century: A Survey*, edited by Raymond Klibansky, Vol. I, Firenze: La Nuova Italia Editrice, 1961, pp. 5-44.

Fielding, Henry, *The History of Tom Jones: A Foundling*, Introduction by George Sherburn, New York: Modern Library, 1950.

Fogarty, Daniel, *Roots for A New Rhetoric*, New York: Bureau of Publications, Teachers College, Columbia University, 1959.

Frye, Northrop, *Anatomy of Criticism: Four Essays*, Princeton, New Jersey: Princeton University Press, 1957.

Gallie, W. B., "Essentially Contested Concepts," in *The Importance of Language*, edited by Max Black, Englewood Cliffs, New Jersey: Prentice-Hall, 1962, pp. 121-146.

Gilson, Etienne, *The Philosophy of St. Bonaventure*, translated by Dom Illtyd Trethowan and F. J. Sheed, New York: Sheed and Ward, 1938.

Gomperz, Heinrich, *Sophistik und Rhetorik: das Bildungsideal des εὖ λέγειν*, Berlin: B. G. Teubner, 1912.

Gueroult, Martial, "Logique, architectonique et structures constitutives des systèmes philosophiques," in *Encyclopédie Française*, Vol. XIX, Paris: Librairie Larousse, 1957.

Hall, Everett W., *Philosophical Systems*, Chicago: University of Chicago Press, 1960.

Hamberger, Peter, *Die rednerische Disposition in der alten τέχνη ῥητορική* (Korax-Gorgias-Antiphon), Paderborn: F. Schöningh, 1914.

Hardison, O. B., Jr., *The Enduring Monument: A Study of the Idea of Praise in Renaissance Literary Theory and Practice*, Chapel Hill, North Carolina: University of North Carolina Press, 1962.

Hare, R. M., *The Language of Morals*, Oxford: The Clarendon Press, 1952.

Harrah, David, "Science and the Rhetorical Aspect of Communication," *Methodos*, Vol. IX, 1957, pp. 113-122.

Havet, Ernest, *Étude sur la Rhétorique d'Aristote*, Paris: J. Delalain, 1846.

Hawkins, Sir John, *A General History of the Science and Practice of Music*, Introduction by Charles Cudworth, 2 vols., New York: Dover Publications, 1963.

Hayakawa, S. I., *Language in Thought and Action*, New York: Harcourt, Brace, 1949.

Heidegger, Martin, *Unterwegs zur Sprache*, Pfullingen: Neske, 1959.

Hendrickson, G. L., "Origin and Meaning of the Characters of Style," *American Journal of Philology*, Vol. XXVI, 1905, pp. 249-290.

———, "The Peripatetic Mean of Style and the Three Stylistic Characters," *American Journal of Philology*, Vol. XXV, 1904, pp. 125-146.

Herrick, Marvin T., "The Place of Rhetoric in Poetic Theory," *Quarterly Journal of Speech*, Vol. XXXIV, 1948, pp. 1-22.

Hochmuth, Marie K. (also see Marie Hochmuth Nichols), "The Criticism of Rhetoric," in *A History and Criticism of American Public Address*, edited by Marie K. Hochmuth, Vol. III, New York: Longmans, Green, 1955, pp. 1-23.

———, "I. A. Richards and the 'New Rhetoric'," *Quarterly Journal of Speech*, Vol. XLIV, 1958, pp. 1-16.

———, "Kenneth Burke and the 'New Rhetoric'," *Quarterly Journal of Speech*, Vol. XXXVIII, 1952, pp. 133-144.

Holland, L. Virginia, Counterpoint: Kenneth Burke and Aristotle's Theories of Rhetoric, New York: Philosophical Library, 1959.

Howell, Wilbur Samuel, Logic and Rhetoric in England: 1500-1700, Princeton, New Jersey: Princeton University Press, 1956.

———, "Renaissance Rhetoric and Modern Rhetoric: A Study in Change," in The Rhetorical Idiom, edited by Donald C. Bryant, Ithaca, New York: Cornell University Press, 1958, pp. 53-70.

———, Rhetoric of Alcuin and Charlemagne, Princeton, New Jersey: Princeton University Press, 1941.

Howes, Raymond F. (editor), Historical Studies of Rhetoric and Rhetoricians, Ithaca, New York: Cornell University Press, 1961.

Hudson, Hoyt H., Educating Liberally, Stanford University, California: Stanford University Press, 1945.

Hunt, Everett Lee, "Ancient Rhetoric and Modern Propaganda," Quarterly Journal of Speech, Vol. XXXVII, 1951, pp. 157-160.

———, "Plato and Aristotle on Rhetoric and Rhetoricians," in Historical Studies of Rhetoric and Rhetoricians, edited by Raymond F. Howes, Ithaca, New York: Cornell University Press, 1961, pp. 19-70.

———, "Rhetoric and General Education," Quarterly Journal of Speech, Vol. XXXV, 1949, pp. 275-279.

———, "Rhetoric and Politics," The Pennsylvania Speech Annual, Vol. XXI, 1964, pp. 10-16.

———, "Rhetoric as a Humane Study," Quarterly Journal of Speech," Vol. XLI, 1955, pp. 114-117.

Huxley, Aldous, The Devils of Loudun, New York: Harper, 1952.

Huxley, T. H., Lay Sermons: Addresses and Reviews, New York: D. Appleton, 1870.

Hyman, Stanley Edgar, The Armed Vision: A Study in the Methods of Modern Literary Criticism, rev. ed., New York: Vintage Books, 1955.

———, The Tangled Bank: Darwin, Marx, Frazer and Freud as Imaginative Writers, New York: Atheneum, 1962.

Isocrates, translated by George Norlin in the Loeb Classical Library, Vol. II, New York: G. P. Putnam, 1929.

———, Discours, translated by Georges Mathieu and Émile Brémond, Vol. I, Paris: Collection des Universités de France, 1928.

Jaeger, Werner, Paideia, translated by Gilbert Highet, 3 vols., New York: Oxford University Press, 1944.

Jameson, Frederic, Sartre: the Origins of a Style, New Haven, Connecticut: Yale University Press, 1961.

Jebb, R. C., Attic Orators From Antiphon to Isalos, 2 vols., New York: Russell and Russell, 1962.

———, "Rhetoric," in Encyclopedia Britannica, Vol. XIX, 1954, pp. 247-248.

Jensen, O. C., The Nature of Legal Argument, Oxford: B. H. Blackwell, 1957.

Johnson, Wendell, "The Spoken Word and the Great Unsaid," *Quarterly Journal of Speech*, Vol. XXXVII, 1951, pp. 419-429.

Johnstone, Henry W., Jr., "Can Philosophical Arguments be Valid?," *Bucknell Review*, Vol. XI, 1963, pp. 89-98.

————, "The Law of Non-Contradiction," *Logique et Analyse*, Vol. III, 1960, pp. 3-10.

————, "The Methods of Philosophical Polemic," *Methodos*, Vol. V, 1953, pp. 131-140.

————, "The Nature of Philosophical Controversy," *Journal of Philosophy*, Vol. LI, 1954, pp. 294-300.

————, "New Outlooks on Controversy," *Review of Metaphysics*, Vol. XII, 1958, pp. 57-67.

————, *Philosophy and Argument*, University Park, Pennsylvania: The Pennsylvania State University Press, 1959.

————, "Philosophy and *Argumentum ad Hominem*," *Journal of Philosophy*, Vol. XLIX, 1952, pp. 489-498.

————, "Reason Limited," in *Essays in Philosophy*, University Park, Pennsylvania: The Pennsylvania State University Press, 1962, pp. 115-132.

Jouhandeau, Marcel, *Un Monde*, Paris: Gallimard, 1950.

Karns, C. Franklin, "The Usefulness of Mill's Canons of Causation to Rhetoric," *The Pennsylvania Speech Annual*, Vol. XXI, 1964, pp. 50-55.

Kennedy, George, "Two Problems in the Historical Study of Rhetoric," *The Pennsylvania Speech Annual*, Vol. XXI, 1964, pp. 17-22.

Ibn Khaldûn, *The Muqaddimah: An Introduction to History*, translated by Franz Rosenthal, 3 vols., Bollingen Series, New York: Pantheon Books, 1958.

Kierkegaard, Sören, *Philosophical Fragments*, translated by David F. Swenson, Princeton, New Jersey: Princeton University Press, 1944.

Korzybski, Alfred, *Science and Sanity*, 3rd ed. rev., Lakeville, Connecticut: The International Non-Aristotelian Library Publishing Co., 1948.

La Drière, Craig, "Rhetoric as 'Merely Verbal' Art," in *English Institute Essays—1948*, edited by D. A. Robertson, Jr., New York: Columbia University Press, 1949, pp. 123-152.

Langer, Susanne K., *Philosophy in a New Key*, Cambridge, Massachusetts: Harvard University Press, 1951.

Lee, Irving, "General Semantics[1952]," *Quarterly Journal of Speech*, Vol. XXXVIII, 1952, pp. 1-12.

Leibniz, G. W., *Discours de métaphysique*, Paris: Vrin, 1929.

————, *Die philosophischen Schriften*, edited by C. J. Gerhardt, Vol. VI, Leipzig: A. Lorenz, 1932.

————, *Selections*, edited by Philip P. Wiener, New York: Charles Scribner's Sons, 1951.

Leites, Nathan, "Interaction: The Third International on Its Changes of Policy," in *Language of Politics: Studies in Quantitative Semantics*, edited by Harold D. Lasswell, New York: George W. Stewart, 1949, pp. 298-333.

Liebrecht, Henri, *Les Chambres de Rhétorique*, Brussels: La Renaissance du Livre, 1948.

Lippmann, Walter, *Public Opinion*, New York: Macmillan, 1922.

Locke, John, *An Essay Concerning Human Understanding*, London: Routledge, 1894.

———, *Works*, with a Preliminary Essay and notes by J. A. St. John, 2 vols., London: Henry G. Bohn, 1854.

Logique et Analyse, Nouvelle Série, 21 à 24, Decembre 1963. Issue devoted to "La Théorie de L'Argumentation." Includes contributions by L. Olbrechts-Tyteca, Thadée Kotarbinski, H. W. Johnstone, Jr., Nynfa Bosco, Eduard Nicol, Jacques Ruytinx, Paul Gochet, Max Loreau, Pierre Verstraeten, Maurice-Jean Lefebve, Nathan Rotenstreich, Robert Blanché, Joseph Moreau, Paul Lorenzen, Izydora Dambska, Gerhard Frey, Leo Apostel, Arnould Bayart, Karl Döhmann, Ilmar Tammelo, J. Miedzianagora, Zygmunt Ziembinski, Jerzy Wroblewski, Hans Georg Gadamer, Martial Gueroult, Victor Goldschmidt, Émile Janssens, R. Dekkers, François Masai, Alessandro Giuliani, Robert T. Oliver, Jean Laitat, Bernard Guilemain, and a bibliography of the works of Ch. Perelman.

Longinus, *On the Sublime*, translated by W. Rhys Roberts, Cambridge: University Press, 1907.

McBurney, James H., "The Place of the Enthymeme in Rhetorical Theory," *Speech Monographs*, Vol. III, 1936, pp. 49-74.

McKeon, Richard, "Communication, Truth, and Society," *Ethics*, Vol. LXVII, 1957, pp. 89-99.

———, "Philosophy and Method," *Journal of Philosophy*, Vol. XLVIII, 1951, pp. 653-682.

———, "Rhetoric in the Middle Ages," *Speculum*, Vol. XVII, 1942, pp. 1-32 (reprinted in *Critics and Criticism: Ancient and Modern*, edited by R. S. Crane, Chicago: University of Chicago Press, 1952).

McLuhan, H. M., "Poetic vs. Rhetorical Exegesis: The Case for Leavis Against Richards and Empson," *Sewanee Review*, Vol. LII, 1944, pp. 266-276.

Madden, Edward H., "The Enthymeme: Crossroads of Logic, Rhetoric and Metaphysics," *Philosophical Review*, Vol. LXI, 1952, pp. 368-376.

Maloney, Martin J., "Some New Directions in Rhetorical Criticism," *Central States Speech Journal*, Vol. IV, 1953, pp. 1-5.

Malraux, André, *Saturne: Essai sur Goya*, Paris: Gallimard, 1950.

Mannheim, Karl, *Ideology and Utopia: An Introduction to the Sociology of Knowledge*, with a Preface by Louis Wirth, New York: Harcourt, Brace, 1949.

Maritain, Jacques, "Action: The Perfection of Human Life," *Sewanee Review*, Vol. LVI, 1948, pp. 1-11.

Marx, Werner, "Heidegger's New Conception of Philosophy: The Second Phase of 'Existentialism'," *Social Research*, Vol. XXII, 1955, pp. 451-474.

Matthews, Jack, "A Behavioral Science Approach to the Study of Rhetoric," *The Pennsylvania Speech Annual*, Vol. XXI, 1964, pp. 56-60.

Mead, George H., *Mind, Self and Society*, edited by Charles W. Morris, Chicago: University of Chicago Press, 1934.

Melanchthon, Philipp, *Elementorum Rhetorices*, Argentorati, apud Cratonem Mylium, 1546.

Merleau-Ponty, Maurice, *In Praise of Philosophy*, translated with a Preface by John Wild and James M. Edie, Evanston, Illinois: Northwestern University Press, 1963.

————, *Signes*, Paris: Gallimard, 1960 (English translation: *Signs*, translated by Richard C. McCleary, Northwestern University Press, 1964).

Mills, C. Wright, *White Collar: The American Middle Classes*, New York: Oxford University Press, 1951.

The Monist, Vol. 48, October, 1964. Issue devoted to "Philosophical Argument." Articles included by Henry W. Johnstone, Jr., Duane H. Whittier, D. C. Yalden-Thomson, Ian Philip McGreal, Sid B. Thomas, Jr., Arnold Levison, and William Sacksteder.

Montaigne, Michel de, *The Essays of Montaigne*, translated by E. J. Trechmann, New York: Oxford University Press, 1927.

Murphy, Richard, "Preface to an Ethic of Rhetoric," in *The Rhetorical Idiom*, edited by Donald C. Bryant, Ithaca, New York: Cornell University Press, 1958, pp. 125-143.

Murray, Elwood, "The Semantics of Rhetoric," *Quarterly Journal of Speech*, Vol. XXX, 1944, pp. 31-41.

Myrick, Kenneth Orne, *Sir Philip Sidney as a Literary Craftsman*, Cambridge, Massachusetts: Harvard University Press, 1935.

Natanson, Maurice, "The Privileged Moment: A Study in the Rhetoric of Thomas Wolfe," *Quarterly Journal of Speech*, Vol. XLIII, 1957, pp. 143-150 (reprinted in Maurice Natanson, *Literature, Philosophy, and the Social Sciences: Essays in Existentialism and Phenomenology*, The Hague: Martinus Nijhoff, 1962 and in *The World of Thomas Wolfe*, edited by C. Hugh Holman, New York: Charles Scribner's Sons, 1962).

————, "Rhetoric and Counter-Espionage," *Reflections: The Free South Review*, Vol. III, 1964 (forthcoming).

Nichols, Marie Hochmuth, *Rhetoric and Criticism*, Baton Rouge, Louisiana: Louisiana State University Press, 1963.

North, Helen F., "Rhetoric and Historiography," *Quarterly Journal of Speech*, Vol. XLII, 1956, pp. 234-242.

Olbricht, Thomas H., "The Self as a Philosophical Ground of Rhetoric," *The Pennsylvania Speech Annual*, Vol. XXI, 1964, pp. 28-36.

Ong, Walter J., *Ramus: Method, and the Decay of Dialogue*, Cambridge, Massachusetts: Harvard University Press, 1958.

Pareto, Vilfredo, *Traité de sociologie générale*, translated by Pierre Boven, 2 vols., Paris: Payot, 1917-1919 (English translation: *The Mind and Society*, translated by Andrew Bongiorno and Arthur Livingston, edited by Arthur Livingston, 4 vols., New York: Harcourt, Brace, 1935).

Parrish, W. M., "The Tradition of Rhetoric," *Quarterly Journal of Speech*, Vol. XXXIII, 1947, pp. 465-467.

Pascal, Blaise, *Œuvres Complètes*, texte établi et annoté par Jacques Chevalier, Paris: Gallimard, 1957.

———, *Pensées and the Provincial Letters*, New York: Modern Library, 1941.

Passmore, John, *Philosophical Reasoning*, New York: Charles Scribner's Sons, 1961.

Paulhan, Jean, *Entretien sur des faits divers*, Paris: Gallimard, 1945.

Peacham, Henry, *Compleat Gentleman*, with an Introduction by G. S. Gordon, Oxford: The Clarendon Press, 1906.

Penfield, Wilder and Lamar Roberts, *Speech and Brain-Mechanisms*, Princeton, New Jersey: Princeton University Press, 1959.

Perelman, Ch., *The Idea of Justice and the Problem of Argument*, translated by John Petrie, with an Introduction by H. L. A. Hart, New York: Humanities Press, 1963.

———, "La Quête du rationnel," in *Études de philosophie des sciences en hommage à Ferdinand Gonseth*, Neuchâtel: Édition du Griffon, 1950, pp. 135-142.

———, "Sociologie de la connaissance et philosophie de la connaissance," *Revue Internationale de Philosophie*, Vol. IV, 1950, pp. 309-317.

———, and L. Olbrechts-Tyteca, "Logique et rhétorique," *Revue Philosophique de la France et de L'Etranger*, Vol. CXL, 1950, pp. 1-35 (reprinted in Perelman and Olbrechts-Tyteca, *Rhétorique et philosophie*).

———, ———, *Rhétorique et philosophie: pour une théorie de l'argumentation en philosophie*, Paris: Presses Universitaires de France, 1952.

———, ———, *Traité de L'Argumentation: La Nouvelle Rhétorique*, 2 vols., Paris: Presses Universitaires de France, 1958 (English translation to be published).

Plato, *Collected Dialogues of Plato*, edited by Edith Hamilton and Huntington Cairns, Bollingen Series, New York: Pantheon Books, 1961.

———, *The Dialogues of Plato*, translated by B. Jowett, 2 vols., New York: Random House, 1937.

Plautus, *Trinummus*, translated by Alfred Ernoult, Paris: Collection des Universités de France, 1940.

Polanyi, Michael, *Personal Knowledge: Towards a Post-Critical Philosophy*, Chicago: University of Chicago Press, 1958.

Priestley, Joseph, *A Course of Lectures on Oratory and Criticism*, edited with an introduction by Vincent Bevilacqua and Richard Murphy, Carbondale, Illinois: Southern Illinois University Press, 1964.

Reid, Loren D., "The Perils of Rhetorical Criticism," *Quarterly Journal of Speech*, Vol. XXX, 1944, pp. 416-422.

Révész, Géza (editor) *Thinking and Speaking—A Symposium*, Amsterdam: North-Holland Publishing Co., 1954.

Revue Internationale de Philosophie, Vol. VIII, Nos. 27-28, 1954. Issue devoted to "Théorie de la Preuve." Papers included by Charles Frankel, G. Morpurgo-Tagliabue, and Gilbert Ryle.

——————, Vol. XV, No. 58, 1961. Issue devoted to "L'Argumentation." Papers included by Ch. Perelman, Yvon Belaval, Henry W. Johnstone, Jr., A. J. Ayer, Norberto Bobbio, Paul Foriers, and Jérôme Grynpas.

Richards, I. A., *The Philosophy of Rhetoric*, New York: Oxford University Press, 1936.

Rogge, Eberhard, *Axiomatik alles möglichen Philosophierens: Das grundsätzliche Sprechen der Logistik, der Sprachkritik und der Lebens-Metaphysik*, Meisenheim: Westkulturverlag, 1950.

Ryle, Gilbert, "Philosophical Arguments," in *Logical Positivism*, edited by A. J. Ayer, Glencoe, Illinois: Free Press, 1959, pp. 327-344.

——————, "Systematically Misleading Expressions," in *Essays on Logic and Language*, edited with an Introduction by Antony Flew, New York: Philosophical Library, 1951, pp. 11-36.

Santayana, George, *Scepticism and Animal Faith*, New York: Dover Publications, 1955.

Sartre, Jean-Paul, *Being and Nothingness: An Essay on Phenomenological Ontology*, translated with an Introduction by Hazel E. Barnes, New York: Philosophical Library, 1956.

——————, *What is Literature?*, translated by Bernard Frechtman, New York: Philosophical Library, 1949.

Scanlan, Ross, "The Nazi Party Speaker System," I and II, *Speech Monographs*, Vol. XVI, 1949, pp. 82-97 and Vol. XVII, 1950, pp. 134-148.

——————, "The Nazi Rhetorician," *Quarterly Journal of Speech*, Vol. XXXVII, 1951, pp. 430-440.

——————, and Henry C. Youngerman, "Propaganda and Public Address," *Today's Speech*, Vol. I, 1953, pp. 15-17.

——————, ——————, "Two Views of Propaganda," *Today's Speech*, Vol. I, 1953, pp. 13-14.

Schopenhauer, Arthur, *Sämtliche Werke*, edited by Arthur Hübscher, 6 vols., Leipzig: Brockhaus, 1937-1939.

——————, *Sämtliche Werke*, edited by Paul Deussen, Vol. VI, Munich: Piper, 1932.

Schutz, Alfred, *Collected Papers*, Vol. I: *The Problem of Social Reality*, edited and Introduced by Maurice Natanson, with a Preface by H. L. Van Breda, Phaenomenologica 11, The Hague: Martinus Nijhoff, 1962.

Schwartz, Joseph, and John A. Rycenga, (editors) *The Province of Rhetoric*, New York: Ronald Press, 1965.

Sears, Lorenzo, *History of Oratory: From the Age of Pericles to the Present Time*, Chicago: Scott, 1908.

Sherry, Richard, *A Treatise of Schemes and Tropes* (1550) and his translation of *The Education of Children* by Desiderius Erasmus. A Facsimile Reproduction with an Introduction and index by Herbert W. Hildebrandt. Gainesville, Florida: Scholars' Facsimiles and Reprints, 1961.

Shorey, Paul, "What Teachers of Speech May Learn From the Theory and Practice of the Greeks," *Quarterly Journal of Speech Education*, Vol. VIII, 1922, pp. 105-131.

Simon, Clarence, "Speech as a Science," *Quarterly Journal of Speech*, Vol. XXXVII, 1951, pp. 281-298.

Spiegelberg, Herbert, *The Phenomenological Movement: A Historical Introduction*, 2 vols., Phaenomenologica 5 and 6, The Hague: Martinus Nijhoff, 1960.

Stechert, Julius, *Handbuch der Rhetorik Komparativ*, Berlin: Springer-Verlag, 1961.

Stevenson, Charles L., *Ethics and Language*, New Haven, Connecticut: Yale University Press, 1945.

Strawson, P. F., review of Perelman and Olbrechts-Tyteca, *Traité de L'Argumentation*, *Mind*, Vol. LXVIII, 1959, pp. 420-421.

Stroux, Johannes, *Römische Rechtswissenschaft und Rhetorik*, Potsdam: Stichnote, 1949.

Studies in Rhetoric and Public Speaking in Honor of James Albert Winans, New York: Century, 1925.

Symposium on Philosophy and Rhetoric, held at Pennsylvania State University, February 20-22, 1964. Papers presented by Hubert G. Alexander, Donald C. Bryant, Wayne Brockriede, Lloyd F. Bitzer, Douglas Ehninger, Henry W. Johnstone, Jr., Richard McKeon, Maurice Natanson, Thomas H. Olbricht, Ch. Perelman, Karl R. Wallace, and Otis M. Walter (unpublished).

Symposium sobre la Argumentación Filosófica, Mexico City: Universidad Nacional Autónoma de México, Centro de Estudios Filosóficos, 1963. Papers by Jean Wahl, Nathan Rotenstreich, John Passmore, and Julián Marías.

Tate, Allen, *The Forlorn Demon: Didactic and Critical Essays*, Chicago: Henry Regnery, 1953.

Taylor, A. E., *Plato: The Man and His Work*, London: Methuen, 1937.

Taylor, Henry Osborn, *The Classical Heritage of the Middle Ages*, 4th ed. augmented, New York: F. Ungar, 1957.

Thompson, Wayne N., "A Conservative View of a Progressive Rhetoric," *Quarterly Journal of Speech*, Vol. XLIX, 1963, pp. 1-7.

Thonssen, Lester, "Recent Literature in Rhetoric," *Quarterly Journal of Speech*, Vol. XXXIX, 1953, pp., 501-505.

————, and A. Craig Baird, *Speech Criticism*, New York: Ronald Press, 1948.

Toulmin, Stephen E., *The Uses of Argument*, Cambridge: at the University Press, 1958.

Untersteiner, Mario, *The Sophists*, translated by Kathleen Freeman, Oxford: B. H. Blackwell, 1954.

Ushenko, Andrew Paul, *Power and Events: An Essay on Dynamics in Philosophy*, Princeton, New Jersey: Princeton University Press, 1946.

Vayson de Pradenne, Andri, *Les Fraudes en archéologie préhistorique: avec quelques examples de comparaison en archéologie générale et sciences naturelles*, Paris: Nourry, 1932.

Vivas, Eliseo, *Creation and Discovery: Essays in Criticism and Aesthetics*, New York: Noonday Press, 1955.

Voegelin, Eric, *Order and History*, Vol. III: *Plato and Aristotle*, Baton Rouge, Louisiana: Louisiana State University Press, 1957.

Waismann, Friedrich, "How I See Philosophy," in *Contemporary British Philosophy: Personal Statements*, edited by H. D. Lewis, London: George Allen and Unwin, 1956, pp. 447-490.

Wallace, Karl R., "Aspects of Modern Rhetoric in Francis Bacon," *Quarterly Journal of Speech*, Vol. XLII, 1956, pp. 398-406.

———, *Francis Bacon on Communication and Rhetoric*, Chapel Hill, North Carolina: University of North Carolina Press, 1943.

———, "Rhetoric, Politics, and Education of the Ready Man," in *The Rhetorical Idiom*, edited by Donald C. Bryant, Ithaca, New York: Cornell University Press, 1958, pp. 71-95.

Wallerstein, Ruth, "Rhetoric in the English Renaissance: Two Elegies," in *English Institute Essays—1948*, edited by D. A. Robertson, Jr., New York: Columbia University Press, 1949, pp. 153-178.

Walter, Otis M., "On Views of Rhetoric, Whether Conservative or Progressive," *Quarterly Journal of Speech*, Vol. XLIX, 1963, pp. 367-382.

———, "Toward an Analysis of Ethos," *The Pennsylvania Speech Annual*, Vol. XXI, 1964, pp. 37-45.

Weaver, Richard M., *Ethics and Rhetoric*, Chicago: Henry Regnery, 1953.

———, *Visions of Order: The Cultural Crisis of Our Time*, Baton Rouge, Louisiana: Louisiana State University Press, 1964.

Weil, Eric, *Logique de la Philosophie*, Paris: Vrin, 1950.

Weil, Simone, *L'Enracinement*, Paris: Gallimard, 1949 (English translation: *The Need for Roots: Prelude to a Declaration of Duties Towards Mankind*, translated by A. F. Willis, with a Preface by T. S. Eliot, London: Routledge and Paul, 1952).

Whately, Richard, *Elements of Rhetoric*, New York: Sheldon, 1867.

———, *Elements of Rhetoric*, edited by Douglas Ehninger, Carbondale, Illinois: Southern Illinois University Press, 1963.

Wichelns, Herbert August, "The Literary Criticism of Oratory," in *Studies in Rhetoric and Public Speaking in Honor of James Albert Winans*, New York: Century, 1925, pp. 181-216.

———, "Public Speaking and Dramatic Arts," in *On Going to College: A Symposium*, New York: Oxford University Press, 1938, pp. 235-256.

Wieman, Henry Nelson, and Otis M. Walter, "Toward an Analysis of Ethics for Rhetoric," *Quarterly Journal of Speech*, Vol. XLIII, 1957, pp. 266-270.

Wilder, Amos N., *The Language of the Gospel: Early Christian Rhetoric*, New York: Harper and Row, 1964.

Williams, B. A. O., "Metaphysical Arguments," in *The Nature of Metaphysics*, edited by D. F. Pears, London: Macmillan, 1957, pp. 39-60.

Windelband, W., *A History of Philosophy*, translated by James H. Tufts, 2nd ed., New York: Macmillan, 1901.

Windt, Theodore O., Jr., "The Classical Concept of Ethos—A Perspective," *The Pennsylvania Speech Annual*, Vol. XXI, 1964, pp. 46-49.

Wittgenstein, Ludwig, *Tractatus Logico-Philosophicus*, with an Introduction by Bertrand Russell, London: Kegan Paul, Trench, Trubner, 1947.

Woolbert, Charles Henry, *The Fundamentals of Speech: A Behavioristic Study of the Underlying Principles of Speaking and Reading, a text book of Delivery*, New York: Harper, 1920.

INDEX

action (*see also* conduct, behavior), 1-6, 43, 76, 78, 83, 91, 95, 98
advertising, 7, 22, 23, 32, 52 f, 55
agreement, 8 f, 18, 103 f
analogy, 74, 77
analysis, x, xi, 36, 47, 51, 54, 56-61, 94, 113, 132, 136, 156
Aquinas, Saint Thomas, xii, 110
Aristotle, ix f, xii, xiii, 21 f, 24, 25, 28, 30, 33, 34, 35-39, 41 42, 48 f, 56, 60, 72, 81 f, 84-88, 89, 90 f, 93-101, 103, 110, 127, 133, 136 f
Atkins, J. W. H., 60, 89 n, 90 n
audience, universal, 103, 128, 130, 131-133, 137, 147 f, 152
Augustine, Saint, xii, 25, 123

Bacon, Francis, 25, 46, 48, 49, 55, 82
Baldwin, Charles S., 35, 38, 89, 91 n
behavior (*see also* action, conduct), ix, xi, 2-6, 45 f, 62, 93
belief, 1-6, 15, 17, 23, 49, 94
Bentham, Jeremy, 120
Bossuet, Jacques Bénigne, 43, 118, 123
Bryant, Donald C., 32 n, 93, 94 n, 101 n
Burke, Edmund, 43 f, 55
Burke, Kenneth, 32, 33, 37, 53, 60, 61, 76

Calvin, John, 109, 110 f, 112
Campbell, George, 50
certitude, certainty, 81, 86
Cicero, 24, 25, 29 f, 35, 38, 41, 82, 87 f, 91, 95, 99, 114, 115 n, 124 n
closed mindedness, 3, 12, 16
conduct (*see also* action, behavior), 3-6, 17, 46, 98
Cope, E. M., 83 n, 86 n, 94 n
control, 1-3, 4, 5, 18, 58
contingency, 38, 41, 46, 96, 99
convincing, 11, 17 f, 50, 102

deliberation, 5, 10 f, 103
Demosthenes, 24, 87, 88, 123 f
dialectic, 10, 15 f, 18, 38 f, 69, 70, 72-74, 76, 79, 86, 88, 94-101, 133 f, 136 f, 153, 155
Donne, John, 26, 61
Duhamel, P. Albert, 63 n, 96 n

elocutio, elocution, xiii, 30, 35, 81, 82, 87, 90
epistemology, 39, 81, 100, 125, 128, 131, 155, see also xii, 153
ethics (*see also* morality), x, 33, 34, 47, 50, 63, 77 f, 78, 91, 97, 98, 102, 106 f, 115, 120
exposition, 36-38

fact, factuality, x, 2, 8, 18, 99, 103, 104, 119 f, 128, 129, 131
freedom, 16, 19, 156

immediacy, 3, 6, 8, 15-17, 19
information, ix, 36, 38 f, 40 f, 43, 44, 45, 47, 50, 52, 53, 56, 57
inventio, invention, xiii, 29, 54 f, 81, 87, 90

Hochmuth, Marie (Marie Hochmuth Nichols), 33
Howell, Wilbur S., 59 f, 88 n
Hudson, Hoyt, 32, 33, 34, 42 n, 49, 59, 93 n
Hume, David, 132, 155
Hunt, Everett L., 33, 53 n, 56, 58
Husserl, Edmund, 154, 156

Isocrates, 25, 40, 55, 90, 108, 110

Jaeger, Werner, 83 n, 90 n, 95 n
Johnstone, Henry W., Jr., 135-137, 150-152, 156
Kant, Immanuel, 99, 155
Kierkegaard, Sören, 153-156

La Bruyère, Jean de, 119, 128
language, linguistics, x, 32, 62, 65-79, 96, 98, 100 f, 106
Leibniz, G. W., 117 f, 131, 139
logic, xii, xiii, 12-14, 32, 35, 39, 45, 46, 49, 55, 78, 81, 94, 95 f, 102, 118, 126, 127, 128, 135 f, 149, 155

man, 1 f, 9, 10, 19, 83
Maritain, Jacques, 76, 78 n